MICROCOMPUTERS, CORPORATE PLANNING, AND DECISION SUPPORT SYSTEMS

MICROCOMPUTERS, CORPORATE PLANNING, AND DECISION SUPPORT SYSTEMS

The WEFA Group,
David J. Gianturco
and Nariman Behravesh, EDITORS

Q Quorum Books
New York • Westport, Connecticut • London

This book contains a small number of programs and details computer applications. Every effort has been made to see that these programs and applications are error free. However, the authors and publisher make no warranty of any kind, express or implied, with regard to these programs and applications or any documentation contained in this book. The authors and publisher shall not be liable in any event for incidental or consequential damages in connection with the use, furnishing, or performance of these programs and applications.

Library of Congress Cataloging-in-Publication Data

Microcomputers, corporate planning, and decision
     support systems.

     "The WEFA Group."
     Includes index.
     1. Corporate planning—Data processing.   2. Micro-
computers.   I. Gianturco, David J.   II. Behravesh,
Nariman.   III. WEFA Group.
HD30.28.M498   1988   658.4′012′0285416   88–6011
ISBN 0–89930–164–9 (lib. bdg. : alk. paper)

British Library Cataloguing in Publication Data is available.

Library of Congress Catalog Card Number: 88–6011
ISBN: 0–89930–164–9

First published in 1988 by Quorum Books

Greenwood Press, Inc.
88 Post Road West, Westport, Connecticut   06881

Printed in the United States of America

The paper used in this book complies with the Permanent Paper Standard issued by the National Information Standards Organization (Z39.48–1984).

10   9   8   7   6   5   4   3   2   1

Contents

Illustrations and Tables

ILLUSTRATIONS

TABLES

Acknowledgments

Several people contributed time and effort to this project. The authors wish to extend their sincere appreciation to the following individuals: Beth Barter and Judy Katz for their proofreading and patience, Debera Sullivan for early editorial contributions, Charles Brunner for illustrations, Tim Harrison, Albert Dorr, Albert Scheeler, Jack Katz, Robert Carver, and Hugh Ganser for help with content, and Donald Dutkowsky for help with content and as an ever-present source of encouragement.

About the Contributors

DAVID J. GIANTURCO is a business analyst for the Presidents Support Group at Marine Midland Bank in Buffalo. Before joining Marine Midland Bank, Mr. Gianturco served as manager of microcomputer applications for the U.S. Services Division of The WEFA Group, and as an analyst for the Business Research Group of AT&T Communications in Basking Ridge, N.J. He holds a graduate degree in economics from the State University of New York at Buffalo.

NARIMAN BEHRAVESH is the Senior Vice President for Macroeconomic Forecasting for The WEFA Group and has been with the firm since 1980. Dr. Behravesh manages both the U.S. and International Services divisions at The WEFA Group. He has published several books and articles on various topics in business and economics and holds a doctorate in economics from the University of Pennsylvania.

WILLIAM GERLACH is a consultant with Alphametrics Corporation in Philadelphia. Mr. Gerlach spent several years as a data analyst and consultant with The WEFA Group —U.S. Services Division. He has worked extensively on the development and application of macroeconomic models, including versions of The WEFA Group's Quarterly Model.

MARTIN KATZ is an associate professor of management informations systems at Kennesaw College in Marietta, and holds a doctorate in business administration from Kent State University. Dr. Katz has served as a consultant for several major U.S. corporations. He has also served as an analyst with both the Analytical

Support Center at AT&T in Basking Ridge, N.J., and with the Business Research Group at Bell Communications Research in Livingston, N.J.

JAMES TSITANIDIS is a senior economist with the Canadian Medical Association in Ottawa. He formerly served as an economist with the Saskatchewan Medical Care Insurance Commission in Regina. Mr. Tsitanidis holds a graduate degree in economics from Queens University at Kingston, Ontario, and has published several articles in the areas of health economics and taxation.

JAMES G. WILBER is president of Dynaflow Enterprises in Northridge, Calif. Dynaflow develops graphics-based programming productivity enhancement applications. Mr. Wilber was formerly with Teradyne Corporation in Los Angeles where he held positions in hardware and software development and applications engineering. He has a degree in electrical engineering from M.I.T.

KENNARD T. WING is a management consultant with INTERACT: The Institute for Interactive Management. Previously, he spent five years with The WEFA Group developing microcomputer strategy and planning applications, and two years with Chase Econometrics as a systems consultant.

ROBERTA WHOL is a representative for The WEFA Group and a specialist in the application of the AREMOS software system. She has been active in the development of AREMOS and other products.

Trademarks and Related Information

Several hardware and software products are mentioned in this book. The following is a list of trademarks and their owners. Other product names mentioned may also be trademarks.

Apple, Macintosh: Apple Computer Corporation

AREMOS: The WEFA Group

AT&T: American Telephone & Telegraph

UNIX: American Telephone & Telegraph (Bell Laboratories)

Bernoulli Box, IOMEGA: IOMEGA Corporation

BOEING: The Boeing Company

CA-TELLAGRAF: Computer Associates International, Inc.

Compaq, Compaq Deskpro, Compaq Deskpro-286, Compaq Deskpro-386: COMPAQ Computer Corporation

CP/M: Digital Research Inc.

dBASE, Framework, Ashton-Tate: Ashton-Tate Inc.

Ethernet, Xerox: Xerox Corporation

IBM, Personal Computer, IBM PC, IBM PC-XT, IBM PC-AT, PS/2, PC-DOS, Micro Channel: International Business Machines Corporation

Intel: Intel Corporation

Interactive Financial Planning System, IFPS: EXECUCOM Corporation

Javelin: Javelin Corporation

Lotus, 1-2-3, HAL, Symphony, VisiCalc: Lotus Development Corporation

Microsoft, MS-DOS, MS-OS/2, Multiplan: Microsoft Corporation

Minitab: Minitab Inc.

ORACLE, SQL*Star: Oracle Corporation

Paradox: Ansa Software

R:BASE: Microrim Inc.

SAS: SAS Institute

SPSS: SPSS Inc.

SuperCalc: Sorcim/Computer Associates International Inc.

Toshiba: Toshiba America, Inc.

TRS-80: Tandy Corporation

X-Y-Z: INTEX Solutions Inc.

Z80: Zilog Inc.

The names of most software packages, computers, and computer components are trademarked by their authors or manufacturers. Greenwood Press and Quorum Books are not affiliated with any manufacturer and do not endorse any of the products mentioned in this book.

Preface

Many books cover corporate planning methods, and many others discuss the use of microcomputers in business. However, little is written on the use of microcomputers by corporate planners. This book attempts to fill this void. It offers insight and perspective on the application of microcomputers in planning and the impacts microcomputers have had on large organizations.

The WEFA Group was a leader in converting macroeconomic models to microcomputer-based applications. It was the first major econometrics firm to migrate versions of its large models to microcomputers. In fact, The WEFA Group distributed PCMark7 to clients as early as 1984. The elimination of time-sharing costs enabled clients to run macroeconomic scenarios cheaply and easily on IBM PC-XT class microcomputers. The marginal cost of running scenarios essentially became zero.

Because of the success of the PCMark7, The WEFA Group became aware and involved in other business planning projects. The shape and nature of computing in our clients' planning departments was changing rapidly. Perhaps more important, our consultants and staff began interfacing with people who had very little computing experience. These people were asked to fill new roles. Equipped with microcomputers, these people had the responsibility to complete and support computerized applications. Most have succeeded, and some have become advanced microcomputer users.

Many factors are changing the nature of computing in support groups today. Applications and applications development software are becoming easier to use. This is true across all ranges of computers. The independence that this phenomenon has bestowed on users has rocked many organizations. It has wrenched power from systems groups and allowed end-users to accept responsibility for computer operations. These include applications development. In the past, large corporations witnessed turf battles over the computing portions of many projects. Systems groups selected programming languages and the computers on which applications would reside. Business area specialists became frustrated by their own lack of control. Applications also took a long time to complete. The first step entailed the drafting of formal program specifications. After business area specialists prepared requests, programmers and systems analysts prepared formal specifications. Revisions were difficult. The inflexible process added to development delays and to the frustration of business area specialists. Finally, miscommunication between systems and business professionals caused errors, which increased testing periods and further delayed the implementation of needed applications. After implementation, programmers retained maintenance roles.

New computing environments allow business specialists to develop their own applications. The distance between computing and business disciplines is narrowing. This gives business professionals new freedom and also diminishes or changes responsibilities of systems professionals and groups.

This book will help planners better understand applications, applications development, advancing microcomputer technologies, and related topics. The objective is to provide users with the knowledge and perspective they need to better utilize the microcomputer for project work.

Most planners do not make efficient use of available computing tools. They lack specific knowledge about particular software packages and lack perspective on which type of package is appropriate for a particular set of problems. For example, should financial planning applications be developed with a spreadsheet package or a package that employs an equation modeling framework? Other factors also hinder productivity. Most users do not properly structure their applications. This increases development time and hinders application acceptance by users other than the builder. It also reduces the range of problems that a given application can analyze. This book provides valuable information on these topics. It provides a bridge between the systems world and the planner or end-user responsible for running, maintaining, and building planning applications.

Planners come from many kinds of organizations and have varying responsibilities. Consequently, this book will discuss many types of applications and software. Discussions cover spreadsheet, database, and equation-based modeling packages and other types of application development software. The expertise of The WEFA Group gives a bias to economic analysis, and this bias will be clear in examples. However, themes covered will be common to a broad variety of planning operations and applications development. To that end, this book should be valuable to planners of many cloaks and colors, no matter what their responsibilities, backgrounds, and sponsoring firms.

Nariman Behravesh

Introduction

DAVID J. GIANTURCO

This book will help planners from diverse backgrounds and organizations better use the microcomputer to do their jobs. The book takes a unique approach by concentrating on the application of microcomputing technology in solving common planning problems. The reader will gain specific knowledge concerning microcomputer technology, planning analysis, and microcomputer-based applications development. The reader should form a framework for characterizing analysis and applications and for assessing the impacts of future technological advances.

Decision support is the analysis of issues confronting a firm or other organization and the reporting of findings concerning those issues. Typically, planners and other analysts develop and employ computer-based decision support applications to provide the best available information for managerial decisions. Utilization of decision support analysis and applications is inherent in planning operations. The design, development, maintenance, and use of computer-based applications make up a significant portion of the activities undertaken by planners. Employed applications analyze risks associated with varying market and regulatory scenarios, offer valuable information concerning competitor operations, and forecast demand for services, revenues, inventory, tax payments, cash flow, and a host of related variables. This book will help planners optimize their use of microcomputers, especially in relation to the design and construction of decision support applications.

Because of the authors' backgrounds, marketing and economic examples are stressed. However, this book does not exclude professionals working in other areas. Financial planners should also find concepts and example applications useful and enlightening. Managers can use this book to gain a better understanding of microcomputers and the work microcomputers can perform. Students should find the book useful, especially for understanding business problems and finding efficient computing solutions for those problems. Systems analysts should gain perspective on the problems facing planning departments.

The introduction of the microcomputer changed the nature of analysis and general tasks for many classes of workers. This is as true for employees of small firms as it is for employees of corporate giants, for-profit and non-profit firms, and private and public organizations. The microcomputer revolution has brought about tremendous changes. Microcomputers are accessible to a large user base. They have brought computing closer to users who do not have formal systems training, and they have increased the control users have over analysis and applications. In addition, microcomputers have changed the way in which planners and systems personnel deal with each other. The reason is straightforward. Microcomputers have changed the nature of the way planners, however defined, do their work. The data processing cycle has been broken. More than ever before, users define their computing and analytical needs, build applications, and interpret reports without the help of programmers and systems analysts. Users have more control over their data and applications development and now must shoulder greater responsibility for data and applications integrity.

Microcomputers have changed specific responsibilities for planners and their managers. Managers must understand the new computing environment before they can effectively manage personnel who perform analysis and build applications using new technology. Managers must also understand how this rapidly changing technology will shape planning activities, costs, and managerial responsibilities in the exciting years ahead.

To be sure, the nature of responsibilities of information services organizations has radically changed. These groups are struggling with a host of issues confronting them. Connectivity issues, data duplication, application integrity, software and hardware support, and a myriad of related topics come to mind.

Yet for all this change, in many other ways planning and planners have not been affected by the microcomputer revolution. The microcomputer offers many advantages, but it cannot replace the fundamental knowledge needed by planners and their managers. The microcomputer can be an excellent tool for completing the computing portion of planning analysis and decision support operations. It can help bring imagination to analysis and presentations and reduce the computing skills needed by users. However, it does not replace the need to understand data structures, data integrity, variable relationships, and analytical methodology. While the specific responsibilities of managers have changed, the most basic managerial responsibility has not. As always, managers are responsible for properly assessing the risks and benefits of employing new technologies and insuring the efficiency of operations.

This book discusses the application of the microcomputer to solve common planning problems. In so doing, data, database structure, variable relationships, modeling, and a host of similar topics are discussed. There are two objectives. The first is to offer a framework for conceptualizing planning problems. The second is to provide insight on computer-based applications and how to best employ microcomputer technology to solve these problems.

In developing material for this book, the following approach was taken. An introduction considers the organizational impacts of the microcomputer, especially as they relate to planning operations. These impacts have been significant, with sweeping changes implied for planning and systems professionals. The evolution and popularization of the microcomputer and other computing trends are driving computing responsibilities much closer to end-users. This has precipitated major shifts in responsibilities for computing tasks for both planners and systems personnel. Management's objective is to realize the full productivity benefits offered by new technologies. This will take a careful and creative management effort that recognizes the changing responsibilities of planners and systems staffs.

The rapid pace of technological development is a driving force behind the popularization of the microcomputer in planning and other departments. It becomes imperative to develop a framework for evaluating technological change at the user level and to discuss specific technologies shaping microcomputing today. The framework offered for evaluating technology views the microcomputer as the analyst's assistant. The qualities of a good assistant are paralleled with the capabilities offered by various technological innovations available for integration into the user's microcomputer system. By employing this framework, users can increase productivity by evaluating and imaginatively applying new technologies as they become available. Next, specific technologies are defined. Hardware and operating systems developments are critical factors determining the nature and speed of change in microcomputer capabilities. A review of microcomputer technology evolution and expected advances in near-term technological developments offers insight into the efficient use of microcomputers. Available and soon-to-be-available technologies are discussed at length.

Decision support applications are fundamental tools for conducting planning analysis. Planners build their own applications and can also take advantage of applications written by consultants or other departments within their firm. Employed applications consist of database management systems, spreadsheet applications, large-scale planning models employing traditional equation-based modeling formats, and industry, regional, and macroeconomic models. The middle sections of this book discuss these environments and how to design and use associated applications.

Day-to-day operations often center on the use of database management and spreadsheet products. While widely applied, these products are not well understood by most planners and other users. A section of this book provides a further evaluation of database and spreadsheet environments. First, the three paradigms of database models are discussed: the hierarchical, network, and relational models. By achieving a better understanding of these paradigms, analysts can make more efficient use of a broader range of databases. Two related topics are also discussed: distributed database operations, and the use of fourth-generation systems. There is an important controversy in computing: the evaluation of centralizing and decentralizing database operations. Discussion will shed some light on the issues surrounding this topic. Fourth-generation systems are becoming popular in many large organizations, and planning departments are no exception. Fourth-generation systems provide nonprocedural languages and analytical facilities to aid applications developers in the design and construction of efficient databases. They also provide users with advanced tools to perform simple and complex query operations and data analysis.

The ubiquitous spreadsheet is perhaps the most misunderstood tool used by analysts. Spreadsheets are applied to a wide variety of data analysis and applications development projects. However, only some of these projects are efficiently completed in this popular environment. Ancillary tools and alternative environments may offer superior facilities for completing many projects now performed in the spreadsheet environment. Material here will interest planners from almost every discipline and should provoke thought on the best means to complete various projects. Information concerning expected developments in future releases of spreadsheet products offers insight on the proper use of this environment as capabilities expand.

Advanced applications come in one of two forms: (1) complex applications built by planning or various other departments to analyze corporate operations and markets, and (2) industry, regional, and macroeconomic models. These models are usually constructed by consultants or by vendors (such as The WEFA Group). The main use for both forms of applications is risk analysis. By changing assumptions, the analyst can evaluate the risks associated with varying scenarios. Both groups of applications may also be used for forecasting. Forecasting is a difficult proposition at best, and yet forecasts are necessary for planning. Together, forecasting and risk analysis studies help corporations and other organizations prepare for uncertainties in revenues, service and product demands, costs, cash flow, and many related variables.

Two sections of this book discuss complex applications. In the first of these sections, the PCMark8 macroeconomic model of the United States economy is presented in detail. An example shows the far-reaching effects of an oil price increase. Scenario studies employing regional and industry models are performed similarly to the PCMark8 example presented here. The book's next section discusses the design and construction of spreadsheet applications, traditional planning models, and modular planning systems. Planning systems can consist of several stand-alone applications and a myriad of other applications. For example, spreadsheet-based financial applications, traditional planning models, and industry or macroeconomic models may be combined in a single planning system. Such systems provide a synthesis of diverse analysis. There can be tremendous analytical and political advantages to leveraging existing applications in the formation of modular planning systems. There are also organizational and technical concerns to weigh against these benefits.

Forecasting and econometric methods are important topics in planning. Many of the examples presented in this book have econometric foundations, and a final section serves as a general reference for topics in econometric analysis and forecasting.

The book takes a menu approach, and readers should select sections and chapters relevant to their needs. While chapters presume varying familiarity with computing concepts, most chapters are accessible to readers with limited backgrounds. Each chapter is written by an individual with significant expertise in appropriate subject matter. Chapters blend theory and practical examples to make subject matter relevant to readers' immediate needs.

Specifically, there are six sections: Section 1 explores the popularity of microcomputers and the organizational impacts precipitated by the microcomputer revolution. Microcomputers have changed responsibilities for both planners and systems personnel. This chapter offers perspective on changing attitudes and organizational structures.

Section 2 includes two chapters dedicated to the review and evaluation of advances in microcomputer-based technology. The first of these chapters does not center on specific technological advances, but instead offers a framework for evaluating technological trends. This information will aid in the evaluation of future technological developments. By properly evaluating new technologies, planners can make intelligent decisions concerning the integration of new technologies into current systems and operations. The second chapter offers a high-level review of specific developments relating to hardware and operating systems evolution. Changes in these areas greatly affect the quality, capacity, speed, and versatility of microcomputer systems and peripherals. A basic understanding of these fundamentals will aid users in the evaluation of near-term technological advances.

Section 3 offers an overview of the application of database- and spreadsheet-centered products in planning environments. Database and spreadsheet activities make up a large portion of computerized planning. The information contained in this section will help users better understand database and spreadsheet environments so they can take full advantage of available products. The first chapter reviews database theory including the structure of functional and relational databases. Further investigation centers on the use of fourth-generation systems, distributed database operations, and other selected topics. The second chapter discusses spreadsheets and their application to common planning problems. Traditional spreadsheet products are appropriate for many data analysis and applications development projects, but they are often inappropriate for complex analysis and applications.

Section 4 reviews AREMOS and PCMark8. AREMOS is an advanced econometric modeling system used for data analysis and to construct planning and other models. AREMOS is capable of solving large simultaneous equation models, and many economic and financial models are AREMOS-based. PCMark8 is the AREMOS-based microcomputer version of The WEFA Group Mark8 model of the United States economy. Macroeconomics can play a large role in determining important variables affecting firms, government agencies, and other organizations. PCMark8 scenario studies investigate simple and complex macroeconomic scenarios.

Section 5 covers the design and construction of spreadsheet applications and planning models. Detailed spreadsheet and planning applications are developed from the ground up to illustrate important concepts. Examples use Lotus 1–2–3 and AREMOS. The first chapter illustrates the need for structure in designing and building spreadsheet applications. The second chapter details the construction of a traditional planning model. A product-line forecasting equation is merged with a simplified financial model to form this traditional planning application. The third chapter uses examples from previous chapters to illustrate the construction of modular planning systems. Such systems are composed of any number of integrated stand-alone applications. Information on application prototyping and user interfaces are found in this section.

Section 6 reviews econometric modeling and forecasting. This chapter serves as a reference for econometric concepts discussed in previous chapters. For those with limited formal training in econometrics, the chapter can serve as an excellent primer. For those with more background, the chapter can serve as a review of important concepts.

ORGANIZATIONAL IMPACTS

The popularity of the microcomputer has grown for many reasons, not all related to cost. This popularity has meant changing roles for planners and systems personnel, with planners shouldering responsibilities formerly the domain of systems professionals. The data processing cycle has been broken for many management information system (MIS) projects, with users providing the computing component of decision support operations for themselves.

The planning and systems professions were changing rapidly during the introduction of the microcomputer in large organizations. These changes contributed to the popularity of the microcomputer in planning and other departments. Some of this popularity was due to cost savings, but a greater source of popularity was the independence offered by the microcomputing environment. By eliminating systems professionals from applications development, planners and analysts established their independence and accepted responsibility for data and applications integrity.

In addition to organizational impacts, Chapter 1 discusses the evolution of MIS applications and the difficulties they present. At the outset, MIS applications were treated like traditional data processing and information systems applications. Because MIS applications are fundamentally different from data processing and information systems applications, this approach failed. Understanding the differences in these types of applications is key to understanding the role of technology in the planning process.

To optimize the benefits of new technology, firms must limit discord among systems groups and other departments within the organization. Management must seek imaginative solutions to new issues brought about by the microcomputer revolution. Improper management fosters antagonism for systems support personnel, results in high computing costs, and offers little payoff for the investment made in microcomputer technology.

Organizational Impacts of Microcomputer Technology

KENNARD T. WING

Organizations are changing as a result of the introduction of the microcomputer. Making the best use of microcomputer technology requires understanding these organizational changes and the conditions that helped bring them about. This chapter discusses the planning profession, developments in computing, the role of centralized computing groups, and productivity as it relates to the introduction of the microcomputer.

PLANNING

The planning profession began changing even before the introduction of the microcomputer. Before World War II, planning could hardly have been considered a profession. The typical planning exercise consisted of managers aggregating plans created at the next lower level of the organization, changing a priority here, and padding a pet project there for a margin of safety. Because most corporations confined themselves to their core business and were not dispersed geographically, the people involved tended to have similar objectives and assumptions about the operating environment. Hence this planning format was adequate.

Following World War II, U.S. corporations experienced unparalleled growth. They grew not only in dollar terms but through diversification and multi-national expansion. The old planning method no longer worked. Groups operating in different countries or in different businesses did not share similar objectives and assumptions. Planning required the integration of diverse objectives and assumptions.

Centralized planning developed in this period and came into its own during the 1960s. An economic forecast provided a consistent set of assumptions for planning. While line managers used these assumptions to create the usual bottom-up plan, the central planner created a top-down plan. The two groups would then face off before management and defend their numbers. Typically, the central planner's numbers would be less optimistic than those of the line manager, because the line managers hoped for increased budgets based on aggressive plans. The central planner would then demonstrate why the aggressive plan was inconsistent with the required economic assumptions.

The central planning department's power was dependent on the accuracy of economic forecasts. During the halcyon sixties, centralized planning was embraced by company after company. However, beginning in the 1970s the dramatically increased volatility of the economy ruined forecast reliability and tarnished the credibility of centralized planning groups.

Many companies have expressed their disillusionment with centralized planning by eliminating once-powerful economics and planning staffs. Diversified, multi-national corporations have not yet mastered planning in a volatile world. Hence, the microcomputer entered the market when the planning function was in disarray.

COMPUTING

Planning was not the only profession experiencing changes when the microcomputer appeared in offices. MIS groups also faced fundamental difficulties. To understand this, it is first necessary to understand the nature of the evolution of technology. José Ortega y Gasset has developed a useful taxonomy to draw upon. Technological evolution can be divided into three phases: the accidental, artistic, and design phases.

In the accidental phase, the discovery of utility is unplanned—for example, Sir Alexander Fleming notices that bacteria do not grow around a speck of green mold; the manager finds that the report created to verify that accounting entries cross-foot is also useful in tracking performance.

In the artistic phase, such discovery is a starting point to extend technology. Hence, each user of a technology is a craftsman, both applying and extending the art. The potter's wheel and the woodworker's knives are examples of technology in this phase. This phase is clear in the early days of computing, when only those who could write programs were able to obtain information from computers.

A technology has matured when it reaches the design phase. In this phase the creator of the technology is not the operator of it. For example, the engineer designs a Jacquard loom, but a less skilled worker runs it. Since one weaving machine can replace many hand looms, it is in this phase that technology displaces a worker.

Corporate computing technology climbed the evolutionary ladder quite quickly. Hardware was so expensive that the emergence of specialized application designers was simultaneous with corporate computer acquisition. The early emergence of designers masked the fact that computer technology climbed the evolutionary ladder three times in response to the different types of tasks computers have performed.

The nature of these tasks is traced by the names computer groups have used to refer to themselves. When data processing (DP) was the dominant term, most applications were simply that. Basic accounting and clerical functions were moved to the computer, thereby replacing or displacing legions of clerks. The computer was a bigger and faster adding machine. The so-called high-level languages of the time were adequate for this task, and the problem solutions were well understood. It was not difficult for a systems analyst or programmer to create accounting applications which were run repetitively by computer operators. Applications generated reports that were usable by those who lacked knowledge of computers and programming.

Potential productivity gains made possible by computerization were absorbed by new armies of data entry staff. This led to a new kind of problem for computers and the requirement to once again climb the evolutionary ladder. The problem was to eliminate the need for large data entry staff by having users input the required data directly. This was the development of information systems (IS). Automated branch transactions systems and computerized cash registers are examples of this technology. The existence of the accidental and artistic phases is masked because these phases were carried out primarily by systems analysts. Nevertheless, the earliest attempts to create information systems required the intuitive and trial-and-error methods of these phases. The tremendous growth in information systems applications demonstrates the success that systems analysts had in solving this type of problem. Data processing departments evolved into information systems organizations.

The next change was the transition to management information systems (MIS). This reflected a new kind of computing problem. With the development of information systems, a tremendous mass of data was being stored electronically. Managers wanted to use computers to manipulate that data to help them make better decisions. Database management systems used to query and present data in a variety of ways provided a solution to this new problem.

While MIS applications were the most glamorous computer applications, they comprised a small fraction of the applications supervised by centralized computing departments. Data processing and information systems applications continued to dominate and grow, in part, because the new problem was not proving as tractable as its predecessors.

In both the data processing era and the information systems era, the computerization of a function meant the elimination of a job for a person performing that function. Technology had reached the design phase. Sometimes a new but different job was created in the computing function, but this changed the story only in detail. Computers were applied similarly to equipment on a shop floor to improve and automate some human function.

Systems analysts and programmers had enjoyed great success developing com-

puter systems that were repetitively run by computer operators in the data processing era and operated by employees such as bank tellers and clerks in the
information systems era. Management information systems crossed a boundary
into very different territory.

The development of management information systems proceeded under the
assumption that the design phase had been reached. Systems analysts attempted
to identify the important information needed by management and then attempted
to capture that information in applications. An example might be a linear program
created to schedule plant operations. Under the assumption that MIS was in the
design phase, one would expect that the management position of production
scheduler would be eliminated. In fact, not only do MIS programs fail to displace
management decision makers, managers tend not to rely very heavily on the
computer output.

At the time of the introduction of the microcomputer, MIS groups were organized for the design phase of technology. MIS problems were perceived to
be similar to data processing and information systems problems. Unfortunately,
management had not yet reached the design phase. Suddenly, the computer
program did not replace a human function. Rather, the user had exactly the same
job as before, presumably with some assistance in performing it. This was the
computing environment into which the microcomputer was introduced.

THE POLITICS OF COMPUTING

Intra-company politics also played a role in fostering the success of microcomputers in firms. Every human organism and organization strives for survival
and security. For a firm, the ultimate security is monopoly. This is the motivation
behind calls for government intervention such as international trade restraints,
licensing and certification, and legally mandated insurance coverage. Centralized
computing groups have typically been very successful at creating computing
monopolies within firms. These groups are usually treated on a cost-center basis—an overhead item. The business units who have made use of them do not
pay a proportional share of the support group's costs. More accurately, all
business units pay for support groups whether they use them or not. Like most
successful monopolies, computing groups developed certain characteristics. They
became bureaucratic. Backlogs in applications development became the norm.
MIS groups developed a tendency to grow, absorbing ever greater amounts of
resources. Many of their users and potential users became antagonistic toward
them, which was compounded by the limited growth of data processing and
information systems applications. As most of these had already been computerized, MIS applications appeared to represent the growth area for future electronic computing. Into this political situation, the microcomputer was introduced.

THE INTRODUCTION OF THE PERSONAL COMPUTER

The introduction of the IBM PC in 1981 marks the beginning of the large-scale use of microcomputers in major corporations and other organizations. The earliest microcomputer purchases were justified without reference to the MIS group. Typically, the return on investment was justified by staff reductions or reduced expenditures on outside services such as time-share computing. Because of the low price of the microcomputer, payback periods were seldom more than a year and sometimes less than a month.

Early microcomputer users were not transferring applications that were currently the responsibility of the MIS group. Rather the first microcomputers were used for tasks previously performed by hand or by outside services.

Early users had considered computerizing some of these functions on the in-house mainframe. Typically they had not been able to do so for a variety of cost-related considerations. For example, economic modeling required expensive software and data support, and supplemental programming was often needed. Many early microcomputer applications were either too small for MIS group computerization or of interest to too small a group relative to the costs involved.

The low cost of the microcomputer changed the economics of these decisions dramatically. Small size and specialization no longer limited the computerization of an application. At this early stage in the corporate use of microcomputers, no conflict existed between the microcomputer user and the MIS group. Each appeared to have a comparative advantage for different kinds of applications. Several trends have combined to upset this happy situation.

First, microcomputers are becoming more powerful. For example, The WEFA Group's PCMark8 model of the U.S. economy solves faster on a Compaq Deskpro-386 microcomputer than it does on an IBM 3081 mainframe computer under low usage conditions. Perhaps more than any other single item, this continued technological development threatens MIS group control.

Second, the nature of developing microcomputer (and minicomputer and mainframe computer) software is bringing computing closer to end-users. This is especially true for those involved with MIS applications and support analysis. A wide variety of advanced products are available to a broad base of users. Spreadsheet packages like Lotus 1–2–3, Boeing Calc, and SuperCalc, statistical and econometrics packages like AREMOS, Minitab, SAS, and SPSS, financial modeling packages like Javelin and IFPS, and database products like Paradox, the R:BASE and dBASE series, ORACLE, and FOCUS are just some of the products responsible for bringing computing closer to end-users. New computing products allow the user to interact with the computer. Most include interactive environments and nonprocedural programming languages, and some include natural language interfaces. MIS activities are well served by these capabilities.

Third, users and managers are consciously attempting to satisfy their computing needs without the help of systems groups. DP methods did not serve well in the MIS environment. Systems personnel interfaced with users, obtained application specifications, controlled applied software and related systems decisions, and so on. This frustrated users and their managers. Business managers perceive the microcomputer as a way to get out from under the DP backlog and out from under the thumb of MIS support groups. Microcomputer-based software is capable of handling a large proportion of analytical and applications development projects. The microcomputer itself represents complete independence from computer group control. In addition to offering simplified environments for applications development, microcomputers can operate off-line. There is no need to connect to mainframe computers for processing capabilities. Consequently, there is no need to interface with computer support groups or pay time-sharing costs and so on.

Fourth, the availability of microcomputer-based software to run specialized applications has increased. This is especially true in the banking and financial services industries.

The introduction of the microcomputer and related technology is akin to deregulation. Suddenly, consumers of computing services don't have just one place to shop. For a few thousand dollars they can have in a few weeks what they might have had to wait years for previously.

Another way of looking at this phenomenon is to think of end-users applying make-versus-buy logic to applications development. Instead of going outside for developed systems, the microcomputer allows end-users to construct applications using off-the-shelf software. This reduces both cost and completion periods. In this framework, not only has the microcomputer lowered the price of the make option, but every decision to make instead of buy gives the using group the opportunity to develop computing skills. This skill base increases the attractiveness of the make option. It also insures that the MIS group cannot continue a monopoly based on knowledge once the hardware and software monopoly has ended.

THE ROLE OF CENTRAL COMPUTING GROUPS

The role of MIS groups is uncertain, and this changing role continues to be debated at length in computing trade journals. MIS groups have fought hard and, in the main, successfully to control all computing within their organizations. Yet in the space of a few short years, microcomputers and related technology are destroying that control. Naturally, MIS groups wish to retard that trend.

Like any victim of deregulation, the computing monopolist has limited choices. One is to clamor for re-regulation. This is the approach of those MIS groups that have sought power from management to control the microcomputer and related support activities. Their plausible arguments discuss the benefits of standardization. These include system compatibility, reduced training and support costs, quantity discounts on purchases, and reduced duplication of effort. In return for these benefits, the centralized computing group wants complete control over microcomputer distribution, hardware and software selection, and support offerings.

While some of the points offered by MIS groups are valid, their approach is a cure worse than the disease. Because of the current economic environment, companies cannot afford to continue the bureaucratic monopoly in computing. They must become more competitive, and that includes making the best use of the latest information technology. Consequently, when conflicts occur between business managers who want microcomputers and centralized computing groups that want to control microcomputers, most companies will look for ways to satisfy business managers.

Some centralized computing groups employ a more enlightened approach. They accept the make-versus-buy logic of the microcomputer user and counter by increasing the desirability of buying services, products, and support from their group. Such groups may recommend, provide, and support microcomputer hardware and software; offer courses and seminars; publish a newsletter; organize user groups; and provide consultants to users. A less energetic variant of this approach merely provides advice to users when requested. Executive managements favor this approach because users get the microcomputers and support they desire, and centralized computing gets at least some of the control it desires. However, the great variation in levels of support provided by different organizations suggests there is a problem determining the optimal level of support.

Usually the MIS group remains a cost center organizationally. Hence, there is theoretically no limit to the amount of services it will seek to provide or the bargains it will offer users to keep them from going outside the firm for microcomputers and related support. Instead of economies of scale, the company can end up paying much more than necessary for microcomputer technology. Alternatively, there is no guarantee that MIS groups will be responsive to user needs. Companies are faced with a dilemma: If they give MIS groups the monopoly they desire, best advantage will not be made of the new technology. If management allows the microcomputer to break the MIS monopoly but subsidizes the MIS group's efforts to offer microcomputers and related support, the firm may spend more than necessary without guarantee of quality support.

A solution—implemented by a few firms and in fact applied to some centralized computing departments decades ago—is to make centralized computing groups profit centers, possibly allowing them to solicit business outside the corporation. Users have the freedom to acquire microcomputer technology and support either inside or outside the corporation. In either case, they must pay for what they get. In this environment there is no incentive for centralized computing groups to offer more services than users are willing to pay for. The choice users have to go elsewhere provides the guarantee of quality support—a characteristic lacking in a cost-center approach. Under this structure, companies are likely to get the greatest productivity from their investment in microcomputer technology.

MICROCOMPUTERS AND PRODUCTIVITY

How much has the investment in microcomputer technology raised productivity? This is difficult to measure. General studies measuring white-collar productivity compare the amount of capital invested per office worker to the amount of capital invested per manufacturing worker. Surprisingly, the former is beginning to approach the latter. Those who expect tremendous increases in white-collar productivity similar to that experienced in the manufacturing sector will be disappointed.

The productivity increases in the design phase are much greater than in the artistic phase. Because manufacturing has matured while management is still an art, increases in productivity like those witnessed during the industrial revolution are still in the future. A more appropriate model for microcomputer productivity would be the rise of the crafts. There are definite productivity increases over the accidental phase of technology. However, productivity increases fall short of those that would be experienced if certain aspects of management could be designed.

Further, the potential productivity of the artistic phase will not be realized until a broader base of planning group and line department personnel employs the microcomputer. Departmental computing should not belong to computing specialists, a concept adopted from the MIS group. These groups must recognize the current artistic stage of management. It is no accident that the microcomputer was introduced at a time when the design approach to MIS had revealed its weakness and hence the need to bring the individual into an artistic symbiosis with the computer.

The microcomputer would have been of limited usefulness if a professional systems designer was needed to use it. Like the potter and his wheel, the user can have a creative interaction with the microcomputer. Over time, the user learns more about both his art and his tools.

SUMMARY

In the early 1980s, economic trends forced American management to cut costs, increase productivity and competitiveness, and spark earnings growth. Tremendous increases in economic volatility led to disillusionment with centralized planning, but no new planning paradigm developed to replace it. MIS groups experienced great difficulties extending the benefits of computerization to the practice of management while new data processing and information systems applications were scarce. Centralized computing groups had evolved into large bureaucratic monopolies.

The microcomputer gained its foothold with applications that did not displace systems professionals. Over time, this technology has been applied to complex applications. Technological enhancements have deregulated computing by breaking the monopoly enjoyed by centralized systems departments. Users can choose to create applications with off-the-shelf software instead of relying on centralized computing groups to build them.

There are two basic responses available to MIS groups. The first is to try to control microcomputer technology and support and to reestablish the computing monopoly. The second is to try to accommodate users and provide them with incentives to purchase products and support from the MIS group. The former approach stunts the use of microcomputers, while the traditional cost-center status of centralized computing groups undermines the benefits of the latter approach. Perhaps the best policy is to reorganize computing groups as profit centers and let users buy products and support from whomever they please.

Even in companies with enlightened microcomputer policies, the microcomputer has not yet delivered on its promises of boosting office productivity. It will not live up to the extravagant promises now being made, for two basic reasons. First, management is in the artistic phase, not the design phase where capital equipment leads to large productivity increases. Second, most companies have fallen into the trap of relegating microcomputers to microcomputer specialists.

Microcomputers have and will continue to have organizational impacts. Analysts, managers, and firms who wish to benefit from technological change must understand new technologies and recognize the organizational impacts that result from their introduction. Policies can then be implemented to best use new technologies and manage and structure organizations to maximum advantage.

REFERENCES

Gerrity, Thomas, and Rockart, John. "Wanted: Effective Leaders to Manage End-user Computing," *Computerworld,* (September 8, 1986), 83, 86–91.

Gold, Jordan. "Models of Inefficiency, Demons of Productivity," *Computer Decisions* (May 20, 1986): 70, 72, 73, 75.

Karten, Naomi. "REMark: MIS in Eclipse." *PC World,* (June 1986): 59, 62, 66, 70.

Ortega y Gasset, José. "Man the Technician," *History As a System.* New York: W. W. Norton & Co., Inc., 1961, pp. 87–164.

Martin, James. *Applications Development Without Programmers.* Englewood Cliffs, N.J.: Prentice Hall, Inc., 1982.

MICROCOMPUTER TECHNOLOGY, EVALUATION, AND EVOLUTION

Section 1 described the organizational changes precipitated by the introduction and popularization of the microcomputer in large organizations. The rapid expansion in microcomputer capabilities was identified as a key factor affecting changes in planning and business groups. Technological advances have enabled a growing number of applications to be developed, run, and maintained by end-users on microcomputers. The complexity of some microcomputer-based applications is impressive.

The pace of technological change presents two problems: It is difficult to define and evaluate current technologies, and users face confusion in deciding just what technologies are relevant to them. How does the user evaluate new technologies as they become available? Which technologies can be integrated into the user's microcomputer system, and how? What expenditures in money and time will have the highest productivity payoffs?

To cope with the two problems presented by technological change, planners and other analysts must equip themselves with two weapons. First, these users must develop a methodology for evaluating new technologies. This methodology must provide a framework for evaluating any new technology and must be applicable over time. Next, these users must develop specific knowledge bases covering currently available technologies. This is a difficult and ongoing task. To get up to speed, the interested individual must invest a disproportionate amount of time up front. Staying current then requires a sustained effort.

This section dedicates one chapter to the development of an evaluation methodology, and another to a high-level review of current technologies. Together, these chapters define the boundaries of current technology, provide an evaluation methodology to maximize the benefits offered by technology, and discuss advances that may affect the way planners and analysts work in the future.

Chapter 2 offers a framework for evaluating technological trends. The micro-computer is seen as an assistant, and the qualities of a good assistant are discussed in relation to technological change. What changes will improve the performance of the microcomputer as assistant and in what ways? This chapter does not anthropomorphise the microcomputer, but offers an intelligent set of questions that users and managers should ask themselves when evaluating coming trends. It is also argued that maximization of benefits accruing to existing technology requires users to tailor the technology they use. The microcomputer can become a better extension of the user if the user obtains more than passing knowledge of available technology and customizes the working environment. In addition to increasing productivity, the incorporation of evolving technologies becomes easier.

Chapter 3 provides a high-level overview of currently available technologies. The chapter includes information on the evolution of these technologies and offers insight into research and new products that will affect microcomputer capabilities in the near future. The chapter centers on hardware development, but also offers information on the evolution and characteristics of relevant op-erating systems. UNIX, DOS, and the OS2 operating systems are discussed. The information in this chapter delineates the capabilities of the various classes of microcomputers employed in planning and business groups. Speed, capacity, and price/performance trade-offs are common themes.

When it comes to technological change, planners must meet the same chal-lenges as other users. The same factors affect all users, and the same approach must be taken by all users who wish to maximize the benefits of new technologies. Planners and financial analysts waited somewhat longer for their applications to migrate to microcomputers. The size and special nature of these applications slowed this migration. However, the capability to build and run large planning models on microcomputers has become feasible in the last few years. Appli-cations are the subject of later sections.

2

Beyond MIPS, MHz, and Mbytes

Interpreting Developments in Microcomputer Technology

JAMES G. WILBER

Advances in microcomputer technology documented in the trade press blaze a trail to the future. Chronicled are endless research results and new product introductions, all beckoning us to a world of more MIPS, MHz, and Mbytes, as well as new architectures, protocols, interfaces, networks, standards, buses, semiconductor processes, and so forth. All of this dynamism can be unsettling, particularly to those microcomputer users lacking a clear view of where it is taking them.

Is there any way to determine where these developments are headed? Should the microcomputer user even be concerned? A person who routinely employs microcomputers in planning should, at least as a matter of pride, have some expectations regarding the future evolution of this tool. Such expectations, based on a knowledge of microcomputer technical fundamentals, will enable the user to make this tool a more effective part of the planning process. In essence, the user will benefit from an ability to plan about planning.

What follows is an approach to interpreting microcomputer technology developments and thinking critically about the effectiveness of the microcomputer as a productivity-enhancing tool. While a few specific developments are mentioned, the intent is to avoid delivering such perishable information and instead focus on conveying a perspective—something more representative of durable goods. The best source for specific developments is, of course, periodical literature.

The balance of this chapter will present motivations for tracking technology developments, a specific set of criteria for critiquing a microcomputer environment, and insight into how certain types of developments affect the efficacy of this environment.

THE NEED TO INTERPRET MICROCOMPUTER TECHNOLOGY DEVELOPMENTS

Microcomputers are gradually infiltrating the workplace. Offering numerous advantages over mainframes and terminals, microcomputer networks appear to be inexorably gaining ground. Perhaps the primary reason for the success of the microcomputer in the office is the freedom it offers users to customize their computing environments. To the extent this freedom is not limited by contrary policies, users can select from hardware and software options to satisfy their particular preferences.

This freedom was instrumental in allowing the end-user of computing services to skirt what was typically a hopelessly backlogged corporate computing department. Having accomplished this skirting—maybe turning out a few simple spreadsheets or database searches—end-users now find themselves in a brave new world.

The first microcomputer hardware and software products have been followed by a torrent of others, each claiming to be a better mousetrap, at every conceivable combination of price and performance. Unmanaged, rapid product proliferation can transform the boon into a bane—the necessity to stay current. In this fast-paced environment, the user still turning the crank on a Model-T word processor is liable to be passed by a competitor with a keyswitch and starter motor-equipped alternative. All manner of pitfalls lay before users in evaluating products for capability, reliability, compatibility, and ease of use.

Among business managers, there is growing disillusionment with microcomputers for their perceived failure to deliver promised increases in white-collar productivity. The aforementioned freedom can also amount to a length of rope with which users can hang themselves—individually or collectively. Unsuccessful negotiation of the various pitfalls and poor integration of the microcomputer into the main flow of office work can quickly cancel potential productivity gains.

The microcomputer user can no longer be, in truth or by pretense, a naive beneficiary of computing services. Along with newfound productivity and freedom, the microcomputer user has acquired the responsibility to actively manage the computing environment. Users should not resignedly accept the specific form and function of their machines; they must continually recognize room for improvement. Realizing the microcomputer's potential for improving productivity will require an understanding of how the technology at its current level affects the tool's efficacy. To maintain optimum utilization the user will be required to follow and interpret the impact of ongoing developments.

MEET YOUR NEW ASSISTANT—THE MICROCOMPUTER

The first computers, like most machines, were basically idiots with functional specialties in which they were vastly superior to humans. A power lawnmower is terrific for cutting grass, but it must be directed every inch of the way, and it certainly can't trim hedges. The great virtue of the first computers was their speed and accuracy in performing calculations, but they were difficult to program and couldn't carry on a very good game of Space Invaders. Furthermore, they were expensive to build and operate.

Back in those early days, IBM's chief executive officer predicted that the world demand for computers would be satisfied by about six machines. What he failed to anticipate was the astounding progress to follow in electronics—the invention of the transistor and its eventual integration on a very large scale resulting in today's integrated circuits. This progress reduced the cost of raw computing capability by many orders of magnitude and thereby made many additional applications economically feasible.

This economic revolution in computer manufacturing has gradually transformed the computer-based model for solving nonscientific problems from a compucentric orientation to an anthropocentric orientation. In other words, today we have computers huddled around an individual rather than humans huddled around a single computer. The erosion in computing cost, coupled with improvements in peripheral technology, has led to the decline of batch and time-shared mainframe utilization and created today's common scenario: a dirt cheap ($5), yet powerful, microprocessor twiddling its silicon thumbs, waiting as a human reads a manual or searches for characters on a keyboard.

Economic and technological factors have shifted the computer's role from machine to assistant. Broader acceptance of microcomputers in the office will require that they become more functionally balanced than a fast idiot and become true automaton assistants.

Microcomputer Anatomy 101

Before evaluating the efficacy of our microcomputer assistant as a whole, it will be valuable to look at its physical makeup. A general understanding of the basic functional subsystems will be helpful in evaluating a specific component and its contribution to, or detraction from, the whole.

Technical discussions concerning microcomputers are inescapably peppered with abbreviations which can be baffling to the uninitiated—take MIPS, MHz, and Mbytes, for example. These three abbreviations stand for millions of instructions per second, megahertz, and megabytes. They measure performance associated with the three primary subsystems of all computers: those which process, communicate, and store information. (There also exists a fourth subsystem to do things like supply power to the other subsystems, but it will be ignored in this discussion.) The following is a description of these primary subsystems.

Processing

The core of the processing subsystem is the central processing unit or CPU. This hardware, often a single microprocessor chip, applies rules of Boolean logic to binary data elements ("1"'s and "0"'s) to compute useful results. Adding two numbers together is an example of one basic instruction (process) in a CPU's repertoire. A processor capable of computing the sum of two numbers one million times in one second is said to have 1 MIPS of computing power. This is not necessarily useful but is a hypothetical benchmark.

The computing power of a discrete microprocessor chip is sometimes misleadingly defined in terms of megahertz. What this figure actually defines is the microprocessor's characteristic clock rate, say 6 or 8 megahertz. Loosely analogous to a human heartbeat, a microprocessor's clock governs the internal operations of the device. Just as the foot speed of a human cannot be inferred from heart rate, the computing power of a microprocessor cannot be determined from its clock rate. It is true, however, that higher clock rates generally correlate with greater computing power.

A MHz figure can only be properly used to compare the computing power of different speed versions of otherwise identical processors. Different processors can require different numbers of clock pulses to execute the same instruction. For example, different processors, both clocked at 10 MHz, one requiring 4 and the other 5 clock pulses to perform a basic instruction, possess 2.5 and 2 MIPS of processing power, respectively.

Increasingly, microcomputers are being equipped with one or more additional, specialized processors, called coprocessors. Arithmetical coprocessors are optimized for performing computations on floating point (noninteger) numbers. They are often gauged in Mflops—millions of floating point operations per second.

Communication

The communication subsystem is essential to transfer information from the outside world to the processor and relay back computed results. Individual lines of communication are often referred to as channels. An important aspect of a communications channel is its bandwidth. Bandwidth is often measured in megahertz and refers to the maximum rate at which information can be transferred over the channel.

One megahertz means 1 million cycles per second, not 1 million rental cars. (Heinrich Hertz was a radio pioneer.) These cycles are some repetitive event in a continuous process such as rotation of the earth (0.0000115 Hertz) or the electrical signal oscillations that carry Channel 2 broadcasts to your television set (55.25 MHz).

The following is a list of different communications channels arranged in order of increasing bandwidth or information-carrying capacity per unit of time: smoke signals, mail, telegraph, telephone, television. The quest for channels of ever-increasing bandwidth should be evident.

Communications channels transmit information with the help of a carrier. In the case of smoke signals, for example, smoke is the carrier; the information is "blankets on sale—cheap." Carriers limit the maximum rate at which information can be transmitted. For example, the message, "teepee on fire—bring water," was probably never transmitted via smoke signals. The human voice channel, with an audio frequency carrier, would have been instinctively recognized as more suitable. For the same reason, optical fibers, which employ light as a carrier, are becoming the channel of choice for applications which require the rapid transfer of large amounts of information. The frequency of a light-wave carrier is in the hundreds of millions of MHz.

It is important to distinguish between the bandwidth of a communications channel and the actual information rate. Both can be measured in MHz. In the case of night-time morse code signaling using light pulses, the light carrier permits a high maximum rate of transfer (bandwidth), but the realized information transfer rate is much lower. (In this example, the actual rate is limited by the operator's ability to code and decode the alphabet.) Some computer-related references use the terms baud (bits per second) or data transfer rate to explicitly refer to the actual rate of information transfer.

Microcomputers process and transmit information in the form of bits (the binary digits "1" and "0"). Internally, the carriers for these transmissions are electrical signals. At the microcomputer's boundary with the outside world, various devices change the information carrier. For example, a modem modulates with information bits an audio frequency carrier suitable for telephone transmission to another, demodulating modem. (Modem is a contraction of the words modulate and demodulate.) A video display modulates visible light (electromagnetic radiation, if you must) suitable for transmission to human eyes, using information bits.

As a final point, the bandwidth of a channel can be increased by paralleling multiple channels. For example, if one wire has a bandwidth of 1 MHz, thirty-two identical wires over the same path have a combined bandwidth of 32 MHz.

Storage

The storage subsystem consists of electrical or magnetic memory components which hold information before and after processing. Two subtypes of storage are primary and secondary memory. One megabyte is 1,048,576 (2 to the 20 power) bytes or eight times that many bits of information.

Individual storage locations in primary memory, commonly known as random access memory (RAM), can be accessed quickly—on the order of one ten-millionth of a second—to either accept or supply bits of information. Individual storage locations in secondary memory, commonly either floppy or hard disk peripherals, can take over 10,000 times longer (30 milliseconds versus 100 nanoseconds) to randomly access.

A microcomputer contains both types of memory to optimize overall system performance. RAM is fast but expensive; magnetic media storage is slow but inexpensive. Frequently accessed information is kept in RAM as much as possible to speed processing. An incidental benefit of magnetic storage is its nonvolatility; unlike RAM, it remembers information after power is removed.

Components

The following list sorts commonly known microcomputer hardware components into the three subsystem categories:

Processing

    central processing unit (8086, 80286, 80386, 68020 microprocessor chips)

    arithmetical coprocessor (8087, 80287, 80387, 68881 chips)

    graphics coprocessor (TMS34010, 82786)

Communication

    video display

    keyboard

    mouse

    light pen

    digitizing tablet

    audio speaker

    printer

    optical scanner

    modem

    network links

Storage

    RAM

    hard disk drive

    floppy disk drive

    optical disk drive

    tape drive

Note that the floppy disk, optical disk, and tape drives, although listed as storage devices, are often used to communicate information to and from the microcomputer. The attractive features of these peripherals are their low cost per bit of data stored and the convenient portability of their media.

ASSESSING YOUR ASSISTANT

Evaluating the contribution to worker productivity offered by any computer is difficult because there are so many variables involved. Some of these variables can be objectively measured or compared, such as the megaquantities—MIPS, MHz, and Mbytes in their various manifestations. Others, such as ease of use and ergonomics, are more subjective and therefore harder to measure, but no less important.

In following the progress of technology developments (that is, increasing megaquantities at reduced cost), it is easy to get drawn into the thrill of the battle and forget that these are means to an end, not ends in themselves. One particular ergonomic factor may dispose a user against using some microcomputer, whatever that machine's megaquantities, thereby canceling its potential benefits. Real improvements in productivity depend on how well the user and machine are integrated into an effective whole.

It was pointed out before that the early perception and usage of computers as machines is steadily giving way to a more personal role as assistant. It is only natural as this evolution continues that efforts intended to assess the microcomputer's power gradually change their orientation. Such efforts should begin to rely less on a performance yardstick that simply measures megaquantities and adopt one that is capable of assessing human qualities. At some point, this change of yardsticks will be required to realize continued increases in the microcomputer's effectiveness.

Individuals formally evaluate one another often in terms that are appropriate for our purposes. In the following cases, the subject is evaluated relative to qualities that contribute to productive and responsible behavior: report cards, job interviews, promotion reviews, and so on. Listed below is a proposed set of criteria for evaluating automaton assistants.

1.0 WORK HABITS

    1.1 Works efficiently

       1.11 works quickly

       1.12 works accurately

    1.2 Communicates well

       1.21 expresses self clearly

       1.22 follows instructions

    1.3 Easily adapts to solving new problems

    1.4 Shows initiative

2.0 SOCIAL SKILLS

    2.1 Gets along well with others

    2.2 Is dependable

    2.3 Has high integrity

Additional criteria apply to machines.

3.0 MACHINE ATTRIBUTES

    3.1 Is inexpensive

    3.2 Is portable

LINKING MEGAQUANTITIES TO YOUR ASSISTANT'S VALUE

Preceding sections have explained the fundamental relevance of the mega-quantities—MIPS, MHz, and Mbytes—and proposed a set of criteria for evaluating the performance of a microcomputer assistant. These two ideas will be tied together by exploring the causal links between a microcomputer's endowed megaquantities and its likely performance vis-à-vis the criteria.

This section would be remiss if it failed to point out the preeminent role of software in determining the level of productivity enhancement a user may realize with any set of microcomputer hardware. At its base level of operation, a microcomputer appears a meaningless whir of binary ones and zeroes shuttling back and forth between various peripherals, storage locations, and processors. If forced to work at this level, even the most intrepid computer expert would find the microcomputer a productivity drain rather than an enhancement tool. It is only the system and application software that suppress this complexity and harness the machine's raw computing power.

The lucidity of the software creator's understanding of a problem and implementation of a corresponding solution ultimately determine the ease with which the user achieves work objectives. The application software, however, can only operate within the confines of the host microcomputer's capabilities with regard to processing, communication, and storage—the characteristics measured by the megaquantities.

Most users realize that there is a catch-22 that involves buyers and software developers for new microcomputers. Potential buyers want software available in abundance before investing in a microcomputer, and developers seek to minimize their risk by only creating software for microcomputers already sold in large numbers. For this reason, the appearance of superlative software products can lag a new hardware introduction by several years. Thus, increased mega-quantities are not necessarily important to the new microcomputer buyer for what they offer immediately but for the latitude they grant software developers to eventually create superior applications.

1.0 WORK HABITS

1.1 Works efficiently

1.11 works quickly
1.12 works accurately

Most neophyte users have no complaints about how quickly their microcomputers work. Giving someone computing power, however, is like giving a child an allowance—no matter how much you give, the child will always want more. As the user moves up the learning curve and heaps more complex and extensive problems onto the assistant, response time and attendant finger drumming grow.

Slow response time can indicate a microcomputer that is CPU bound or I/O (Input/Output) bound. The former is a case of MIPS shortage, and the latter, MHz shortage. On a single microcomputer these effects vary with the nature of the application being run.

A microcomputer is CPU bound when its communications and storage subsystems are idle during the majority of a response delay. More MIPS can be added in a variety of ways. The simplest is often to increase the CPU microprocessor's clock rate. Ordinarily, however, this will require a new chip representing improved semiconductor fabrication technology. An arithmetical coprocessor can alleviate the CPU bottlenecks that can occur in applications which require extensive calculations involving nonintegers.

Within the same semiconductor fabrication technology, processors with increased bit width—say 8 to 16 to 32 bits—possess more MIPS because they can process more bits simultaneously. The more compelling reason to increase the bit size of a 16-bit processor (for instance the de facto standard 8086 and 8088 microprocessors) is to facilitate working with expanded storage. A 32-bit design easily handles references to 4295 Mbytes (2 to the 32 power), while Rube Goldberg extensions must be added to a 16-bit design as soon as RAM exceeds 65,536 bytes (0.066 Mbytes).

Various processor architectures are being explored as means of increasing MIPS. Reduced instruction set computer architectures (RISC) are based on the premise that a few, seldom-used instructions designed into a processor's repertoire unduly slow the execution of all instructions. Using leaner, faster-running hardware, RISC designs implement the purged complex instructions when needed as sequences of simpler instructions. RISC designs can achieve a performance advantage with existing semiconductor technology without rewriting software. Parallel processor architectures seek to solve problems faster by decomposing them into subproblems which can be solved simultaneously by several processors. The problem decomposition is nontrivial and typically must be considered as the software is being written. This approach is in its infancy, but holds promise.

A microcomputer is input/output (I/O) bound when its processing and storage subsystems are idle during the majority of a response delay. Typically this problem occurs when an inherently fast processor must communicate with a slow peripheral device such as a 300- or even 1200-baud modem. If the communication need not be interactive, the CPU can be freed for other tasks by simple storage buffer hardware which slowly dispenses or accumulates bits to or from slow peripherals.

In general, I/O bottlenecks can be avoided by taking advantage of higher bandwidth communications channels. High-bandwidth coaxial cables in an Ethernet local area network, for example, permit faster data transfer than wires carrying RS-232 protocol signals. Often the higher cost of high-bandwidth channels precludes their use unless I/O bottlenecks are severe.

I/O bottlenecks can result from slow-responding storage devices. A fast processor may be forced to wait one or more clock cycles (wait states) during every access to RAM if that memory is slow to look up and store information. Similarly, a hard disk drive's response time (disk latency) may be slowed by a lumbering, mechanically driven read/write head. A mechanical drive is a very low bandwidth segment of the communication channel connecting the magnetic media to a processor. Magnetic bubble memories do not share this mechanical problem but have lower capacity at a higher cost per bit stored. These bottlenecks are MHz limitations inextricably linked to the performance of primary and secondary storage.

So-called cache memory goes primary storage one better by connecting several hundred or thousand bytes of RAM to a processor with a very high bandwidth link. Typically this bandwidth is achieved by minimizing the physical distance between the two—when possible, by placing them on the same microprocessor chip.

When speaking of digital computers, work accuracy comes with the territory. An erroneous result signals some sort of hardware or software defect. The computer's propensity for precision is not necessarily an unmitigated blessing: it can be a curse when the user is unable to precisely state the problem to be solved. This point will be covered under items 1.3 and 1.4.

1.2 Communicates well

1.21 expresses self clearly
1.22 follows instructions

Careful attention to these items is vital to the productive use of microcomputers. Communication is the glue needed to integrate the human and microcomputer assistant into an effective whole. Effective communication depends on two factors: a high-bandwidth communications channel and a common language.

To better understand the role of high-bandwidth communications, consider a face-to-face meeting between two persons. Tones of voice, rates of speech, facial expressions, gestures, postures, and physical contacts all convey information. Several channels are open simultaneously (recall that overall bandwidth is the sum of paralleled channels). The examples cited employ three of the five senses—sight, sound, and touch. Employing multiple channels is an effective way to communicate. Ask any sharp-looking, dulcet toned, firm-handshaking, fragrant, salesperson who knows a lot of good restaurants.

Look at how the typical microcomputer cripples the person trying to communicate with it: It expresses information by displaying words and numbers which must be read, and accepts information in the form of pressed keys. The primary reason for this primitive behavior has historically been the microcomputer's paucity of MIPS, MHz, and Mbytes relative to the demands of equipping it with humanlike capabilities.

The highest bandwidth input channel to a human is visual. Whoever said a picture is worth a thousand words was only talking about a rough sketch. Assuming an average of seven letters per word, each followed by a space, 1,000 words translates to 8,000 bytes. Constructing a television frame (512 x 380 pixels, with three bytes per pixel to specify color) demands closer to 4.5 Mbytes. (Pixels are the indivisible picture elements used to create an image on a video display.) In terms of computer storage, one of these pictures is worth 580,000 English words! A 10-Mbyte hard disk, which many users never fill with words, could not hold even three different still television pictures.

Adding storage capacity to the microcomputer is only part of the visual solution. High-bandwidth data paths (many MHz) are needed to update displayed images quickly and transfer them from point to point. Optical fiber networks, just being developed, will go a long way toward meeting this need. Furthermore, tremendous processing power (many MIPS) is required to alter or move parts of a single frame while keeping delays short enough for interactive applications.

The highest bandwidth output channel for a person is voice. Making a computer speak is far easier than equipping it to accept voice input. The latter requires translating sounds into words and comprehending the meaning of the words. Current microcomputer add-on systems recognize a limited vocabulary. Natural language research is attempting to manage the formidable problem of accurately extracting meaning from free-form speech.

People cut through much of the ambiguity of casual speech by understanding the context in which remarks are made—effortlessly applying vast amounts of information to separate reasonable from unreasonable conclusions. Comparable behavior by a computer is estimated to require upward of hundreds of MIPS or Mflops, even Gigaflops. The artificial intelligence field, to which this problem belongs, includes in its parlance the term logical inferences per second (LIPS) to specify the computing demands of this and similar reasoning-oriented problems.

With regard to microcomputers and humans speaking the same language, it is time for users everywhere to rise up and rebel against software, particularly applications, that force the user to first learn a cryptic language of any sort. The defense that once you learn the cryptic language, it's easy, is no defense. Paying for cryptic software is a lot like paying to have a book translated from Russian into German, then learning German so you can read it. The computer buyer appears to be voting for an intuitive, graphics-based user interface, typified by Apple Computer's Macintosh. Sales of this hardware doubled in 1986 while the overall personal computer market expanded by only 9 percent.

Microcomputers clearly will need a lot more MIPS, MHz, and Mbytes before they can express themselves on the level of television-grade pictures and can understand speech. Pessimistic and optimistic views of this situation are possible: Human/microcomputer communication is very poor, or it has so much room for improvement. The latter view is recommended and should lead to healthy anticipation of hardware with higher megaquantities.

We will be far along when a computer, listening to your instructions, senses stress in your voice and breaks in with, "Hey, did you hear the one about the

Apple, the IBM, and the clone?'' (Presumably, it would have picked this one up from someone while hobnobbing on the network.)

1.3 Easily adapts to solving new problems
1.4 Shows initiative

''Soft'' in the word software refers to the alterability of instruction sequences stored in electrical memory. This alterability confers functional malleability onto otherwise rigid hardware. Whereas the first computers were often programmed and used by the same person, increasingly complex computer systems and more widespread use have distanced the programmer and end-user. Complex software applications currently require development sequences that consist of definition, design, programming, test, acceptance, and installation phases. When the whole sequence stretches into months or years, the term software is grimly ironic to an end-user who desires a software modification. A software development model such as this makes the computer's functionality very hard. This problem varies in degree with the complexity of the application and the capability of the user.

New software development models, designed to preserve some of the softness of software for the end-user, have been introduced over the past decade or so. Different approaches include shortening the time required to execute an iteration of the development cycle and permitting the end-user to execute more of the development cycle.

Software prototyping is an approach which attempts to achieve a better final result by executing more iterations, with less time per iteration. This objective is accomplished by quickly implementing a skeleton system and then fleshing out the functionality with each iteration. The strength of this approach is that the look and feel of the final product are evident early on when major changes are easier to make.

Other approaches to preserving software softness include spreadsheets, fourth-generation languages, and expert systems. In essence, these approaches all make the computer programmable on a conceptual level that is closer to the problem being solved than the nuts-and-bolts operation of the computer. Here, the end-user creates a what-level expression of the desired results. The application, rather than a conventional programmer, then translates this expression into a how-level instruction sequence demanded by the computer.

The familiar spreadsheet program is a generalized application which permits final definition of tabular accounting solutions by an end-user. Alternatives such as this to the conventional development model do not necessarily represent straight-ahead progress in improving productivity. Here's an excellent illustration of the potential pitfalls: A building contractor used a spreadsheet to prepare a project bid. The contractor made a structural error in developing his spreadsheet and consequently underbid by $100,000. In the end, he lost at least as much as he had saved by not hiring a programmer to prepare the software. Presumably, a programmer would have better understood the necessity to test and otherwise debug the software.

Fourth-generation languages are designed to permit easier access to information stored in database form. They allow the end-user to express information requirements in a simple way. Some, for example, have the user build a pro forma model of a desired financial report which the application fills in with database information and calculations.

Expert systems are an example of artificial intelligence (AI) programming. A simplified explanation of the difference between conventional and AI programming is that, in the former case, all lines of reasoning about the solution of some problem are explicitly coded in advance of program execution. AI software, on the other hand, is equipped with rules of logic which it combines using an inference engine to form lines of reasoning each time it executes. Every expert system has a knowledge base which contains facts and rules for reasoning about a problem domain, such as blood disease diagnosis.

A great strength of the knowledge-base/inference-engine scheme is its easy extendability. For example, the discovery of a new disease would require only simple additions to the knowledge base; whereas a conventional programming approach would require merging newly written code with existing code. This merging activity is dangerous for its potential to adversely affect other sections of code, so it would have to be followed by thorough retesting. Expert systems are, in addition, able to reason forward and backward—in other words, draw conclusions from knowledge or, given a hypothetical conclusion or goal, determine whether facts and rules support it.

These systems are able to incorporate probability factors into their rules so that, like human experts, they can solve problems with imprecise input information and imprecise answers. Such a system, for example, might conclude that, based on available information, there is a 60 percent chance that a patient has disease X; a 30 percent chance the patient has disease Y; and a 10 percent chance that the symptoms are due to other causes.

Returning to criteria items 1.3 and 1.4, we can conclude that software applications, from the end-user's point of view, are growing more adaptable. It is not an exaggeration to state that the adaptability of the spreadsheet which enabled nonprogrammers to solve all sorts of numerical calculation problems helped usher in the age of the microcomputer. AI software techniques promise to endow computers with capabilities approaching initiative. With access to a large knowledge base, and an expression of a user's long-range goals, a reasoning system could independently explore means of achieving those goals. Proponents of AI say this will happen in our lifetime; opponents say it will never happen. All agree that any meaningful reasoning capability will demand substantial amounts of MIPS and Mbytes.

2.0 SOCIAL SKILLS

2.1 Gets along well with others

2.2 Is dependable

2.3 Has high integrity

The social skills are influenced little by megaquantity technology developments but are, nonetheless, important aspects of the microcomputer assistant's performance. The microcomputer's ability to get along well with others refers to the ease with which it is integrated into a heterogeneous world of computers and communications devices.

Summarized earlier was the evolution of the dominant computer-based problem-solving model from compucentric to anthropocentric. This evolution is rapidly progressing toward what might be characterized as an anthropocentric/networked stage. Apparently driven by a philosophy that no computer is an island, a rush is on to link computers around the office, country, and world. Inter-computer communication channels include local area networks (LANs), dedicated microwave channels, the telephone network, satellites, and others.

Compatibility is of primary concern in interconnecting these devices. Standards defining communication protocols are frequently established both by dominant market players and by official standards organizations. Standards can facilitate progress when they bring order to chaotic incompatibility, but standards can also impede progress when they discourage acceptance of superior performance. The microcomputer user must often weigh the need for performance against the need to avoid risk in considering new products or whole new microcomputer systems.

A dependable computer is there when you need it. The reliability of both hardware and software always follows a learning curve with the introduction of new technology. This effect should always be factored into productivity improvement forecasts. The user should be aware of inherent reliability limitations of the system. For example, data backups are an essential discipline; a user should design a microcomputer system that will minimize their inconvenience.

Finally, a high-integrity microcomputer system will support controlled access to the valuable information stored in it. Security is growing in importance with increasing interconnection of microcomputers. Again, the user must assume the responsibility of understanding the vulnerabilities of the computer assistant and take precautionary measures.

3.0 MACHINE ATTRIBUTES

3.1 Is inexpensive

3.2 Is portable

This section deals with criteria associated primarily with machines, although there are remote human parallels. Progress in electronic technology is largely centered today around the manufacture of integrated circuits (IC). Integrated circuit technology might well be called the great facilitator of the computer revolution. It does not simplify electronic circuitry, but rather encapsulates extremely complex solutions into packages of reduced size, weight, and power consumption. In addition, these packages offer greater reliability, durability, and proprietary design protection than conventional circuitry.

The great complexity of these devices typically entails a long, expensive design process that must be amortized with large sales volumes to keep unit prices competitive. Raw material cost per device is just a few cents—the most common IC base material is silicon, the most abundant element on earth. A variety of materials, designs, and fabrication processes are used to create devices with different combinations of performance characteristics. Greater operating speed, for instance, is typically traded off against greater power consumption.

The nature of the integrated circuit design problem is surprisingly similar to that described for software development—a long development cycle that distances specialized implementers and end-users. The common theme is complexity. Not surprisingly, the major thrust in integrated circuit computer-aided design (CAD) today is enabling the circuit end-user to design circuits with a minimum knowledge of IC fabrication. Silicon compilers are an embodiment of this work, translating circuit designs into geometric layout masks—the blueprints used in fabricating ICs. They are the spreadsheets of the IC design world.

LOOKING TO THE FUTURE

Presented here is a list of areas in which microcomputer technology is expanding the frontiers of MIPS, MHz, and Mbytes. The planner needs to better understand how specific developments in these areas will influence the microcomputers of tomorrow.

- Processing
  gallium arsenide
  x-ray lithography
  optical computing
  parallel architectures
  neural networks

- Communications
  fiber optics
  Integrated Services Digital Network (ISDN)
  cellular communications
  voice input and output
  optical scanners

- Storage
  VLSI circuit fabrication
  optical disks
  molecular computer elements

• Software
  expert systems
  natural language interfaces
  graphics-based interfaces

Someone has estimated that 80 percent of the scientists that ever lived are alive today. It would appear reasonable to expect continued geometric expansion of our knowledge of the world around us, including steady progress in computer processing, communication, and storage. With unlimited MIPS, MHz, and Mbytes, what then will limit our productive use of automaton assistants? The answer—with due respect to the microcomputer helping me prepare this text—"Only human imagination."

3

Microcomputer Technology

MARTIN KATZ

Even if you are a veteran programmer or analyst, it is unlikely that the first generation of microcomputers will be familiar. Introduced about 1974, the first machines such as the Altair 8800 had only 1K of memory and came in kit form. Programs were loaded by means of a front panel of switches, and the register lights displayed results. In later models, memory increased to as much as 8K, and programs could be stored on audio cassettes. The software consisted of all that the user was capable of writing—in machine language.

The second generation of hardware was introduced in 1978. These computers included the Apple II, TRS-80, and Commodore PET. They had as much as 64K of memory and were based on 8-bit microprocessors such as the Zilog Z80 and the Intel 8085. A keyboard became the means of input, and a monitor or television screen replaced the register lights. Floppy disk drives became available which could hold about 100K bytes of information. A BASIC interpreter allowed these machines to be used by almost anyone who had knowledge of programming, but the limited memory and slow speed restricted their use to very simple applications. Few microcomputers were found in the business environment.

Three years later, the IBM PC was introduced. This third-generation hardware quickly developed into a machine with a possible 640K bytes of memory, hard disk storage, high-resolution color graphics, and software for almost every application. Within two years, this machine became the standard for both the computer industry and the corporate environment.

Today, microcomputers based on processors such as the Intel 80386 approach the power of large mainframe systems. The microcomputer is as much a part of the manager's desk (at the office and at home) as the calendar and telephone. The corporate planner hardly needs to be a computer scientist to use a word processing package or electronic mail. However, many analysts using spreadsheets or doing forecasting have only a minimal understanding of the technology sitting at their fingertips. A better understanding of microcomputer hardware and software will allow both more efficient data management and the development of effective tools to provide timely information for corporate decision-making.

This chapter provides the material for an understanding of microcomputer hardware and operating systems, especially microcomputers based on the Intel 80386 microprocessor using the OS/2 operating system. The chapter provides the analyst with an awareness of the technological innovations that will affect planning.

HARDWARE FUNDAMENTALS

A computer can be organized into four functional units: central processing unit (CPU or processor), memory, input/output (I/O), and mass storage. The CPU performs the instructions described by a program. Programs and data are held in main memory during execution and are stored permanently on mass storage devices such as a hard disk. The input/output units such as the keyboard and monitor provide communication links between the computer and the outside world. Information is passed between the units of the computer on transmission channels called buses. The microcomputer is distinguished from other computers by its central processing unit, a microprocessor (see Illustration 3.1).

Central Processing Unit

A microprocessor is a central processing unit which is implemented in a single circuit element called a chip. The CPU is composed of two functionally distinct units: the control unit and the arithmetic and logic unit. The control unit (CU) fetches, interprets, and performs the instructions in memory which make up a program. The arithmetic and logic unit (ALU) performs the mathematical functions such as addition and subtraction and the primitive logical operations AND, OR, and NOT.

The microprocessor operates by comparing voltage levels or states. These levels are usually referred to as LOW and HIGH, or OFF and ON. The most elementary unit of electronic memory also stores information encoded as OFF or ON states. The two-state electronic representation of OFF or ON is analogous to the binary number system in which a digit is represented as 0 or 1. Since a binary digit can represent the state of the basic electronic memory element, the binary number system can represent information stored in a computer. Both the binary digit and the elementary memory unit are called a bit. A group of eight bits is called a byte. The notation K represents 2^{10} or 1,024, which is a convenient number in binary mathematics for making notation easier. For example $2^{16} = 65,536$ which is more easily expressed as 64 times 1024 or 64K.

A register is a set of bits within the CPU which serves as a fast-access memory for processor operations. Microprocessors are distinguished by the number of

Illustration 3.1
The Microcomputer System Architecture

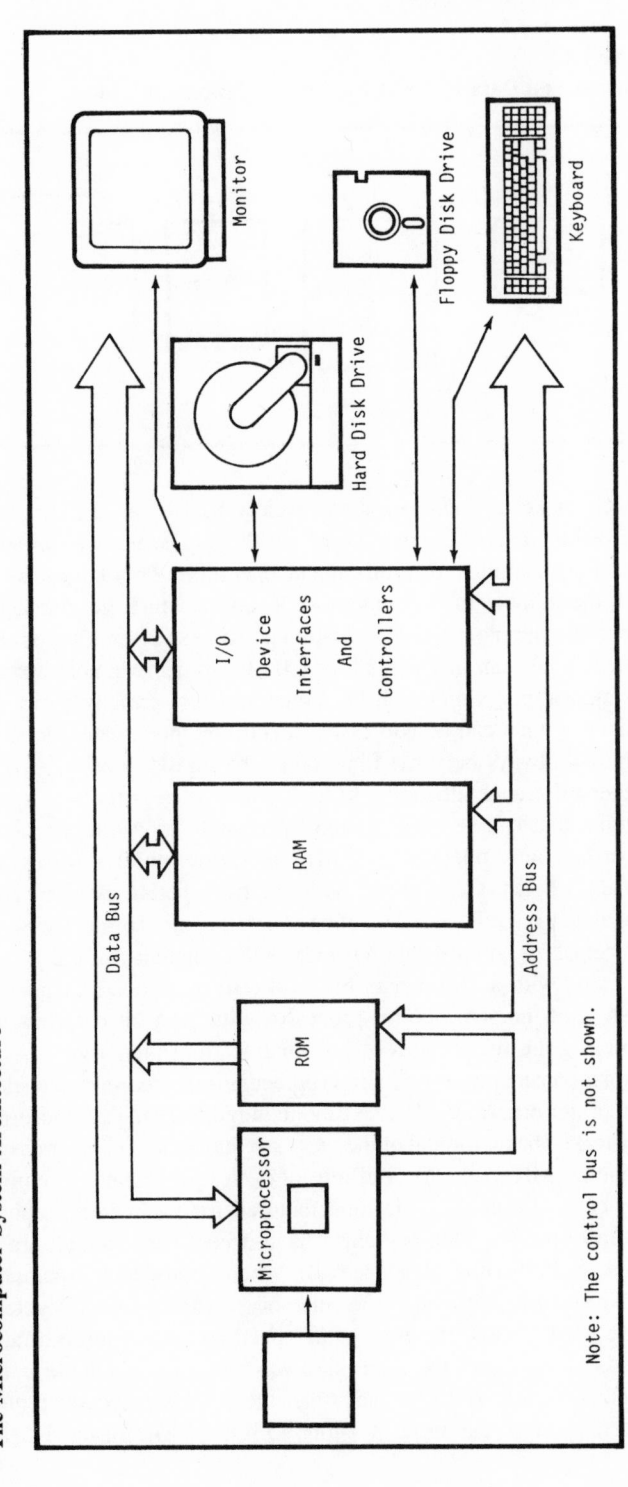

Monitor

Hard Disk Drive

Floppy Disk Drive

Keyboard

Data Bus

I/O
Device
Interfaces
And
Controllers

RAM

Address Bus

ROM

Microprocessor

Note: The control bus is not shown.

Illustration 3.2
Components and Data Flows of the Central Processing Unit

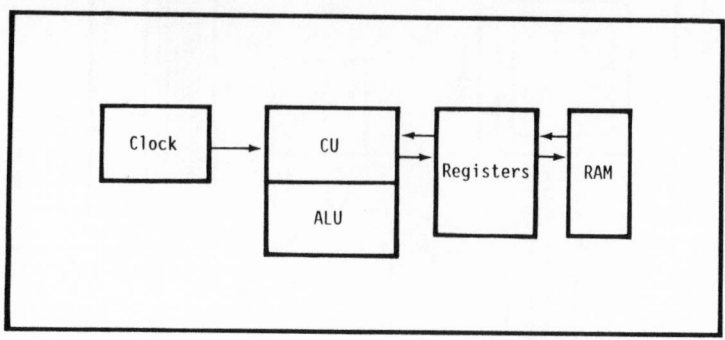

bits which make up their registers, usually 8, 16, or 32. This is because the number of bits a register has determines the largest number which can be represented and manipulated in an integer operation. This largest integer also determines the number of main memory locations which the register can directly address. For example, an 8-bit register can address 2^8 or 256 possible locations. A 16-bit register can address 2^{16} or 64K locations. Memory management and address algorithms, which will be discussed later, actually allow a CPU to use more memory than can be addressed directly by the register alone, but memory capacity will always be some function of the register size.

Another difference attributed to the number of register bits is the amount of information that can be manipulated by a single processor operation. An 8-bit processor can only operate on 1 byte at a time while a 16-bit processor can manipulate 2 bytes. Generally it will take two operations of an 8-bit processor to manipulate the equivalent data of one operation of a 16-bit processor. However, the number of bits on the data bus affects the efficiency of the processor. A 16-bit processor with a 16-bit data bus will retrieve 2 bytes of information in an operation. But the same 16-bit processor with an 8-bit data bus will take two steps to bring the full 2 bytes of information from memory.

The final consideration in the microprocessor discussion is the clock rate. The duration of a processor cycle (the time required to change the information stored in a register) is the reciprocal of the processor clock rate. Clock rates are measured in megahertz (MHz) which is millions of cycles per second. The processor clock rate can be no faster than the time required for the memory chips to store or retrieve information. Memory chips have access times which are measured in nanoseconds (billionths of a second). When a processor operates faster than information can be retrieved from memory, extra processor cycles called wait states are used to slow the processing speed and allow more time for memory access. As an example, the Intel 8086 was originally available in a 5 MHz and an 8 MHz version. With one wait state, the 5 MHz processor requires memory chips having an access time of 440ns to 490ns. The faster 8 MHz processor with one wait state requires 215ns to 265ns access time. Use of the faster processor increases computing speed by 60 percent, but the faster components required by the 8 MHz processor were significantly more expensive when the PC was introduced.

Memory

Although memory can refer to any component of the computer which can store information, this explanation will limit the definition to electronic memory. The term mass storage refers to devices, such as the hard disk, which provide permanent storage of large amounts of information.

Memory is the area where both program and data are stored. Random access memory (RAM) allows for both reading and writing of information. Read only memory (ROM) can only be read and is used to store fixed instructions such as those required to load the operating system from disk. Memory is organized into words based on the number of bits in the CPU registers. Thus the normal word size is 2 bytes for a 16-bit processor, 4 bytes for a 32-bit processor.

RAM is the memory in which a program is stored during execution. The control unit of the processor retrieves the program instructions from RAM for decoding and execution. Data are stored in RAM for processing by the arithmetic and logic unit. Because the direct use of this memory by the central processing unit requires fast read-and-write cycles, RAM is relatively expensive.

Two types of RAM chips are currently available: static and dynamic. Static RAM (SRAM) chips retain data as long as power is supplied. Once data are stored in SRAM, no further action is required by the CPU. In contrast, dynamic RAM (DRAM) chips use capacitors which, like batteries, store electricity—but only temporarily. Before the electric charge is gone, the capacitors need to be recharged. This recharging is called refreshing and must be done every 4 milliseconds with today's chips.

Because refreshing requires additional circuitry and overhead in terms of cycle time, DRAM is slower than SRAM. DRAM chips have been used on most microcomputers until recently because they are smaller and, more important, significantly cheaper than SRAM even with the additional cost of refresh circuitry. However, the speed requirements of the Intel 80386 and most recent 10 and 12 MHz Intel 80286 processors require 70 nanoseconds or faster memory access time that is only available with SRAM.

Coprocessors

Coprocessors are designed for efficiency in a specific task such as managing input/output or performing floating-point mathematical operations. They operate in conjunction with the main processor and can yield dramatic increases in system performance. For example, the Intel 8087 math coprocessor works with the 8086/8088 processor. This 80-bit processor is designed for high speed, extremely accurate floating-point mathematical operations. Without the math coprocessor, these operations are performed by software using logical operations and integer arithmetic to emulate floating-point instructions. The 8087 performs these operations up to 100 times faster than the 8086 and with accuracy greater than most mainframe processors. Intel 80287 and 80387 coprocessors are available for their respective 80286 and 80386 processors.

Many corporate planning functions involving financial or econometric modeling are based on techniques such as multiple regression. These analyses can expect significant improvements in both computational speed and accuracy with the math coprocessor. The actual increase depends on the efficiency of the program code in using the coprocessor and on the nature of the data and data manipulations. Benchmarks are the only method of comparing the performance of alternative software for a specific application.

The Intel 8089 is an input/output coprocessor which works in conjunction with an 8086 or 8088 processor and controls the I/O functions allowing the main processor to perform other tasks. The combination of the 8089 coprocessor with the main processor results in concurrent high-speed processing of data and printing. Coprocessors for graphics, string comparison, local area networking, and communications are currently available. Coprocessors designed for functions such as text processing and database management are expected soon.

Buses

A bus is defined as a set of communication lines which passes information among the units of the computer. The communication lines perform three functions: transmitting data, carrying addresses, and carrying synchronization signals. The data bus transmits data among the components of the computer, for example, between the CPU and memory. The information on the address bus specifies a location which is either the source or destination of the information on the data bus. The control bus carries synchronization signals and status information between the CPU and other devices.

The impact on the efficiency of the CPU by the number of bits transmitted simultaneously on the data bus has been previously discussed. The Intel 8086, a 16-bit processor with a 16-bit data bus, will retrieve 2 bytes of information in an operation. In contrast, the Intel 8088, the same 16-bit processor but with an 8-bit data bus, will take two steps to bring the full 2 bytes of information from memory. IBM built its original PCs with the Intel 8088 processor because it was less expensive to design and build a system using the prevalent 8-bit bus components. The 16-bit processor was needed to support a workable memory size and instruction set. In contrast, the Compaq Deskpro was designed for the 8086 processor and featured a 16-bit bus as do all 80286-based machines.

To tap the power of the 80386 processor, Compaq designed the Deskpro-386 with a 32-bit bus for memory access. This machine retained the 16-bits on other transfers for compatibility with existing hardware. However in designing the new PS/2 series, IBM developed a completely new bus designated as the Micro Channel. The Micro Channel supports full 32-bit transfers on all operations in PS/2 80386-based systems.

The data bus has an even more significant impact because it defines the architecture and therefore the performance of the whole computer system. A CPU may be designed using one, two, or three data buses. The rationale for differing designs lies in balancing the efficiency of the system with cost. A single bus system is less costly to design and build but is slower in transmitting information. The triple bus system provides maximum transmission efficiency but is very expensive to design and build. The following example demonstrates the efficiency of a three bus versus a one bus system.

Recall that the ALU performs arithmetic and logical operations on data which are received on the data bus. In general these operations are performed on two input variables producing an output variable (or result). For example, two variables J and K are added to produce result I as in this line of code: $I = J + K$. The following steps might be performed by the ALU in executing this line of code:

1. FETCH THE VALUE OF J TO THE ALU
2. FETCH THE VALUE OF K TO THE ALU
3. ADD THE TWO VALUES
4. STORE RESULTING VALUE IN I.

With a single bus architecture, all data transfers between CPU registers and the ALU are carried on the same bus which requires that the data bus be multiplexed. Multiplexing is a time-division scheme which allows the bus to perform a different function within an allocated time period, like this:

1. TRANSMIT THE VALUE OF J TO THE ALU IN TIME PERIOD 1
2. TRANSMIT THE VALUE OF K TO THE ALU IN TIME PERIOD 2
3. TRANSMIT THE VALUE OF I TO MEMORY IN TIME PERIOD 3.

The triple bus architecture uses two input buses to the ALU which allows the simultaneous transmission of inputs J and K. The result I is transmitted on a third bus which allows the inputs for the next operation to be transmitted to the ALU on the free input buses.

This architecture is the most efficient in terms of transmission efficiency and speed but requires three sets of physical channels. In a microprocessor this takes up space on the chip and makes production more critical and costly. Most microprocessors have been designed around a single bus. However, as demands for processing speed increase, designs will shift to the triple bus architecture.

Mass Storage

Recall from the previous discussion on memory that RAM is volatile—in other words, information is lost if power is removed. Mass storage devices such as magnetic tape, floppy disks, and hard disks allow permanent, nonvolatile storage of information. Tape and floppy disks also serve as media for the interchange of data between machines.

A floppy disk drive is found on almost every microcomputer and is the standard medium for data exchange and software distribution. The floppy disk is a thin plastic disk with a coating of magnetic material. Two sizes have become industry standards: the 5 1/4-inch disk which is usually encased in thin plastic and the newer 3 1/2-inch disk which has a rigid plastic case.

The 5 1/4-inch disk in the double-sided double-density (DSDD) format can hold about 360K bytes of information while the quad-density format holds about 1.2 megabytes. A megabyte (MB) is one million bytes. The 3 1/2-inch disk in the DSDD format can hold about 720K bytes of information while the quad-density format holds about 1.44MB. Note that when referring to mass storage, K usually means kilo (i.e., 1,000) rather than 1,024 as used with main memory.

The hard disk (fixed disk) is made of aluminum alloy coated with magnetic material and is rigid unlike its plastic counterpart. This technology covers a wide range of devices that hold from 10MB to 350MB or more. To put some perspective on these numbers, a DSDD 5 1/4-inch floppy disk holds about 200 double-spaced pages of text. In comparison, a 350MB drive holds about 193,000 pages. Data stored on the hard disk are accessed between five and twenty times the rate of a floppy resulting in a significant increase in computing speed.

Both types of disks are similar in operation. The floppy disk is inserted into the drive where it is clamped between the pressure pad and the read/write head. It rotates at 300 revolutions per minute while the read/write head moves over the surface, retrieving information. The low number of revolutions per minute (rpm) is required because of the friction and mechanical wear from stabilizing the flexible disk. The hard disk is more rigid and inherently stable allowing 3600 rpm or more which increases the information transfer rate. The read/write head moves just above the surface which, in conjunction with a more sensitive magnetic material on the disk surface, allows for higher density packing of information. Because of the critical tolerances in the hard disk, the slightest amount of contamination or physical shock can cause the system to crash. This sensitivity requires the mechanism to be sealed in an airtight case and shock mounted, thus eliminating interchange among machines.

The sensitivity of the hard disk has made backup essential to maintain data integrity. Considering the constantly increasing capacity of these drives, this is no trivial task. With a small drive, a backup can be accomplished with floppies, but a 10MB drive takes about 25 DSDD floppies for a complete backup. Magnetic tape provides an alternative for archival storage which is easier and may prove more economical.

Reel-to-reel magnetic tape has historically been the mainframe standard for data interchange, backup, and archival storage. Although reel-to-reel tape has been available for the microcomputer, the extremely high cost of both the drive and medium has precluded interest in the user community. In contrast, cassette and cartridge tape drives are relatively inexpensive and reliable. They are excellent devices for the backup of almost any size hard disk.

Cassette tape, 0.15-inch wide, is physically identical to the familiar audio cassette. The tape itself is optimized for digital rather than analog recording. This is generally a low performance medium with a capacity of 1 to 5 megabytes. The tape cartridge uses either 1/4- or 1/2-inch tape with respective capacities of 5 to 60MB and 100 to 350MB. Cartridges are usually preferred because they control tape tension, alignment, and contamination better than cassettes.

A system which combines the advantages of both the floppy and hard disk is the Alpha 10 cartridge developed by Iomega Corporation. This is a plastic cartridge which houses a mylar floppy disk. In contrast to both the floppy and hard disk drives, the Alpha 10 disk spins over a stationary plate. The read/write head protrudes from a slot in this plate. As the floppy disk spins over the stationary surface, it is drawn to the read/write head and stabilized by negative air pressure. Since the disk flies over the head, any disturbance causes the disk to rise and move away from the head. The physical damage caused by a head crash in the traditional drive cannot occur.

The Iomega system based upon the Alpha 10 drive is called a Bernoulli Box. These systems are configured with 5, 10, or 20MB cartridges and either one or two drives per unit. The cartridges provide a medium of data interchange between similarly equipped machines, a secure method of data storage, and an easy method of backup for the smaller hard drives.

The most recent advances in mass storage involve the use of optical rather than magnetic technology. A laser can be used to record and read information on a light-sensitive medium. The laser beam can be focused to a diameter of 1 micrometer which results in a recording density of 100MB on a 12-centimeter disk. This is the same disk and basic technology of the digital audio compact disk (CD) player. Mainframe optical systems are being developed using 12- or 14-inch disks that can store over a gigabyte of data. A gigabyte is 1000MB—about 500,000 double-spaced typed pages.

The drawback to the current optical technology is that it is a permanent write procedure. Once information is written, it cannot be overwritten or erased. This drawback will probably be overcome in the near future as much research appears to be concentrated on the development of an erasable medium.

An interesting alternative to the optical disk is storage on optical cards. A system has been developed that can store 2 megabytes on a credit-card-sized medium. It is expected that 20 megabytes of storage will soon be possible with this system.

ADVANCED CONCEPTS

Microprocessor Design

Several concepts can be incorporated into the microprocessor that will significantly improve performance regardless of the system bus architecture. The

CPU can be designed with instruction-pipelining or look ahead. With this technique the CPU is designed to prefetch a set number of instructions from memory that follow the instruction that is under execution. These instructions are fetched and stored in a special high-speed instruction RAM while the CPU is simultaneously executing instructions. Some processors are capable of simultaneously executing an instruction, decoding the following instruction, and fetching yet another instruction from the high-speed RAM. In either case, if the instruction under execution does not result in a branch, an improvement in speed occurs.

A second technique called memory interleaving organizes memory into logical sections called banks. Consecutive addresses are stored by cycling through the banks (i.e., the first address is stored in the first bank, the second address in the second bank, and so on). Because of the manner in which DRAM chips are refreshed, this technique results in faster effective memory access times. More sophisticated interleaving techniques allow the simultaneous fetching from each bank resulting in very fast access of consecutive memory locations.

The last technique in this discussion is called cache memory, which is the use of a very fast memory buffer directly connected to the CPU. A memory buffer is a temporary storage area which holds data needed for the next operation. The CPU uses the high-speed buffer as a primary memory for both the program under execution and the data accessed by that program. Memory management hardware copies information from main memory into the buffer as required. The contents of the buffer, if changed, are written back to main memory when no longer needed. Again, the result is very high speed execution if the main memory accesses are minimized.

Operating Systems

Advanced concepts such as multitasking and multiprocessing are most easily introduced by tracing the evolution of the mainframe computer. Since each advancement in hardware technology required a corresponding development in the operating system, they will be discussed together in this section.

An operating system is a set of programs that directs the overall processing operations of a computer. The operating system serves as an interface between an application program (such as Lotus 1–2–3) and the microcomputer hardware. In early mainframe computers, one program was executed at a time. As the speed of CPU, I/O, and mass storage increased, hardware resources became idle during the execution of a program. For example, the CPU would wait for printing to finish before resuming computation, and while the CPU was occupied, the printer was idle. In effect, the CPU and I/O devices were idle 50 percent of the time during the execution of a typical program.

Data Channels and Interrupt Structures

The data channel served as the first step to increased efficiency. The data channel is a hardware device that accepts I/O commands from the CPU and then controls I/O operations. The CPU can then proceed with computations until another I/O operation is required. If the data channel has not completed the previous I/O operation, the CPU might still have to stop computation while waiting until the channel is free. The data channel is thus an early and much simpler conceptualization of an I/O coprocessor such as the Intel 8089, and a first step toward simultaneous operations.

The development and implementation of an interrupt structure was required to better use the potential for simultaneous processing. An interrupt is a signal from a device such as a data channel which in this case would indicate that the device is free to accept more printing. If the CPU has been designed with status registers, it can save the task on which it is currently working, respond to the interrupt by sending more output to the printer, and then restore the previous program for continued processing. Even with data channels and interrupts, the CPU will remain idle waiting for a free channel if the program has a large number of I/O operations.

These hardware developments provide the necessary foundation for the development of multiprogramming operating systems which concurrently run two or more programs in memory. With multiprogramming, if the CPU is waiting for the current program's I/O, processing switches to another program. This switching increases the efficiency of both CPU and I/O operations as a whole. However, the execution time for any single program may increase when compared with execution on a dedicated processor.

Multitasking

Multitasking is the concurrent processing of several tasks by a single CPU. (This process was originally termed multiprogramming. The term multitasking is now more generally used in both mainframe and microcomputer literature.) Only one task is being performed by the processor at any given time, but processing is alternating among tasks required by the programs which are under execution. Other forms of multitasking include time-slicing and windowing. With time-slicing, each of a number of users' programs is allowed a given amount of CPU time in succession, thereby creating a time-sharing environment. With windowing, each of a single user's different tasks under execution is given an area on the microcomputer screen. Windowing is especially important in integrated packages where different tasks may include word processing, spreadsheet operations, and graphing.

Multiprocessing

Multiprocessing is the use of more than one processor to simultaneously perform a set of different tasks. The concept of multiprocessing was introduced in the discussion of the Intel 8089 I/O coprocessor. Recall that the 8089 coprocessor works in conjunction with the 8086 processor and controls the I/O functions while the main processor is performing other tasks. The combination of the 8089 with the main processor results in the simultaneous high-speed processing of data and I/O.

Multiprocessing can also refer to the processing of multiple independent tasks by more than one CPU as is often found in the mainframe environment. An example is on-line transaction processing in which two or more CPUs are dedicated to real-time banking transactions. These machines access a common database on shared mass storage, but one CPU may handle teller windows while the other is responsible for automated teller machines.

Parallel Processing

Multiprocessing has just been defined as the use of multiple processors to perform a set of different tasks. Parallel processing, in contrast, is the use of multiple processors to perform a single task. Many scientific and engineering problems consist of sets of computations which can be performed independently. More specifically, most matrix mathematics consist of sets of independent elementary operations—for example, the multiplication of two matrices:

$$C = A \times B$$

where

$$A = \begin{vmatrix} 1 & 2 \\ 3 & 4 \end{vmatrix} \quad \text{and} \quad B = \begin{vmatrix} 5 & 6 \\ 7 & 8 \end{vmatrix}$$

consists of four sets of independent operations:

$$C_{11} = (1 \times 5) + (2 \times 7)$$
$$C_{12} = (1 \times 6) + (2 \times 8)$$
$$C_{21} = (3 \times 5) + (4 \times 7)$$
$$C_{22} = (3 \times 6) + (4 \times 8)$$

Each of the four elements of C can be solved independently and simultaneously by four independent processors speeding computations by a factor of close to four. Now consider the case in which A and B are each 100 x 100 and the multiplication of these two matrices consists of 100 sets of elementary operations. In this situation the use of 100 independent processors would speed the computation by a factor close to 100.

Parallel architecture computers are under development by a number of universities and manufacturers. Some current designs are based on multiple microprocessors sharing a common memory. The coordination of multiple processors both in terms of hardware and software is extremely difficult. Neither a programming language, which will translate mathematical problems to independent parallel computation, nor an operating system, which will manage multiple processors, has been developed. Thus these machines are only useful for a small set of complex scientific problems. However, their applications will broaden.

Virtual Memory

RAM was historically expensive in terms of both real cost and relative cost per bit as compared with mass storage devices. At first, programmers were required to segment code into subroutines and use various techniques to fit large programs into available memory. In the early 1970s, memory management techniques were developed which allow programs to be stored on disk, divided into segments called pages, and swapped in and out of memory automatically. These techniques of virtual memory enable very large programs and very large amounts of data to be processed in a much smaller amount of memory than a completely resident program, yet are transparent to the programmer.

As a simple example of how virtual memory operates, assume a program has been compiled and resides in a disk file. This compiled program requires 300 memory locations—one location for each of 250 instructions and 50 locations for a data array. The instructions would start at address 1 and end at address 250, while the data would start at address 251 and end at address 300. However, our computer only has 100 locations of usable, real physical memory—a classic example of trying to put three pounds of dehydrated cow manure into a one-pound bag.

The virtual memory system must first allocate real memory locations 51–100 for the data array which leaves locations 1–50 available for the program. The first 50 instructions are brought into real memory, and execution is started. Assume that the first 35 instructions are executed and now instruction 36 requires a branch to location 114. Location 114 is a virtual address greater than the 100 locations of real memory available. The virtual memory system readdresses the virtual locations 101–150 as 1–50, brings this segment into real memory, and continues execution.

The price of microcomputer memory is steadily declining, and 32-bit microprocessors make extremely large amounts of real memory easily addressable. Consequently, some argue that virtual memory management is not needed with these new microprocessors. The demands on the microcomputer in terms of more powerful analytical methods and ever-larger data sets historically seem to grow at a faster rate than hardware technology. Increasing demands by users for windowing, complex graphics, and increased speed require not only more memory but faster processors which require expensive high-speed static RAM chips. With a properly designed operating system and hardware, virtual memory can be equivalent in speed to real memory, is far less costly, and insures that there will always be enough memory.

Old proverb: There will always be one more byte of data than there will be gigabytes of physical memory available for the analysis.

MICROPROCESSORS

This section will discuss the salient features of the Intel 8086/8088, 80286, and 80386 which are the most common microprocessors in the business environment. For example, the IBM PC is based on the 8088 microprocessor, and the original Compaq Deskpro and the IBM PS/2 Model 30 are based on the 8086. Both the IBM PC-AT, PS/2 models 50 and 60, and the Compaq 286 series use the 80286 microprocessor. The Compaq 386 series and the IBM PS/2 models 70 and 80 use the 80386.

Intel 8086/8088

The Intel 8086, first produced in 1978, was the first microprocessor designed with 16-bit registers. In order to address more memory than the 64K possible with 16 bits, the address registers are used in conjunction with segment registers. Information from these two registers is combined in a manner which yields a 20-bit physical address. This allows the 8086 a 1 megabyte (2^{20}) address space.

The 8086 microprocessor with an 8-bit data bus became available in 1979 as the Intel 8088 microprocessor. Both processors are designed to use the Intel 8087 coprocessor for floating-point mathematical computations. The original 8086/8088 processors were released in 5 MHz and 8 MHz versions. Current 8086 microprocessors are available at 10 MHz. The IBM PC, IBM PC-XT, and original Compaq computers are based on the 8088 processor. The AT&T 6300 and Compaq Deskpro are 8086-based microcomputers. 8086-based microcomputers were popular because they offered speed increases over 8088-based machines. This speed increase was due in part to the use of a 16-bit bus. These machines became known as "true 16-bit machines," as they tied a 16-bit processor to a 16-bit data bus.

Intel 80286

The Intel 80286 was introduced in 1983 and was used by IBM for the PC-AT marketed in 1984. The 80286 processor has the ability to operate in two different modes which are called "real" and "protected."

In the real mode the processor emulates an 8086 using 16-bit registers and segment registers to address 1 megabyte of physical memory. The 80286 was designed for faster clock rates and was originally available in 6 MHz and 8 MHz versions. However, the 80286 is also more powerful than the 8086 because of a more efficient instruction set. The 80286 performs a comparable instruction in fewer steps.

The protected mode of the 80286 provides for memory management and protection enabling the processor to utilize hardware that supports multitasking and virtual memory. Memory management allows a program or program segment to execute in different areas of memory—the basis of virtual memory. Memory protection prevents a program from accessing memory being used by another program or the operating system. Finally, protected mode operation allows for 16 megabytes of physical memory and 1 gigabyte (2^{30}) of virtual address space.

Unlike the original IBM PC, the PC-AT and similar 80286-based machines have been designed around a 16-bit data bus. The 80286 supports a 80287 math coprocessor which is similar in operation to the 8087. Currently, the 80286 is available with clock rates up to 16 MHz. In addition to the IBM PC-AT, other 80286-based machines include the IBM PS/2 models 50 and 60, Compaq's Deskpro-286, and the Toshiba T3100 laptop. The T3100 was the first major laptop to incorporate an 80286 processor and a hard disk.

Intel 80386

The Intel 80386, first introduced in the Compaq Deskpro-386 in late 1986, is designed around a full 32-bit architecture. The processor is available in 16 MHz, 20 MHz, and 25 MHz versions and supports an 80387 math coprocessor. Like the 80286, the 80386 operates in both a real and a protected mode.

In real mode the 80386 is operating as an 8086, but with 32-bit registers and data bus. The limitations of 1 megabyte of physical memory addressed in 64K segments are still present. But in protected mode the 80386 can address up to 16 megabytes of physical memory and 64 terabytes (2^{46}) of virtual memory. Hardware memory management and protection provide multitasking and virtual memory.

Unlike the 80286, which is limited to 64K segment addressing in protected mode, the use of a linear addressing model in the 80386 allows segments of 4 gigabytes. Hardware memory paging is also present. These features allow programs to be managed in larger segments which yield an increased efficiency in the virtual memory system. The 80386 also provides a virtual 8086 mode which allows multitasking of 8086 programs. This means that the processor can concurrently execute multiple programs developed for the 8086/8088 PC without modification or recompilation. In addition to the Compaq Deskpro-386, other 80386-based microcomputers include the IBM PS/2 models 70 and 80.

OPERATING SYSTEMS

MS/PC DOS

MS-DOS (which IBM calls PC-DOS) was designed for a single-user microcomputer that performs one task at a time. The Intel 8088, the processor for which DOS was specifically designed, has no hardware support for multitasking. Nor was it likely that DOS was conceived with its current sophisticated users and powerful applications software in mind. DOS was chosen over the CP/M operating system, the standard used on 8-bit microcomputers popular at the start of the decade. Peter Norton relates a legend of how DOS became the IBM PC operating system:

As the story goes, when IBM came shopping for CP/M, Gary Kildall, the man who created CP/M, intentionally kept IBM's representatives waiting, and fuming, while he flew his plane for hours in the skies overhead. Kildall, we're told, thumbed his nose at IBM as a customer, while Bill Gates, head of Microsoft, rolled out the red carpet for IBM. Gates donned his rarely-worn business suits for meetings with IBM to demonstrate that he was serious about doing business with them.

In the 8-bit computer world, Gate's company Microsoft had been dominant in programming languages, and Kildall's company Digital Research dominated operating systems—and IBM was prepared to keep it that way, planning to hire each of them for their specialties. But Kildall played hard to get, even after IBM had Bill Gates plead their case for Kildall's cooperation.

In the end, IBM turned to Microsoft for an operating system as well as programming languages, and Microsoft had to come up with one in very short order. It delivered the goods by picking up an existing but little known CP/M-like operating system and polishing it to meet IBM's requirements. That operating system became the DOS that nearly every PC user works with. (1986, 270)

When DOS was modified for the IBM PC, an effort was made to keep the new operating system similar to CP/M both to maximize the ability of users to learn the new operating system and to transfer user software. Many of the sophisticated features of the UNIX operating system have been integrated into DOS as Microsoft has continued to develop and expand the power of the operating system. However, the limitations of the 8086/8088 processor and the need for compatibility with previous releases have limited DOS's expansion.

DOS does the job for which it was designed quite well. It is relatively easy to work with for both the user and systems developer. It is an exceptionally easy system for the tyro. Many complaints against DOS are really hardware limitations. The 8086/8088 processors neither multitask nor support virtual memory and have a maximum 1MB physical address capability. These same limitations apply to the 80286 and 80386 operating in real mode.

Multitasking DOS: OS/2

The Microsoft MS-OS/2 operating system (which IBM will call OS/2) will support advanced features such as multitasking and virtual memory and therefore requires the use of protected mode instructions. Although the real mode of both the 80286 and 80386 emulate the 8086 instruction set, the protected mode instructions and operation are specific to each individual processor. The OS/2 operating system for the 80286 will therefore be very different from that of the

80386. Neither version of the operating system is available as this is being written, however, the major features can be predicted. OS/2 will allow use of the full 16MB of physical memory and gigabyte of virtual memory addressable in the 80286 protected mode. Multitasking and virtual memory will be provided with full hardware support. Applications software will need to be coded in protected mode instructions to take advantage of these features. However, a compatibility feature provides a single 640K partition in which an 8086 real mode application may run.

In contrast, OS/2–386 will provide 4 gigabytes of real memory and 64 terabytes of virtual memory for applications developed in 80386 protected mode. In contrast to the 64KB segment model of the 80286, the 4GB protected mode segment, in conjunction with hardware memory paging functions, provides a superior multitasking and virtual memory environment. Both the development and porting of applications software will be much easier for the 80386 systems. The virtual 8086 mode allows multitasking of 8086/8088 applications software which in turn can be executing concurrently with protected mode applications. However, it appears that 80286 protected mode applications cannot execute on the 80386 without modification because the processor does not support an 80286 virtual mode.

Unix

UNIX is a full multitasking operating system developed in the late 1960s and early 1970's at Bell Laboratories. If the system was not conceived as a multitasking environment from the start, it developed into one rapidly and has not had to suffer the growing pains of DOS. Not surprisingly, the system is mostly written in the C programming language. UNIX was developed with portability across hardware in mind. Although the system was originally installed and continues to be widely used on Digital Equipment Corporation minicomputer systems, the telephone switches being developed at that time by Western Electric were computers which needed operating systems. The switches developed into today's 3B series of AT&T UNIX computers.

As UNIX is generally hardware independent, it is available for both 80286 and 80386 microcomputers. It is also available for the 8086/8088 machines, but the lack of hardware multitasking and memory protection, and the size of UNIX in comparison to DOS, limits its usefulness. A comparison of UNIX (a multitasking system) and MS-DOS (a single-user system) is hardly fair. Neither is questioning which is better. The logical and fair comparison is between UNIX and OS/2–386.

This author is not privy to the inner sanctum of Microsoft, but it is likely that the OS/2–386 system will have many similarities to UNIX in terms of file management and intertask communication. It is also very probable that OS/2–386 will be more efficient in terms of system management and throughput than UNIX, because of the UNIX portability philosophy.

UNIX is designed in modules. The core system code that is common across versions interfaces with hardware-specific modules. But each microprocessor is different in architecture. The most efficient method for management of a particular process or task is different for each processor. As OS/2–386 is specifically designed for the 80386, it will take advantage of every feature of the micropro- cessor. The UNIX system on the 80386 may not take advantage of efficiencies unique to this processor. This is the trade-off with portability. An operating system designed to a specific architecture will usually be more efficient than portable code.

Do you or should you really care? The answer to this question depends on what applications software you intend to use. Many UNIX users are systems developers who are working in multiuser minicomputer environments, and it matters to them. In addition to the expected multitasking operating system soft- ware, UNIX is provided with a large number of utility programs for text and file manipulation. UNIX also provides program performance and analysis ca- pabilities. These utilities and features make life much easier for systems devel- opers, and these features aren't as available in alternative minicomputer environments.

In contrast, almost all business applications (including the tools planners use) are currently available only in MS-DOS. The choice of operating system will probably be dictated by the availability of desired applications software. Other than programmers, most microcomputer users have very little direct interaction (or interest) with the operating system. For example, after entering Symphony, the typical user can work with spreadsheets, word processing, graphics, and communications. The user can also format disks and copy files without leaving the application. Lotus Development Corporation has stated that the typical user should never have to leave the application environment and has indicated plans to extend their products to become a complete operating environment. In the near future, the issue may be Symphony versus Framework or Javelin as an operating environment—not UNIX versus OS/2–386.

Software developers such as Lotus are smoothing the interface provided by MS-DOS and making applications easier to learn and use. But this is a double- edged sword. It is more difficult for the user to become familiar with different "mega-environments" and move between them for different analyses. In con- trast, the Macintosh approach started with an intuitive interface and coerced software developers into integrating it into their applications. The result is that applications are easy to learn, and users find it easy to move among applications.

MS-OS/2 may not provide the strong interface required to keep users "port- able" among different applications environments. The IBM OS/2 will probably quickly diverge from MS-OS/2 as IBM develops the potential communications and database management capabilities which appear to be designed into the PS/2. This may result in significantly different applications environments for OS/2 versus MS-OS/2 applications.

An additional factor has been the lag by Microsoft and IBM in providing a protected mode operating system for the 80286-based PC-AT. This hardware was introduced in 1984, yet the OS/2 operating system has not been released at the time of this writing. The OS/2-386 will probably not be released until the early 1990s. This delay will allow the development of 80386 operating systems by competitors of Microsoft and IBM, which may further confound the issue. The microcomputer environment may resemble that of the mainframe where applications software varies by computer and operating system.

There is one certainty. With the 80386 multitasking environment, the user will have much more powerful and sophisticated applications software. The following chapters will help to apply hardware and software knowledge to data management and the development of decision support systems.

REFERENCES

Morse, S. P., and Albert, D. J. *The 80286 Architecture*. New York: John Wiley & Sons, Inc., 1986.

Norton, P. *Inside the IBM PC*. New York: Prentice Hall, 1986.

Norton, P. *The Peter Norton Programmer's Guide to the IBM PC*. Revised ed. Bellevue, Wash.: Microsoft Press, 1985.

Senn, J. A. *Information Systems in Management*. 3d ed. Belmont, Calif.: Wadsworth Publishing Company, 1987.

Zaks, R. *From Chips to Systems: An Introduction to Microprocessors*. Berkeley, Calif.: SYBEX, Inc., 1981.

SPREADSHEET AND DATABASE MANAGEMENT SOFTWARE

Previous sections provided background material concerning microcomputer technology. These sections discussed organizational impacts, advanced evaluation criteria, and current technologies. These are topics of general interest. Organizational impacts must be understood by all managers, regardless of their personal level of interaction with microcomputers or their specific job responsibilities. Technological change is also a subject of general interest both to managers and the user community at large.

Expertise and the nature of analysis separate various classes of users. Unlike the first two sections, the following sections are tailored to the needs of planners, financial analysts, and professionals with similar responsibilities. These sections describe planning applications. They provide planners with the background needed to build applications and to make use of vended applications like macroeconomic or industry models. These sections will also be of use to planners who find themselves in between these spheres, specifying applications for others to build. In any event, examples provide insight to the marriage of applications development and the microcomputer's role in the development process. The full importance of background material presented in earlier sections will be realized. A focus on organizational impacts and a definition of new technologies will provide perspective on the development of microcomputer applications environments, the popularity of those environments, and the formalization of new roles accepted by planners and other analysts as they divorce themselves from systems groups and take full responsibility for the computing aspects of their own operations.

The new responsibilities accepted by end-users begin with data management. Analysis and applications integrity assume the availability and accessibility of quality data. Therefore it is appropriate to begin the next section of this book with a discussion of database management systems, their evolution, and the developments that will affect database management in the near future.

There is an added incentive for covering this topic early on. Database management systems and spreadsheet packages are among the most widely used products employed by planners and analysts, but they are among the most misunderstood. The goal of this section is to establish basic considerations so that planners and analysts can apply database and spreadsheet products efficiently. Chapter 4 discusses database management systems, and Chapter 5 discusses the use of spreadsheets in planning operations.

Data are the life blood of decision support operations. Database management systems (DBMS) offer efficient means for organizing, storing, retrieving, and manipulating data. Chapter 4 discusses the similarities and differences of hierarchical, network, and relational database models. An understanding of each model may help in optimizing the use of DBMS products in the planning environment. The use of fourth-generation systems is discussed. Fourth-generation systems marry powerful database management capabilities with nonprocedural programming languages. Fourth-generation systems are becoming an integral part of applications developed for planning departments. This chapter also discusses decentralized database operations. This topic has received much attention as firms and other organizations investigate the advantages and disadvantages that various decentralized computing operations offer.

Chapter 5 discusses the use of spreadsheets in planning and identifies limitations not often recognized by spreadsheet users. Spreadsheet products were originally designed to computerize financial and accounting problems formerly completed using pencil and ruled paper. The spreadsheet was used as a large visual calculator. Today's spreadsheet products are more sophisticated. They include programming capabilities, relational database operations, menu construction features, and a host of similar offerings. The spreadsheet is applied to a wide variety of uses including data manipulation, data analysis, and applications development.

The spreadsheet learning curve is steep, and advanced features allow users to continually increase the complexity of tasks. Many users, especially those with limited systems training, apply their favorite spreadsheet product to tasks better completed in an alternative environment. Planners and financial analysts are major abusers of the spreadsheet environment, and they often develop large and unwieldy applications that are best completed using alternative systems tools. By understanding the limitations of traditional spreadsheet products and the advantages of alternative environments, users can select the proper software to complete decision support applications. Predictions are made for features expected in future releases of popular spreadsheet products. These advances will ameliorate some of the difficulties associated with traditional spreadsheet products.

Outside of large planning models developed using traditional modeling software, database and spreadsheet products are used for a great majority of the applications that planners build for themselves. Later sections will discuss commercially available applications and the design and construction of traditional planning models. In addition, several types of applications will be combined to form modular planning systems. Spreadsheet applications are among the applications included in these planning systems.

4

Database Management and Distributed Data Processing

MARTIN KATZ

Decision support systems are computer-based systems designed to provide information and models to support the managerial decision-making process. In contrast to traditional management information systems, decision support systems are designed to provide support for the unstructured or less-formally structured problems such as those faced by the corporate planner. They should also provide adaptability to the different types of problems and the often short time frames faced by the decision maker.

The increasing number of decision support systems being implemented has emphasized the need for timely and efficient access to a wide range of data. The proliferation of microcomputers throughout the organization has also put parts of the corporate data bank on every desk and quickly demonstrated the need for data integrity and security.

Data management is the foundation on which every successful decision support system is built. Without proper data management, essential information will not be readily available for analysis—if available at all. Poor data management may also result in a loss of data integrity which ultimately affects the quality of managerial decisions.

This chapter first discusses the fundamental concepts of database management systems followed by an overview of local area networks and distributed processing. This overview provides an understanding of methods by which information is shared among users of microcomputer-based decision support systems. Finally, fourth-generation languages are discussed as tools for effectively developing decision support systems.

DATABASE CONCEPTS

Data, Records, and Files

A set of related data items is a record. The items in a record are considered a unit. For example, Jack Customer has a checking account, a savings account, and a credit card with the Lost Mountain National Bank. The balance for each individual account is a data item while the set of all account balances for Jack Customer is a record. A file is a set of similar types of records such as all customers whose address is Lost Mountain Township.

The president of the bank decided to institute a new bank card, the OWEALOT Card. The OWEALOT card has silver, gold, and diamond-studded versions with unique services and credit lines for each class of card. The president decided that the diamond-studded class would be offered only to those customers who already held the bank's old credit card and had at least $100,000 on deposit in a savings account. A list of these customers was quickly needed.

The president asked the data processing department for the required list, and, as you might expect, the "it can't be done in less than six months" answer was given. The bank has COBOL applications for processing checking account, savings account, and credit card activities at the end of each day. Each application program generates a unique file with a specified physical representation of data. A special application would have to be written by a programmer to input each of the unique files and generate the list. The alternative was to perform a set of sort/merge runs, but these could not be run while the other applications were running, which was 24 hours a day.

Database Management System

In contrast to the independent files just described, a database is an integrated set of data organized by logical relationships. The database allows information to be easily retrieved for various applications without the necessity of knowing where and how the information is physically stored. A database management system is the software system by which a database is created and managed. The database management system is the vehicle for translating the logical structure by which a user or an application views the data to the physical storage and retrieval of the data. Data from separate files can be joined without developing a new application program.   A database management system usually has a query language which allows nonprogrammers to generate reports and retrieve information with minimal training. If Lost Mountain National Bank had a database management system, the president could have entered the table request himself and had the desired information in minutes. The MIS manager would also still have his job. (And I might not have to wait in line 45 minutes to cash a check!)

There are benefits to database management systems in addition to providing an easy means of accessing data. Generally data are stored once, and separate files for various applications are no longer necessary. This not only reduces the costs involved with entering and storing redundant information but also increases the integrity of the data. A database administration staff is usually charged with designing, updating, and determining access rights to the database. These functions are the key to data accuracy and security.

Schema and Subschema

In a file system such as that used by Lost Mountain National Bank, data are stored in isolated files. Each file contains data but no information about the relationship of that data to other data contained in other files. In contrast, a database integrates files by describing the relationships of data within and between files. These relationships are defined in a schema and subschema.

The schema describes the data and the logical relationships of the data items in the database. The subschema describes the data and logical relationships for a particular user or user application. The subschema is a subset of the schema. The schema and subschema present a logical view of the database. The logical view is concerned with data and data relations (i.e., the data structure). The physical view describes the details of storage and access modes. A database management system allows applications development from a logical view without concern for the physical view of the data. The data dictionary contains the complete description of the database variables, files, and relationships.

Database Models

The schema describes the database in terms of data and data relationships. The database model describes the method of expressing these relationships. The most common models used in database management systems are hierarchical, network, and relational.

The hierarchical model organizes data in terms of a tree structure. Data associations are expressed in one-to-many (superior/subordinate) relationships. Each superior may have one or more subordinate(s), but each subordinate has only one superior. Because the relationship in a hierarchical model is always one-to-many, data in lower levels can only be accessed by following the path starting from the highest level of the tree. Illustration 4.1 shows a hierarchical database for Lost Mountain National Bank. The data are organized in three levels: branch, service, and account. The account records are reached by the path:

branch → service → account.

The structure of a hierarchical database determines the efficiency in which different inquiries are supported. The database in Illustration 4.1 is very efficient in listing the accounts by each service and branch; however, it is not efficient at listing the accounts for each individual customer.

The limitations of the one-to-many relationship are ameliorated in the network model. The network model is similar to the hierarchical model except that it

Illustration 4.1
Hierarchical Database

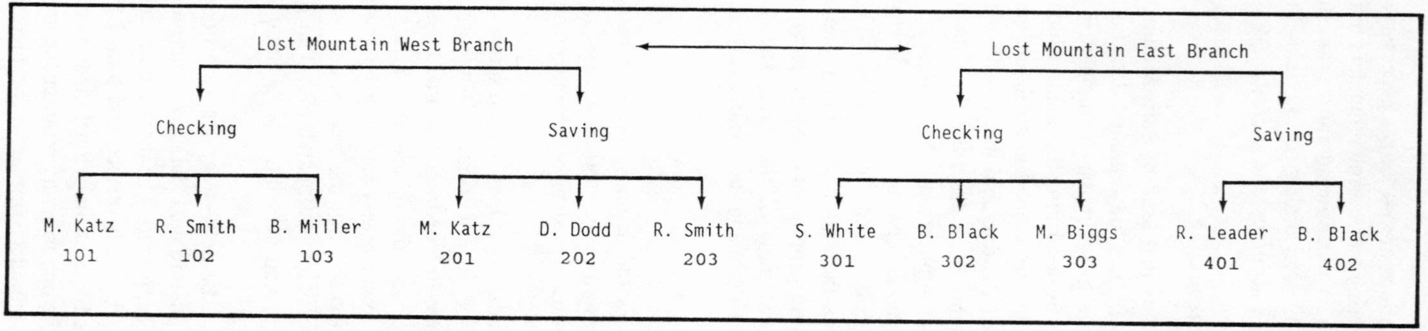

allows many-to-many relationships. Thus each subordinate may have multiple supervisors. A network database for Lost Mountain National Bank is shown in Illustration 4.2. This database is similar to the hierarchical model of Illustration 4.1, but the network model allows the inclusion of a relationship of branches to services. When your account is at the West branch and you cash a check at the East branch, this relationship proves to be extremely important.

The relational model is based on a two-dimensional table called a relation. The columns of the relation are called attributes (or fields) as each represents an attribute of the data. The rows are called tuples (or records) and constitute the records of data. Each cell formed by the attribute by tuple matrix contains a data value. Link fields are data common to a set of tables which are to be logically related. For example, account number could be used as a common data item in two tables and would serve as a link field allowing relationships to be formed between the two tables. Illustration 4.3 shows a relational database for Lost Mountain National Bank. Notice that all account numbers and branch information are available in the relation as shown.

Each of the database models can express any required data relationships. There are, however, advantages and disadvantages for each model. Data relationships must be specified in the design of hierarchical and network models. These models are very difficult to modify since all affected relationships must be reconfigured. However, tree structures have less data redundancy and may have faster access. Certainly less memory is required for storage of a given amount of information.

The advantage of relational models is that links can be easily established allowing all possible combinations of data to be retrieved. New attributes can be added, and relational databases easily stay current with the information needs of the organization. Relational databases do require more memory than hierarchical or network systems. The original implementations of relational database management systems were painfully slow in comparison to the tree structured systems; however, most current systems exhibit good processing efficiency. Most current microcomputer database management systems are based on relational models.

FOURTH-GENERATION LANGUAGES

All database management systems provide a query language which allows the user to extract information from the database. A query language is usually designed for nonprogrammers, and the command structure is very close to conversational English. Query languages allow the extraction of information in the form of tables or allow the information to be stored in a file for further processing.

Fourth-generation languages such as FOCUS and ORACLE provide relational database management and query language capability plus support for a full programming language. These programming languages are nonprocedural and require the user to describe what task is to be accomplished rather than how to

Illustration 4.2
Network Database

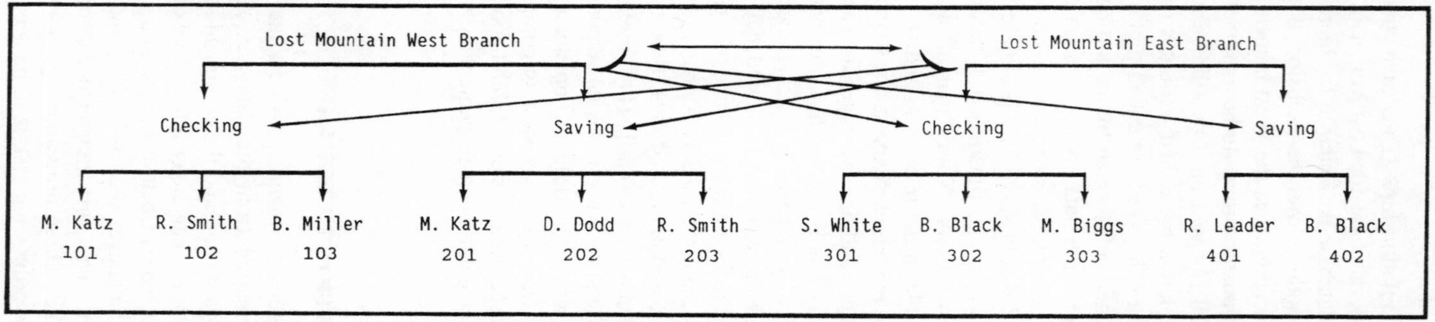

Illustration 4.3
Relational Database

Customer Name	Branch	Checking Acct. #	Savings Acct. #
M. Katz	W	101	201
R. Smith	W	102	203
B. Miller	W	103	
D. Dodd	W		202
S. White	E	301	
B. Black	E	302	402
M. Biggs	E	303	
R. Leader	E		401

accomplish the task. For example, a procedural language program to list the savings accounts with balances greater than $100,000 might look like this:

```
110 READ(3,120,END = 170) IACCT,DOLLARS
120 FORMAT (I4, F10.2)
130 IF ( DOLLARS .LE. 100000 ) GOTO 110
140 WRITE(4,160) IACCT
150 FORMAT(1X,I4)
160 GOTO 110
170 END.
```

A fourth-generation language program to accomplish the same task might look like this:

LIST ALL SAVINGS ACCOUNTS WITH GREATER THAN $100,000 BALANCE.

Fourth-generation languages allow new applications to be produced faster than third-generation languages such as FORTRAN or COBOL. The end-user can often program the application with no assistance from the programming staff. Additional features of many fourth-generation languages such as FOCUS and ORACLE often include statistical and financial analysis functions, graphics, and spreadsheets, which make these languages ideal for developing decision support systems. Many fourth-generation languages are available in both mainframe and microcomputer versions and provide for data transfer between systems.

Although fourth-generation languages increase development productivity, the performance of the application is often poorer than the equivalent application developed in a third-generation language like FORTRAN or COBOL. However, Inmon and Bird (1986) suggest evidence that although well-written third-generation applications outperform fourth-generation applications, a fourth-generation application written by a nonprogrammer will outperform a third-generation application written by a mediocre third-generation programmer. In terms of providing timely answers for managerial decisions, the fourth-generation language is without equal.

NETWORKS AND COMMUNICATION

Distributed Processing

The essential feature of distributed processing is that the computing facilities are at remote sites rather than at one central location. The majority of data processing for a location is done on-site, and the information required for that location is maintained in local databases. These remote locations are linked to the central location by a communications network which allows load sharing—the balancing of the processing load among systems—and provides backup for hardware problems. Large databases need not be duplicated on different systems, and peripherals such as high-speed laser printers and computer output microfilm devices can be shared. If properly implemented, sharing systems and resources in a distributed processing environment can ensure that needed computing power is available to all users. Most major corporations have implemented distributed processing in the mainframe environment.

Local Area Networks

Microcomputers are generally linked in a local area network (LAN) for sharing data, software, peripherals, and electronic mail. LANs are geographically small and often installed in the same office or building. The microcomputers in a LAN can be linked via twisted-pair (telephone) wire, coaxial cable (used for cable television), or fiber optic cable.

The foundation of the LAN is the network server. This is the computer that handles the network commands and functions. The network server thus defines the characteristics of the network operation. It also manages the mass storage devices used to centralize data and software.

The simpler form of a network is based on a disk server. When operating as a disk server, the network server functions as a hard disk that can be accessed by all the microcomputers linked in a network. The shared hard disk of the server appears to each microcomputer as another drive under its control. Usually the shared storage of the disk server is partitioned and allocated to each machine. Generally only one machine is allowed access to a particular file at a time.

The network based on a file server has a network server with software that is more complex, flexible, and powerful than that used by a disk server. The file server usually controls each microcomputer's operating system. The individual machines access the network via files, and more than one user may be allowed access to the same file during a session. Since access via files is more efficient than the space allocation of the disk server, more disk space is available to each machine. Databases may be simultaneously shared and updated. The more sophisticated server software can translate and allow files to be shared among different machines and operating systems.

DISTRIBUTED DATABASE SYSTEMS

The most recent feature of fourth-generation languages such as ORACLE SQL*Star is the ability to access and manage data stored in databases on different processors. This can be accomplished even if the processors are different types and running under different operating systems. To implement this distributed environment, a version of the fourth-generation language must be running on each of the processors. The database is partitioned in a logical manner such that a subset of the database is stored on each processor. Certain processors are designated as having a data dictionary which catalogs the location of all data items. When a request for data is made, the local data dictionary is searched to determine if the data are available in the local database. If the data are not available, a catalog data dictionary is searched. The catalog site determines the location and routes the request to the appropriate processor. To the user, the database appears as if it is a single database on the user's microcomputer.

The distribution of a database over different processors is a very complex process and demands a large amount of hardware and software resources. The benefits become apparent when a decision support system requires data normally used at a remote location. The processing efficiency and data availability required by the users at the remote location are not diminished, yet the data are readily available to decision support applications on other systems or at other locations. Although the distributed architecture does improve efficiency and availability, it also revives the problems of data integrity and security.

SUMMARY

Fourth-generation languages are an excellent tool for developing decision support systems as they combine relational database capability with statistical and financial analysis modules. They also support a nonprocedural language for applications development which allows end-users to develop most applications without technical assistance. Most fourth-generation languages are developing distributed database management capability, allowing access to data on different computers which may have different operating systems. This ability is a two-edged sword. The problems of data integrity and security, which were resolved by implementing a central database, now return.

REFERENCES

Housley, T. *Data Communications and Teleprocessing Systems.* 2d ed., Englewood Cliffs, N.J.: Prentice Hall, 1987.

Inmon, W. H., Bird, T. J., Jr. *The Dynamics of Database*. Englewood Cliffs, N. J.:Prentice Hall, 1986.

McFadden, F. R., Hoffer, J. A. *Data Base Management*. Menlo Park, Calif.: The Benjamin/Cummings Publishing Co., 1985.

Stamper, D. A. *Business Data Communications*. Menlo Park, Calif.: The Benjamin/Cummings Publishing Co., 1986.

5

Spreadsheets: Use and Misuse

DAVID J. GIANTURCO

The success of the microcomputer was certainly tied to the popularization of the spreadsheet. A microcomputer outfitted with a spreadsheet package offered tremendous advantages for completing accounting, financial, and other operations as compared with performing these tasks by hand. The legendary VisiCalc spreadsheet program is still remembered in user circles, and software developers still dream of creating a product as revolutionary and as successful. Since the time of VisiCalc, spreadsheet packages have improved and are employed for many analytical and operational functions. It's rare to find a microcomputer user in a planning environment who does not use a spreadsheet package. In fact, many users become introduced to microcomputers through the use of spreadsheets.

A new user can begin using a spreadsheet with minimal effort. With help from a more knowledgeable office mate, a new user may skip tutorials and can complete simple tasks almost immediately. As the user becomes comfortable and more proficient in the use of a particular spreadsheet package, a tendency develops to employ the spreadsheet for tasks best completed in another environment. The pervasiveness of a particular spreadsheet product within an organization is offered as a motivating factor for developing complex applications with, say, Lotus 1–2–3 or SuperCalc. While the argument has merit, it is overapplied. The argument is only valid for applications that have a high probability of being distributed to a significant number of users.

This chapter will discuss some general characteristics and some limitations of the spreadsheet environment. A general tendency has been to apply spreadsheets to problems best handled in other environments. Understanding the unique characteristics of the spreadsheet environment is fundamental to increasing user productivity and to improving the quality of analysis and constructed applications.

Table 5.1
Customer List

ID#	Customer	City	Representative	Last Called
1	G. Whiz	Toronto	Jones	1/12
2	B. Square	Ottawa	Smith	2/12
3	I. Talian	Buffalo	Smith	2/12
4	G. Lordy	Ottawa	Smith	4/12
5	A. Muck	Rochester	Jones	5/12
6	D. One	Buffalo	Smith	2/12

This chapter is not intended to be an introduction to the use of spreadsheets and assumes the reader has a cursory understanding of spreadsheet basics.

THE SPREADSHEET

Spreadsheets present the user with a row-column display, and the spreadsheet environment is often referred to as a worksheet. Typically, columns are delineated by letter designations, and rows are numbered. Data, including labels and formulas, are stored in the worksheet's cells. Each cell has its own address, as identified by its unique row-column designation. A cell can contain an alphanumeric label, a numeric data entry, or a formula that generates either a label or numeric data based on information located in other cells in the worksheet. A cell might also incorporate predefined financial, statistical, and other functions. This cell orientation represents a major distinction between spreadsheets and traditional systems tools and has ramifications for data dimensioning, programming, modeling, and applications development.

Macro information can usually be incorporated in cells. Macros are used to execute several logical keystrokes sequentially and are invoked by a single keystroke. Macros are also used to incorporate menus—an important feature when developing applications for other users. Macros provide general programming capabilities. Programming logic can usually be incorporated in spreadsheet applications, but included languages are unwieldy and difficult to master.

By the nature of their row-column orientation, spreadsheets lend themselves to two-dimensional problems. Office operations, tabular information storage, certain accounting problems, and other tasks are easily handled in two-dimensions. Examples of office operations include customer (or member) lists, inventory information, and library functions. Many office operations make use of the limited relational database capabilities offered by spreadsheet packages. Consider the customer list in Table 5.1.

Each row of the spreadsheet is a record, and each column heading is called a field. A record owns the fields corresponding to it, for example, the first record owns the identification number of 1, the customer G. Whiz, the city of Toronto, and so forth. If Table 5.1 is declared to be a database, then certain useful operations can be performed. The user can sort the database by any of the field designations. For example, sorting the database by the last called field and using a descending order sort, the database would appear as in Table 5.2

Table 5.2.
Customer List

ID#	Customer	City	Representative	Last Called
5	A. Muck	Rochester	Jones	5/12
4	O. Lordy	Ottawa	Smith	4/12
2	B. Square	Ottawa	Smith	2/12
3	I. Talian	Buffalo	Smith	2/12
6	D. One	Buffalo	Smith	2/12
1	G. Whiz	Toronto	Jones	1/12

The user could also extract records based on field information, sending only records meeting certain criteria to some area of the worksheet. For example, only customers with a Buffalo (city) address could be extracted. Other database operations are possible.

Not all tabular information found in worksheets is declared to be a database. The database example is presented because it is one of the most sophisticated spreadsheet applications normally encountered in an office setting.

Another class of applications essentially uses worksheets as visual calculators. The term worksheet has its origins in accounting applications formerly performed by hand on large sheets of lined paper.

SPREADSHEET LIMITATIONS

Planners encounter spreadsheets at every turn: Data vendors supply files convertable into worksheet files; worksheets are used to store many types of data; simple and complex planning applications are developed in this environment; and so forth. In some situations, the spreadsheet is not the ideal environment for storing or working with data. Further, many planning applications developed with a spreadsheet are better developed using more traditional computing tools. Spreadsheets impose three serious limitations. The first is the difficulty of handling three-dimensional data sets; the second concerns cell versus equation modeling; and the third concerns reprogramming analytical algorithms.

Dimensionality

Concerning the dimensionality problem, consider Illustration 5.1. This illustration contains exhibits of branch bank information. Deposit information is collected for the following type of accounts: certificates of deposit (CD), demand deposits (DD), and time deposits (TD). Different branches are delineated by letters.

Consider Exhibit 1. The objective is to collect deposit information for three types of deposits for three branches for one point in time. This is a two-dimensional problem easily handled in a worksheet. However, if branch deposit information must also be tracked over time, the user is confronted with a three-dimensional problem requiring either multiple matrices in the same worksheet

Illustration 5.1
Branch Bank Deposit Information

```
        Exhibit 1                    Exhibit 2                    Exhibit 3
       2 Dimensions             3 Dimensions, 1 file         3 Dimensions, 2 files

          Time 1                Time 1           Time 2
       CD  DD  TD            CD  DD  TD        CD  DD  TD            CD DD TD
  A    20  40  60       A   20  40  60     A  21  41  61
  B    10  10  10       B   10  10  10     B  11  11  10              CD DD TD
  C     7   8   9       C    7   8   9     C   7   9  10         A   20 40 60
                                                                B   10 10 10
                                                                C    7  8  9
```

Illustration 5.2
Branch Bank Deposit Information

```
              Exhibit 4
             2 Dimensions

              Branch A
           (Quarterly Data)

              CD   DD   TD

      80Q1    20   40   60
      80Q2    21   41   61
      80Q3    21   42   61
      80Q4    22   43   61
      81Q1    22   44   60
```

(Exhibit 2) or multiple worksheet files, (probably) one matrix per file (Exhibit 3).

These exhibits point to a classic division in data used by planners. Exhibit 1 shows an example of cross-section data. It is a snapshot of deposit information by type of deposit by branch. The data are valid at one point in time. The data in Exhibit 1 are essentially no different from the data presented in the customer list example shown earlier. Exhibits 2 and 3 show time-series data, where certain variables are tracked over time—for example, tracking CDs for branch A on a quarterly basis.

Traditional spreadsheet products can handle data across time but only to the exclusion of some other information. Illustration 5.2 shows the level of deposits by instrument for Branch A over time. Quarterly information is shown starting with the first quarter of 1980.

In Exhibit 4, a two-dimensional matrix contains all the needed information concerning Branch A. However, similar matrices are needed for Branches B and C.

Users of traditional spreadsheet packages have two options to solve the data dimensionality problem. They can either create large worksheets that have many matrices, or they can store a large number of small worksheet files, each containing a single matrix of two-dimensional information. With either solution, data manipulation is complicated by the dimensionality problem. Several tasks that would be easy to perform using traditional systems tools become much harder in the spreadsheet environment. For example, obtaining time-series data from cross-section data matrices stored in separate worksheet files is difficult and may require advanced programming skills. The general difficulties of handling data in more than two dimensions is a major limitation of most spreadsheet packages.

Software developers are aware of the limitations imposed by the dimensionality problem, and two approaches have been taken to provide more flexibility. The first approach is to offer consolidation capabilities. This approach uses a separate worksheet file to consolidate data stored in other worksheet files. Multiplan (from Microsoft Corporation) is an example of a product that provides consolidation capabilities. X-Y-Z: Consolidate (from the INTEX Corporation) and Lotus HAL offer some consolidation capabilities for Lotus 1–2–3. The second approach employs a three-dimensional scheme, allowing the user to manipulate data from several logically different worksheets in one file. Boeing Calc, a spreadsheet package released by the Boeing Company, employs this second approach.

A further look at the Boeing Calc product will offer insight into the value of the three-dimensional format. Boeing Calc employs a three-dimensional address scheme. The user can stack worksheets (called pads or workpads in the product's vernacular), and each cell address includes a worksheet designation. For example, cell 1A1 is the address of the first cell on the first worksheet, cell 2A1 is the address of the first cell on the second worksheet, and so on. The stacked sheets are part of the same file. Data are easily passed from worksheet to worksheet. An imaginative use of summary worksheets allows the application of mathematical formulas that refer to data located in logically different worksheets. For example, suppose the user has four spreadsheets, each containing cross-section data for one quarter during the year. Suppose that a quarterly average must be calculated at year's end. A summary sheet, logically the fifth sheet, is used to calculate the year-end average. This operation is shown in Illustration 5.3.

The summary sheet will automatically incorporate data changes made in any of the first four worksheets. Data updates become simplified and easily automated.

The user can also collect and manipulate data in other imaginative ways. For example, a summary sheet could be used to form time-series data from a collection of worksheets each containing cross-section data. This operation is simplified because the user can move, refer, and manipulate data from different worksheets and also because the product allows relative cell addressing across worksheets.

Analysts working with large amounts of financial data will find that three-dimensional schemes will simplify data storage and manipulation. One classic problem is that of looking at a firm by division, and another is looking at a

Illustration 5.3
Collection of Data in Summary Sheet to Compute Quarterly Average

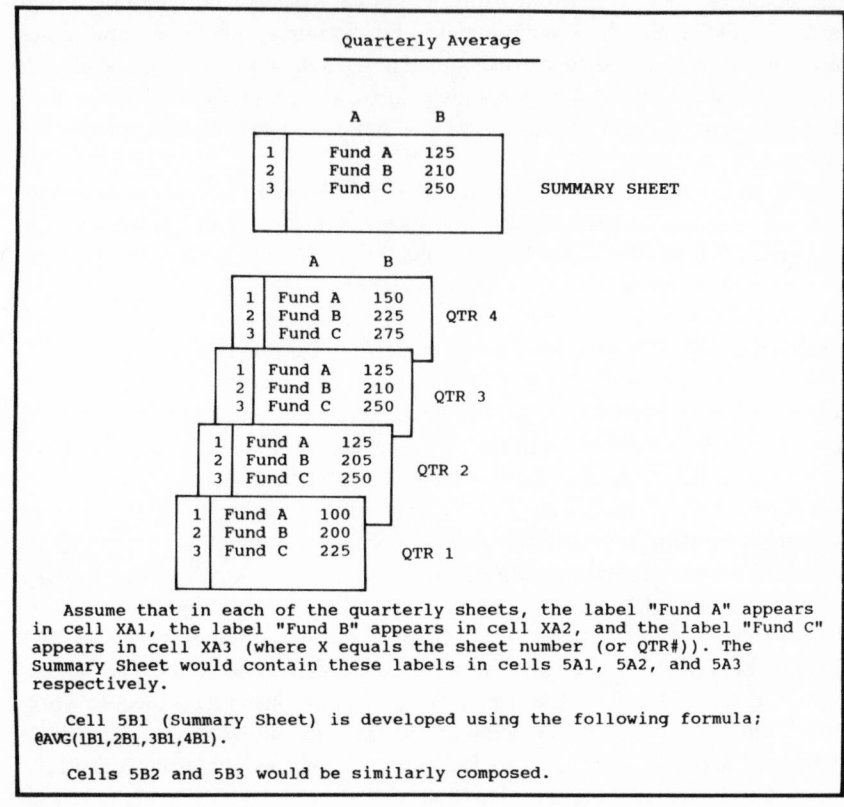

Assume that in each of the quarterly sheets, the label "Fund A" appears in cell XA1, the label "Fund B" appears in cell XA2, and the label "Fund C" appears in cell XA3 (where X equals the sheet number (or QTR#)). The Summary Sheet would contain these labels in cells 5A1, 5A2, and 5A3 respectively.

Cell 5B1 (Summary Sheet) is developed using the following formula; @AVG(1B1,2B1,3B1,4B1).

Cells 5B2 and 5B3 would be similarly composed.

holding company by subsidiary. In these cases, divisions or subsidiaries become the third dimension. Each division or subsidiary is stored on a separate worksheet, and corporate or holding company totals are calculated by summing across sheets. Consider: An analyst stores balance sheet information for each subsidiary of a holding company on separate worksheets. A total for the holding company remains on a summary sheet. In this way, the analyst can move through the subsidiaries and analyze their operations. The analyst can also keep totals by sets of subsidiaries. In this manner, analysis proceeds by peeling back each layer of holding company totals. Like peels of an onion, the analyst moves backward through the corporation analyzing the important pieces comprising the whole.

Many planners and other analysts perform peer group analysis on a regular basis. Because peer group analysis requires the collection of data across firms, three-dimensional schemes lend themselves well to these applications.

Last, the ability to manipulate data in three dimensions can be a valuable aid in day-to-day operations. This is especially true if spreadsheets are used to manipulate data that is later passed to other packages or languages. For example, the user might form a matrix of time-series data from several separate matrices containing cross-section data. This data would then be passed on to traditional packages like AREMOS, the Interactive Financial Planning System (IFPS), Javelin, and others. Modeling using these time-series data can then be performed in these other environments.

In summary, the general difficulties of handling data in more than two dimensions is a major limitation of most traditional spreadsheet packages. Depending on the planners' needs, data may be better stored and manipulated using dedicated database management products or traditional time-series packages like AREMOS, IFPS, Javelin, and others. Imaginative products like Boeing Calc and X-Y-Z: Consolidate may offer the user options for completing applications and collecting and manipulating data. Most popular spreadsheet products will soon incorporate consolidation capabilities if not direct three-dimensional formats. A common format will allow the user to view more than one spreadsheet on the screen at one time. Spreadsheets will be dynamically linked, so that changes in one worksheet will automatically update data in other worksheets.

These advancements will be welcomed by the user community, and users should be encouraged to use the third dimension in data manipulations and applications. This format offers a more natural and logical framework for handling many applications, especially data consolidation across time and organizational divisions. Depending on the format, data manipulations can be greatly simplified. As three-dimensional graphics packages are wedded to new spreadsheet products, users will discover more interesting ways to view data series relationships.

Equation Versus Cell Modeling

Perhaps the most serious limitation of spreadsheets lies in the area of applications development. Spreadsheets employ a cell modeling format. Spreadsheet packages are overapplied to include applications best handled by employing an equation modeling format. Planners have been traditional abusers of spreadsheet products. Planners build financial models and other decision support applications using spreadsheet packages when traditional packages or high-level languages offer superior capabilities. The result is lengthened development time, difficult application maintenance, and error prone applications.

Traditional modeling packages are structured in the following way. Computing is done via equation modeling, with variable names and mathematical operations included in equations. Data series do not appear in the model, with data being assigned to variable names in some previous operation. All of a model's equations are visible. Presuming the modeler uses a reasonable mnemonic scheme, there is no difficulty reading the program code that comprises the model. This simplifies modeling, debugging, and data and application maintenance.

Cell modeling is not conducive to separating data and modeling operations. A worksheet's cells can contain both data and formulas. While range names can

Illustration 5.4
Equation Modeling Format

	DATA SECTION		
TIME	UNIT-COST	MARKUP%	QUANTITY
1980Q1	100	1.5	200
1980Q2	101	1.5	200
1980Q3	102	1.5	210
1980Q4	102	1.5	225

MODEL SECTION

UNIT-COST * MARKUP% = PRICE
PRICE * QUANTITY = REVENUE

Illustration 5.5
Cell Modeling Format

	A	B	C	D
1	TIME	UNIT-COST	MARKUP%	QUANTITY
2				
3	1980Q1	100	1.5	200
4	1980Q2	100	1.5	200
5	1980Q3	102	1.5	210
6	1980Q4	102	1.5	225
7				
8	TIME	PRICE	REVENUE	
9				
10	1980Q1	150	30000	
11	1980Q2	150	30000	
12	1980Q3	153	32130	
13	1980Q4	153	35425	
14				
15				

be used in certain circumstances, most programming is done using cell addresses. Unlike program code generated by traditional modeling packages, cell addresses are not easy to read. They include a blur of letters, numbers, and special characters. Modeling and debugging require much searching in sheets and tracing cell references for definitions. A simple example illustrates the difference between modeling and cell formats. Consider Illustrations 5.4 and 5.5.

The equation modeling format separates the data assignment and modeling steps. The user can change data, pass data to the model, and print reports of any included variables. The user can also change equations in the model section. This will not affect input data but will affect reported results for output variables.

With the cell modeling approach, the data and modeling steps are not inherently separate. For example, it is not clear how the data in the revenue column (cell

Illustration 5.6
Cell Modeling Format

```
C10:   D3*B10

          A            B           C          D

 1      TIME      UNIT-COST     MARKUP%    QUANTITY
 2
 3     1980Q1        100          1.5        200
 4     1980Q2        100          1.5        200
 5     1980Q3        102          1.5        210
 6     1980Q4        102          1.5        225
 7
 8      TIME        PRICE       REVENUE
 9
10     1980Q1        150         30000
11     1980Q2        150         30000
12     1980Q3        153         32130
13     1980Q4        153         35425
14
15
```

range C10 to C13) is generated. The user must verify that the data were generated via a formula. Spreadsheet packages offer various means for the user to view the formula contents of cells. The most common method is to move the cursor to the cell in question and check the editing portion of the screen. The cell contents generally appear in the upper left-hand corner of the screen. The screen would appear as in Illustration 5.6.

By moving the cursor to cell C10 the user can verify that the screen display is generated by a particular formula input. Cells C11, C12, and C13 must also be checked to be sure that their formulas are similar to that input in cell C10. On large spreadsheets, referring to cell addresses is difficult—much more difficult than referring to equations. Changing formulas in a spreadsheet application can also be difficult, and changes in one cell must be replicated properly to all other similar cells.

In the equation modeling format, all changes are complete as soon as the model's equations are adjusted. Properly structuring spreadsheet applications (especially separating data, work, and report sections), using range names where possible, including labels and notes, using protected ranges to inhibit inexperienced users from deleting cell formulas by entering data in formula generated cells, and a host of other suggestions can mitigate some of the difficulties inherent in the cell modeling format. However, in situations where equations can efficiently represent an application's logic, the equation format will offer superior performance. Improvements include reduced application development time, ease of maintenance, fewer errors, and ease of user acceptance. In the extreme, large simultaneous financial and general planning models should be developed using traditional systems tools. Products like IFPS, Javelin, and AREMOS will offer dramatic development advantages.

New products are attempting to bridge the gap between the cell and equation modeling formats. Some products present users with a spreadsheet type interface but actually treat data in variable format. Javelin is such a product and can be used for complex simultaneous equation modeling for time-series applications. X-Y-Z: Model (released by the INTEX Corporation) allows equation modeling using existing 1–2–3 worksheets. Complex modeling logic is translated into an equation format, and this information is stored in separate files.

Reinventing the Wheel

Users are generally comfortable using spreadsheets. Some users exclusively use a spreadsheet package because they are not comfortable with traditional analytical tools. When such users are assigned complex data analysis or applications development projects, they often choose a spreadsheet package. Users reprogram complex statistical and financial functions, even when widely available products include these functions. For example, users can enter data in a spreadsheet and port that data to a statistical analysis package to perform data analysis. Data can be ported by a variety of methods. Also, many traditional packages can read and write data directly to and from spreadsheets. Using appropriate data analysis packages can greatly reduce analysis time and increase the integrity of reported results. Whenever complex algorithms are reprogrammed, the chance of programmer error is high.

Using Ancillary and Alternative Products for Applications Development

A major value in accepting a particular spreadsheet product (usually Lotus 1–2–3) as the standard in large organizations is that everyone owns a copy of the product. Data and applications can be exchanged freely among users. This advantage carries with it the liability that ancillary products or alternative software products will not be owned and employed by a broad user base. Consequently, applications developers cannot assume that end-users will own, know, and use ancillary or alternative products. While both offer solutions for individuals or a small number of users, use by the general community cannot be assumed. To the extent that applications require the end-user to actually understand the workings of these products, further product training and support must be offered by information center organizations. Last, the inertia issue cannot be overlooked. Discovering and using ancillary or alternative products requires effort and possibly a deep understanding of the technical problems associated with analytical applications development or complicated data manipulation. Traditional spreadsheet users have limited systems training and awareness and tend not to be in touch with market offerings. They may also be unaware of the complexity of the applications or data manipulations they wish to build or perform.

For all these reasons, sophisticated and novice developers and analysts tend to use a stand-alone spreadsheet package. And so while ancillary and alternative products offer logical bridges to proper environments, they may not offer practical bridges to those environments. In the worst-case scenario, users developing applications strictly for their own use do not investigate ancillary or alternative products. The result is unwieldy, error-prone spreadsheet applications.

Counter Arguments

Arguments are advanced for developing complex applications in a spreadsheet environment, even when other environments are more appropriate. This is a natural result of the popularity of spreadsheet products like Lotus 1–2–3. Users have become comfortable with such products and have invested significant time and effort in developing related skills. The greater the skill level a user has with an individual product or within an individual environment, the greater the tendency to overapply the product or environment. Many users have developed excellent spreadsheet skills but, at the same time, are reluctant to investigate other tools better suited for specialized or larger projects.

Two reasons are advanced to justify the development of specialized or complex applications within the spreadsheet environment. The first reason is that the developer is proficient only with a certain spreadsheet product. Second, in large corporations, many individuals know and own a particular spreadsheet package. Consequently, development of applications in this familiar environment will help insure acceptance within the organization.

Justifying the use of a spreadsheet package for complex modeling projects based on the comfort level of the developer is a myopic approach. This approach does not force the planner or analyst to improve general systems skills. Most planners and analysts have highly developed skills and knowledge bases in their areas of expertise. They should be encouraged to investigate software products that can best complement their knowledge and skills. Many users argue that corporate information centers provide inadequate support for new products. They would rather go with a known commodity when developing applications and avoid the risks associated with selecting and applying other products. This argument is not without merit.

Information centers are often staffed by individuals with competent systems backgrounds but who lack other specialized expertise. For example, the center may support statistical and financial modeling software but cannot provide a consultant with expertise in statistical or financial analysis and applications development. In these situations, the information center is not a satisfactory source for new product information or software support. The answer to this problem is straightforward. Planners and other analysts must seek alternative sources of information. They must find other users with similar responsibilities and query them on the products they use. Other excellent sources of information include user groups, conferences, and software vendor trade shows. Some firms maintain internal consulting groups. Staff consultants have both systems knowledge and expertise in a specific discipline such as econometrics, statistics, finance, or mathematics. These groups provide excellent information.

There are many sources of product information and support, the information center being just one. Users must become adept at locating alternative sources of information. Further, for most financial, statistical, and econometric applications, packages exist that are not difficult to master and yet offer significant advantages over spreadsheet environments. These packages greatly improve the quality and decrease the development time of applications.

The second justification offered for developing complex applications with spreadsheet packages is the widespread use of a particular package within an organization. The position advanced is that application acceptance is encouraged because users already own a particular spreadsheet package and are comfortable with its use. The argument is over applied and is only relevant for applications that have a reasonable probability of being used by a significant number of individuals within the organization.

If an application stands a reasonable probability of being used by several individuals, the developer should consider two other options before deciding to use a spreadsheet package to complete an application. First, other popular products offer means of user input and do not require knowledge of the specific package employed to develop the application. For example, products like AREMOS and IFPS offer facilities to develop query-type interfaces. The user is prompted for a series of answers before an application is run. Admittedly, the developer must have proficiency with these systems to build such interfaces. The developer should also consider using spreadsheets to front-end applications processed in other environments. The term *front-end* refers to a process where a spreadsheet or other suitable systems tool is used to develop a user interface for an application developed in another package or a high-level language. For example, a spreadsheet menu interface can be used to gather information from a model user. This information is then used to generate a data set that is passed on to an application developed using IFPS, AREMOS, BASIC, PASCAL, or some other package or language.

By using a spreadsheet to front-end a model built with a specialized package or high-level programming language, the applications developer achieves a familiar and user-friendly interface and does not forfeit the power of more traditional systems tools. Usually the user will interface with a spreadsheet in the microcomputing environment, but the final application might reside on a micro, mini, or mainframe computer.

Many managers feel that the microcomputer has set them free—free of computer applications development backlogs, dependence on programmers and other systems personnel, and high computing costs. However, is it wise to ignore the systems review process all together? People who manage planners and analysts must be sure that their staffs are employing reasonably efficient means to complete projects. If applied properly, microcomputer technology offers great benefits, but the tendency to develop applications with improper systems tools mitigates these advantages. While this argument applies in general, the abuse of spreadsheet products is particularly acute. This phenomenon comes as no surprise given the number of planners and other analysts who use microcomputers but lack formal systems training.

The freedom offered by the microcomputing environment—the freedom for end-users to develop applications, the freedom to select specialized software and hardware, and the freedom to customize environments—carries with it the responsibility to have a basic understanding of that environment and available applications development software.

DATA COLLECTION AND MANIPULATION

As discussed earlier, spreadsheets are used for data collection and manipulation. Depending on the manipulations to be performed, the spreadsheet may offer an excellent enviroment. This is especially true of spreadsheet products that offer ways of conquering the dimensionality problem. Several factors suggest that spreadsheet packages will continue to increase as the default medium for exchanging and manipulating data: Worksheet files have become popular for transferring data between users via the exchange of floppy disks; data vendors offer facilities for translating data into worksheet formats; most spreadsheet products are expected to incorporate consolidation capabilities; and indications are that some spreadsheet products will allow users to include sophisticated database commands. This will allow the spreadsheet to become the receptacle of data stored in a number of databases. A common theme is the ability to include Standard Query Language (SQL) commands in spreadsheets. These commands will be used to receive data from DB2 databases. In planned systems, data will reside on a myriad of connected computers, thus allowing the microcomputer user to query mainframe or minicomputer databases.

Lotus HAL offers a common language interface for Lotus 1–2–3, which facilitates data queries and manipulation. The product also has advanced programming features that greatly simplify certain operations formerly completed using macros.

LESS COMMON BUT APPROPRIATE USES FOR SPREADSHEETS

Using Spreadsheets to Front End Applications

As mentioned earlier, spreadsheets can be used to develop front ends for applications written in high-level languages or based in other packages. Such an approach can offer the developer the best of both worlds: a comfortable and familiar user interface and the proper environment for developing complex applications. However, most corporate applications developers do not consider this approach when building applications.

This approach is implemented in one of two ways. The most common method is to use a menu interface to generate a data set. This data set is then passed to programs developed with popular languages or other software packages. The second approach is to use the spreadsheet front end to modify a model's program code. This code is then passed to another environment.

Building menus is a straightforward process with many spreadsheet packages, and users have become comfortable with the point and select process. The menu interface is only one of three interface formats that applications developers can employ. Template and query formats can also be used. Interface formats are more fully discussed in Chapter 9.

Prototyping

Although the general tendency has been to apply spreadsheets to applications best handled by traditional systems tools, the spreadsheet environment is virtually ignored for producing prototype models. This is an area for which the spreadsheet often provides the ideal enviroment. Prototypes are small, simplified versions of large or complex applications. They test algorithms, the suitability of user interfaces, data structures, and so forth. The prototype serves as a means to review the general capabilities and characteristics of proposed applications before they are built. Together, developers and users can test the user interface, discuss data inputs, and review output reports and graphs.

Prototypes generally include a limited set of data, only the most important computing routines and reports, and (usually) a user interface similar to that proposed for the final application. Spreadsheets can be used to develop prototypes for applications that will eventually be built in other environments. The spreadsheet environment is quite flexible and allows several types of user interfaces, graphics, and reporting formats. The developer can mimic other environments easily and efficiently and, therefore, can build a prototype in short order.

Prototypes may or may not be functional—that is, they may or may not actually employ algorithms intended for the final application. Nonfunctional prototypes are appropriate for developing user specifications and for allowing the developer and the user (or manager) to iterate on a design that will be suitable. Functional prototypes include the core algorithms and data structures intended for the final application. Beyond appearing like the final application, they attempt to work like it. As the prototype becomes more complex, the spreadsheet may or may not be the appropriate environment for development. Again, the spreadsheet combined with traditional systems tools might serve as a reasonable means for developing complex functional prototypes.

SUMMARY

The spreadsheet environment is popular for data collection and manipulation and certain operations requiring lists, data tables, and limited databases. It can be ideal for certain accounting and financial applications. Developments such as consolidation and database query capabilities will contribute to the spreadsheet's popularity in these areas.

The spreadsheet has been overapplied. Users should consider completing complex data manipulations and applications using ancillary tools or alternative environments. Many applications built using popular spreadsheet products are better developed using a product employing an equation modeling format. Complex data analysis is more efficiently completed using existing analysis packages. User resistance to ancillary and alternative products is high. Reasons include the number of users who are comfortable with specific spreadsheet products that are widely known and supported in large organizations, and inertia. Managers should encourage experimentation using alternative systems tools that best complement the employee's current knowledge base.

AREMOS AND PCMark8

Planners often use sophisticated econometric and financial modeling systems to build models. Some planning departments employ models built by outside consulting firms, and these include macroeconomic, regional, and industry models. AREMOS is an example of a software system that can be used to build a variety of models. The chapters in this section describe the AREMOS system and review an example of a vendor-supplied macroeconomic model—The Wefa Group's PCMark8 model of the U.S. economy.

Chapter 6 provides a high-level overview of AREMOS. The system offers powerful database management and advanced programming capabilities. Simple and sophisticated models can be built using a traditional equation modeling format. A variety of statistical and graphical methods can be used to analyze time-series data.

Chapter 7 discusses the PCMark8 model. PCMark8 is an AREMOS-based macroeconomic model used to investigate simple and complex scenarios. The WEFA Group's staff economists developed and maintain PCMark8, but users can investigate macroeconomic scenarios on office microcomputers. Users are provided multiple sets of forecast data that incorporate optimistic, pessimistic, and most likely assumptions about near-term economic conditions. General economic conditions can affect variables that are important to organizations. Changes in macroeconomic conditions can influence such variables as sales, prices, manufacturing expenses, consumer sentiment, and demand for social services. Examples in later chapters will illustrate the use of macroeconomic variables in firm-level planning models.

The example presented in Chapter 7 illustrates the far-reaching effects resulting from a change in imported oil prices. This scenario affects diverse sectors of the U.S. economy and illustrates the value of macroeconomic models. Regional and industry models have similar properties to the PCMark8, both in operation and in the richness of agent interactions evident in scenario studies. Chapter 7 will have special value for analysts considering the use of macroeconomic, regional, and industry models.

An important theme emerges during this discussion of the PCMark8 model. Planners are maligned when forecasts prove inaccurate. The thrust of planning analysis is moving away from forecasting and toward risk analysis. Defining the risks associated with plausible scenarios is the key objective of planning analysis. Most planning applications include a baseline forecast incorporating the planner's best information concerning future conditions. Scenario analyses use this baseline forecast as a benchmark, and the risks of each scenario are measured against the baseline case. Of course, the results of multiple scenario studies can be compared against each other. The reporting format used in Chapter 7 will re-surface in later chapters when planning models and functional planning tools are discussed. The format shows scenario, baseline, and delta (scenario minus base-line) results.

6

AREMOS
An Overview

ROBERTA WHOL

AREMOS is a fully integrated decision support system which allows the user to store, modify, analyze, and present time-series data in a single environment. AREMOS is an acronym for Advanced Retrieval and Econometric Modeling System. There are both mainframe and microcomputer versions of AREMOS, and each version supports a large user population. Several models built by The WEFA Group are AREMOS-based. These include versions of the Mark8 macroeconomic model of the U.S. economy, the Long-Term Model of the U.S. economy, and individual models of all Organization for Economic Cooperation and Development (OECD) countries.

AREMOS offers a structured, nonprocedural command language, and command syntax is easy to learn. Because of its powerful database design, ease of use, analytical functionality, and inclusion of a high-level programming language, AREMOS can be used for a variety of modeling and data analysis projects. These can include large economic and financial simultaneous equation models.

AREMOS uses can be roughly divided into three categories: data storage, analysis, and presentation.

DATA STORAGE

AREMOS is designed around a powerful database structure, and data can be accessed from a variety of files. Data series can also be directly entered into the system, and many operations require limited manual data entry.

Most operations involve the access of demographic, economic, and proprietary data series from data files. Data series are often accessed from data interchange format (DIF) and time series format (TSD) files. Many microcomputer-based packages can write and convert DIF files, and this facilitates data exchange between AREMOS and other packages. Data vendors often make data available in DIF files.

TSD files are generated by AREMOS. These allow the user to store and transfer descriptive information in addition to data values.

AREMOS can read print files (also known as ASCII, text, flat, and PRN extension files). These can be generated using word processors and spreadsheet, database management, and other specialized packages. For example, it is common practice to use spreadsheet packages to produce data tables in print file format. These data tables are then read into AREMOS. AREMOS can also produce print files so that data can be exchanged to and from spreadsheet files, word processors, and other software packages. Because of the popularity of the Lotus 1–2–3 spreadsheet package, a special data exchange capability has been added to the microcomputer-based version of AREMOS (AREMOS/PC) allowing the package to both read and write 1–2–3 worksheet data information without the need to create print files.

Data can be transferred between the microcomputer and mainframe versions of AREMOS (AREMOS/PC and AREMOS/VM). This data communication is bi-directional—that is, data can be downloaded to the microcomputer from the mainframe and uploaded from the microcomputer to the mainframe.

While data can be accessed from many different types of data files, and from both the microcomputer and mainframe environments, most data are ultimately stored in an AREMOS databank. By this process, data accessed from a variety of file formats and locations become homogeneous. For example, after being stored in an AREMOS databank, a data series that is hand entered in AREMOS and a data series extracted from a 1–2–3 worksheet are treated identically by the AREMOS system.

An existing AREMOS databank file can be expanded in several ways. Existing data series can be revised, and new data series can be added. New data series are often derived as transformations of existing data series. Descriptive information concerning stored data series can also be added or changed.

AREMOS databases are flexible both conceptually and physically. The actual size of an individual databank file is limited only by the system's storage medium. Data series can have a variety of frequencies: annual, semiannual, quarterly, monthly, biweekly, weekly, lunar, and periodic. A data series' frequency is indicated by its extension. For example, GNP.A and GNP.Q denote gross national product with annual and quarterly frequencies, respectively. Series with identical names but different frequencies can coexist in the same databank file. While the bulk of most databank files will consist of data series, other information can also be stored in a databank. Scalars, matrices, equation specifications, model specifications, functions, lists, and other information can be stored in a databank file.

ANALYSIS

AREMOS includes facilities for analyzing individual data series and relationships between data series. Analysis capabilities begin with such standard measures as mean, variance, and correlations and extend to multivariate regression analysis and simultaneous equation models. This range of capabilities is important because it allows the user a great deal of power and flexibility within a single system. AREMOS can be used for simple data analysis or to solve complex systems of equations such as large financial models or macroeconomic models of the U.S. economy.

AREMOS/PC can offer great savings over traditional time-sharing methods of analysis. For example, a subscriber to The WEFA Group's AREMOS-based PCMark8 model can run macroeconomic scenarios on a variety of microcomputers. The marginal computing cost of running such scenarios is virtually nonexistent. The PCMark8 model contains several hundred equations. While superior speed performance is offered by 80286- and 80386-based microcomputers, individual scenario studies can be completed in a few moments using a simple 8088-based (IBM PC-XT class) microcomputer.

PRESENTATION

The presentation of results is an important aspect of business analysis, both for investigative and reporting purposes. Analytically, graphic and tabular presentation of results is important in data and scenario analysis. For reporting purposes, graphic and tabular presentation of results affects an audience's ability to grasp key findings. Graphic presentation is becoming increasingly popular because of several factors: the sophistication of output devices (laser and color printers, plotters, video displays, for example), the falling cost of generating sophisticated presentation materials, and the unwillingness and inability of audiences to study tabular reports.

AREMOS offers a sophisticated report generator that gives the user control over the presentation of tabular material. AREMOS also offers a variety of graphic formats for presenting data and allows the user options over labels, footnotes, and so on. AREMOS offers the following graphic formats (some of which are shown in Illustration 6.1): stacked bar chart, histogram, pie chart, X-Y plot, multiple series against time, line graphs, connected and unconnected symbols, and step graphs.

MICROCOMPUTER AND MAINFRAME VERSIONS
OF AREMOS

The microcomputer and mainframe versions of AREMOS are functionally identical—that is, the same analysis can be accomplished in either environment, but the steps involved in accomplishing the analysis can be somewhat different. Specifically, the two systems differ in graphics, keyboard/screen capabilities, and user interfaces.

AREMOS/VM runs under the Conversational Monitoring System (CMS), and AREMOS/PC runs under PC-DOS and MS-DOS. AREMOS/VM makes use of CA-TELLAGRAF software (from Computer Associates International) in pro-

Illustration 6.1
Examples of AREMOS Graphics

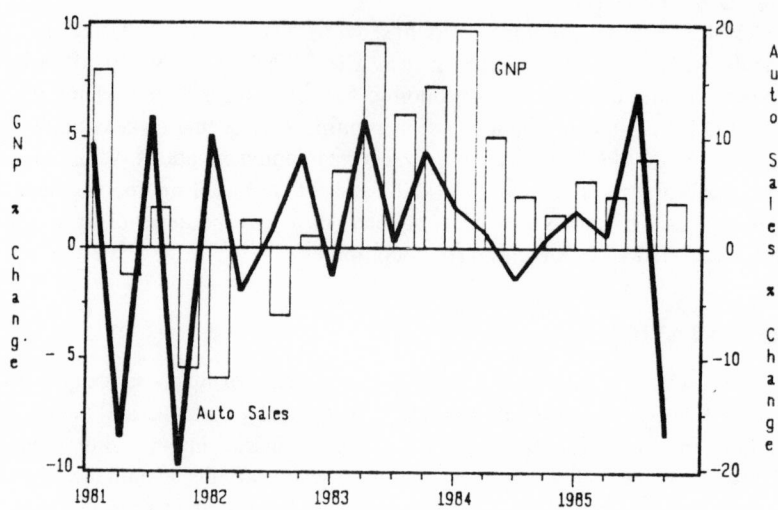

Growth in GNP
and Auto Sales

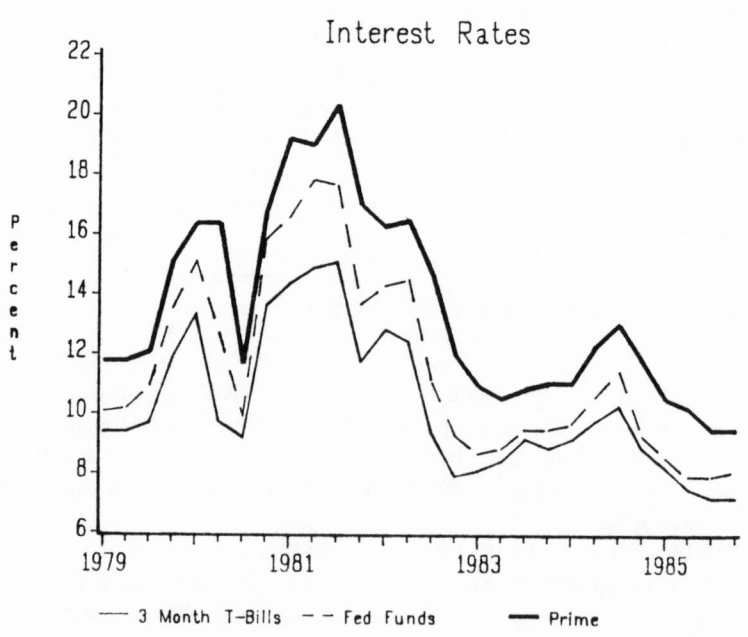

Interest Rates

Illustration 6.1 (continued)

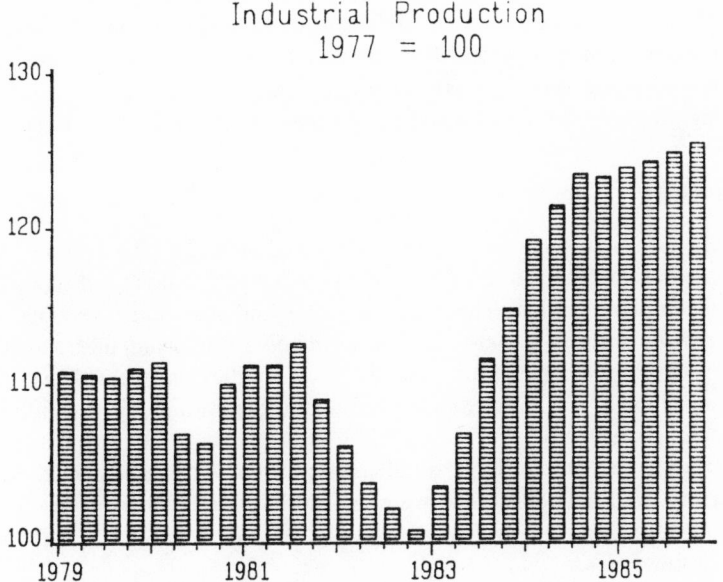

Industrial Production
1977 = 100

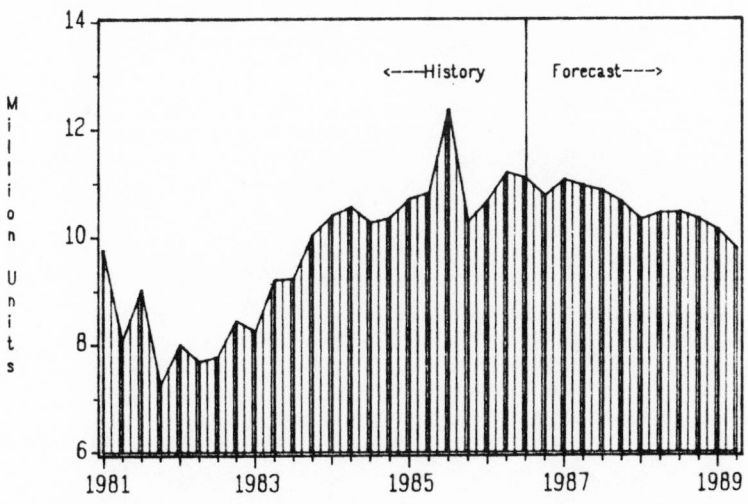

Auto Sales
History and Forecast

ducing presentation-quality color graphics. AREMOS/PC has advanced capabilities for printing and plotting presentation-quality graphics and produces output in less time than graphics generated via the mainframe.

Keyboard and screen handling are other areas where the mainframe and microcomputer versions of AREMOS diverge. Microcomputer keyboards include function keys and very fast screen-handling. AREMOS/PC uses these features offering graphics and tabular formatting capabilities and full-screen data entry.

SUMMARY

AREMOS is an integrated system developed around a powerful yet flexible database design. The system offers varied analytical functions and sophisticated presentation capabilities. The microcomputer and mainframe versions of the software do differ, but most differences involve microcomputer capabilities. Efforts have been made to exploit these capabilities and provide users with superior graphics and tabular data presentation facilities along with full-screen data entry forms.

AREMOS can support large simultaneous econometric and financial models, and many WEFA Group models are AREMOS-based. Most of these models offer menu or template-driven user interfaces, but models can easily be run without these aids.

7

PCMark8

WILLIAM GERLACH

PCMark8 is a 427 equation, quarterly frequency, simultaneous, macroeconomic model used by economists and business planners to forecast short-term economic activity in the United States. PCMark8 is the eighth quarterly U.S. model developed by The WEFA Group under the guidance of Nobel Laureate Lawrence Klein. The PCMark8 is the second version of these models available for use on microcomputers. The initial quarterly model, known as the Wharton Model, was constructed by Klein in 1963 at the behest of business leaders interested in improving the corporate planning process through more accurate forecasts of economic activity.

The original Wharton Model contained fewer than 100 equations and could be solved on a mechanical desktop calculator by a nimble-fingered statistician in roughly one day! The rapid development of mainframe computer technology during the 1960s and 1970s dramatically reduced solution time, which in turn allowed for larger, more detailed models, broader scenario analysis, and more consistent and accurate forecasts. An unfortunate by-product of powerful mainframe model-solving packages was exorbitant time-sharing costs. Before the advent of microcomputer-based macroeconomic models, model solvers were constrained by the balances of their computer accounts. Today's microcomputer-based models, such as PCMark8, combine the speed of mainframe computers with the expense of the old mechanical calculators. Models containing as many as 1,000 equations can be solved in minutes with little cost. Inexperienced users can now afford to experiment with microcomputer-based macroeconomic models without fear of huge computer expense. If microcomputer advances continue at their current pace, most, if not all, econometric forecasting will be moved from the mainframe to the microcomputer within two years. By 1988, the twenty-fifth anniversary of the development of the first quarterly model, even the most sophisticated econometric modeling and forecasting will be performed on a microcomputer.

The PCMark8 model consists of many distinct sectors which together comprise the U.S. economy. Each sector is made up of four components: exogenous assumptions, behavioral equations, add factors, and identities.

Exogenous assumptions are data inputs with values determined outside of the PCMark8 model. Exogenous assumptions are embodied in behavioral equations, and associated forecast values for exogenous data series are derived from other econometric models or analysis. PCMark8 employs a host of exogenous assumptions, such as the price of oil, which serve two purposes: First, some economic concepts, oil prices in particular, are very difficult to predict using standard regression analysis. Given the power of OPEC to manipulate world oil prices through abrupt changes in supply, a reasonable forecast of oil prices is dependent on a thorough understanding of OPEC's strategy and market reaction to that strategy. This sort of collusive and potentially arbitrary behavior is not easily predicted solely by econometric analysis. Instead, an exogenous data series is developed by a WEFA Group energy economist employing a variety of techniques to shape a forecast. Other exogenously developed data series are output by separate specialized models, and, in this way, forecast output from one model may be used as exogenous input to the PCMark8 model. Second, exogenous assumptions are used as policy levers to ease forecast manipulation. PCMark8 users can measure the effects of decreases in defense spending or hikes in the federal funds rate simply by altering the exogenous series for these concepts and resolving the model.

Behavioral equations are derived through regression analysis using time-series data. Typically, a model builder will start the specification of an equation by selecting the variables believed to be fundamental determinants of the equation's behavior. Next, different forms of the equation are regressed and variables are dropped or added to achieve the best possible fit. The final version of an equation will contain coefficients for each explanatory (independent) variable. Optimally the equation will predict the historical values of the dependent variable with very small error, say within 1 to 2 percent. The difference between the actual value and the predicted value generated by the equation is called the residual. All behavioral equations have at least a small residual. Behavioral equations are the core of a simultaneous macroeconomic model. They represent the basic strength of econometric theory: the ability to predict future economic interactions based on past economic interactions. Here is a simple equation for total consumption expenditures:

$$CONSUMPTION = 0.922 \times DISPOSABLEINCOME +$$
$$0.622 \times CONSUMERSENTIMENT - 82.355$$

In this equation, consumption is the dependent (or explained) variable, and disposable income and consumer sentiment are the independent (or explanatory) variables. Coefficients associated with the explanatory variables measure the individual effects attributed to these variables. For example, 0.922 is the coefficient for disposable income, implying that each $1 billion increase in disposable income will increase consumption by $922 million. (For more information on the interpretation of econometric equations, see Chapter 11.)

There are two ways to adjust the forecast of a behavioral equation: exclude the equation from the model and peg the forecast values, or change the equation's add factor. For example, a user interested in the effects of a $2 billion increase in automobile consumption could exclude the behavioral equation, CEDA (Consumer Expenditures for Durable Goods—Automobiles), and raise its forecast values for all future periods.

EXCLUDE AUTO;
CHANGE{INCREASE}AUTO = 2,2,2,2,2;

By excluding the equation, the user has literally taken the equation out of the model. The value of CEDA is now an exogenous assumption; it is an explanatory component of other behavioral equations, but its forecast values are no longer determined by the model.

Alternatively, a user can modify the add factor for the behavioral equation without excluding the behavioral equation from the model solution process. An add factor is similar to a residual for the forecast period. Over the estimation period, a residual is also referred to as an error term for an equation. The error term is the difference between the actual historical value for the dependent variable and the predicted values for the dependent variable generated by the behavioral equation. As mentioned previously, no behavioral equations predict their historical values exactly, so naturally the unadjusted forecast for a behavioral equation is also subject to error.

Add factors were created to compensate for nonrandom errors and to simplify policy analysis. An add factor is applied to the output of the behavioral equation, increasing or decreasing its natural value. For example, suppose the equation for consumption of autos and parts predicts a value of $144 billion for the first quarter of 1987. The forecaster decides that based on the rate of 1986 fourth-quarter sales, rising consumer debt, and tax law changes, auto consumption will be roughly $142 billion. To effect that change, the forecaster would set the add factor for the equation equal to -2. When the model is re-solved, this time using the add factor, the auto consumption result in the first quarter of 1987 will be:

$$142 = 144 + (-2)$$

In short, add factors enable forecasters to better reflect prevailing economic conditions and shape alternative forecasts. Modifying add factors is the most commonly employed method of forecast adjustment for large, complex models.

The final component of an econometric model is an identity. An identity is a simple arithmetic statement, aggregating or disaggregating several economic concepts. Identities are not the result of regression analysis and do not have residuals. Rather, identities are economic accounting tools. An example of an identity is:

CONSUMP = DURABLE + NONDURABLE + SERVICES

That is, total consumption is the sum of durable consumption, nondurable consumption, and service consumption. While identities can be excluded and modified, it is more common to change behavioral equations or exogenous components.

MODEL SECTORS AND LINKAGES

The PCMark8 model can be conceptualized as ten major sections: consumption, investment, government, personal income, prices, financial, profits and capital, employment and demographics, foreign sector, and energy. Individual planners have more interest in sectors relevant to their markets. For example, firms producing various consumer goods have a heightened interest in the consumption and personal income sectors of the model because these sectors will determine the willingness and ability of consumers to purchase goods. For general discussion, a detailed understanding of the elements comprising each sector are not necessary. However, those with further interests will find a detailed explanation of each of the model's ten sectors in an appendix to this chapter.

PCMark8 is a highly simultaneous model, implying that shocks imposed on one sector will have effects in other sectors. For example, if interest rates fall, consumption and investment will rise. Unemployment will fall, labor compensation costs will increase. As labor costs rise, so will prices, triggering a possible increase in interest rates and a drop in consumption and investment and so on. The utility of a macroeconomic model is the ability to simulate economic events that occur when the economy is thrown into disequilibrium. Econometric models rely on integrated equations and sectors to reproduce the complexity and diversity of economic activity.

This chapter includes a PCMark8 scenario study. The example details macroeconomic responses to increases in OPEC oil prices. PCMark8/AREMOS (the AREMOS-based version of the PCMark8 model) is used to analyze macroeconomic responses to a steep rise in crude oil prices. The exogenous series for oil prices is increased over the forecast period. The model is resolved to yield a forecast of economic conditions. Scenario results are then compared to the original (baseline) forecast. The impact is substantial and pervasive: prices, incomes, consumption, car sales, tax receipts, the deficit, labor costs, investment, and interest rates are significantly and explicably different from the original forecast.

PCMark8 SOLUTION EXAMPLE

To access AREMOS, first move to the AREMOS directory. This is accomplished by entering:

CD \AREMOS   (Change Directory, AREMOS)

Once in the AREMOS directory, enter:
When the AREMOS banner and prompt appear, the user is ready to work with the PCMark8 model. The user enters the key word:

→ PCQTR (Right arrows indicate user entered AREMOS commands. The user need not enter the arrow.)

This key word is the name of a procedure stored in the AREMOS support bank. A procedure is a series of AREMOS commands stored in a databank and executed when the procedure name is entered. The AREMOS support bank contains error messages and procedures, such as this one, for various WEFA Group models. In general, databanks contain time-series data, documentation, lists, procedures, and models. This particular procedure consists of just two commands:

OPEN{PROTECT}PCQTR;

PCQTR:PCQTR;

The first command opens the PCMark8 procedure bank, PCQTR, protected from user modification. The second command directs AREMOS to execute the procedure PCQTR stored in the bank PCQTR. The procedure, when executed, displays the forecast menu in Illustration 7.1.

Selection number one copies the baseline forecast into the bank MYSIM, opens MYSIM as the primary bank, sets the forecast period, the model to be used, and a variety of solution options. When the procedure ends, the AREMOS solution environment is fully prepared. Selections two and three enable users to generate the high and low alternative forecasts based on The WEFA Group's changes or the user's changes to the baseline forecast assumptions. Selection five provides an overview of the model structure and descriptions of all model-related procedures.

The next example tracks the impact of four successive OPEC oil price increases. The price of OPEC oil is increased over baseline levels for four consecutive quarters, starting in the first quarter of 1987. To limit the solution to

Illustration 7.1
The Forecast Menu

```
WELCOME TO WHARTON'S PCMARK8 QUARTERLY MODEL OF THE U.S. ECONOMY.

    Selections 1-4 copy the forecast of your choice into the databank MYSIM
and prepare AREMOS for model simulation. Selection 5 displays useful
information pertaining to the model, policy analysis, and printing of
standard tables.

1. WHARTON'S BASELINE FORECAST
2. WHARTON'S HIGH ALTERNATIVE MENU
3. WHARTON'S LOW ALTERNATIVE MENU
4. OTHER FORECAST
5. MODEL OVERVIEW, POLICY ANALYSIS HELP-FILES, AND STANDARD TABLES
6. QUIT

(ENTER 1, 2, 3, 4, 5, OR 6 TO QUIT) => 1
```

four quarters, the period is reset. The exogenous series for OPEC oil prices is increased $5, $8, $12, and $15, using the CHANGE command.

→ SET PERIOD 87Q1 87Q4;

→ CHANGE{INCREASE}OPECPRICE = 5,8,12,15;

To compare how the new oil price path differs from the actual forecast, a procedure called SCOM is invoked. SCOM, short for solution comparison, prints the level, absolute difference, and percentage difference for like-named series in different banks. A version qualifier is a tag given to each AREMOS data series. Normally the tag is used to denote frequency. For example, GNP.Q would be gross national product at a quarterly frequency. The version SOL is used to identify forecast or solution data series. The user enters:

→ SCOM

The following prompts appear:

ENTER SERIES FOR COMPARISON → OPECPRICE

ENTER FIRST BANK NAME → MYSIM

ENTER SECOND BANK NAME → QTRBASE

ENTER FIRST VERSION QUALIFIER → SOL

ENTER SECOND VERSION QUALIFIER → SOL

After this information is supplied, the information in Table 7.1 will appear on screen.

By the fourth quarter of 1987, the increase of oil prices is nearly 100 percent above baseline values. The changes to OPECPRICE will feed directly into several

Table 7.1.
PCMark8 Solution Comparison: OPEC Oil Price

	OPECPRICE MYSIM	OPECPRICE QTRBASE	DIFFERENCE	% DIFFERENCE
1987				
Q1	21.5	16.5	5.00	30.30
Q2	23.5	15.5	8.00	51.61
Q3	27.0	15.0	12.00	80.00
Q4	30.5	15.5	15.00	96.77

Units: Price per barrel, current U.S. dollars.

equations including investment in domestic drilling structures, three import deflators, and the refiner cost of crude oil. The equations for import deflators and the refiner cost of crude oil distribute the effects of the price shock throughout the PCMark8 model, directly affecting trade, producer and consumer prices, and indirectly affecting consumption, investment, income, and government expenditures and receipts. For this example, only a single modification was made to this PCMark8/AREMOS simulation. However, users may change many exogenous variables or add factors and exclude many behavioral equations. With the OPEC oil price increase complete, the PCMark8 model is ready to be solved. The key word SIM is entered. Like PCQTR and SCOM, SIM is a procedure which solves the simultaneous and recursive parts of PCMark8.

→SIM

When the AREMOS prompt appears, the solution is complete, and the results have been stored in the primary bank, MYSIM.

Next is a command which will create a list of data series. A list is AREMOS shorthand for storing frequently used series names. For example, if a user always compares the same data series after solving a new forecast scenario, the list obviates the need to enter long strings of data series names. Lists, like data series, are stored in databanks. This particular list is to be used as the variable name input to the SCOM procedure. When the prompt "ENTER SERIES FOR COMPARISON" appears, the list name is entered preceded by a pound sign(#). The pound sign lets AREMOS know that a list is forthcoming. The SCOM procedure will print the comparison for each series contained in the list.

→ LIST OIL = GASPRICE, CONPRICE, DISPINC, SAVINGRATE, CONSUMPTION,

    . . . TOTCOMP, USCARS, FORCARS, PROFITS, RECEIPTS, DEFICIT,

    . . . OILSTRUC, STRUCOTH, UNITLABOR, PRIME, %GNP;

→ SCOM

Table 7.2.
PCMark8 Solution Comparison: Gasoline Price Index

	GASPRICE MYSIM	GASPRICE QTRBASE	DIFFERENCE	% DIFFERENCE
1987				
Q1	311.8	278.9	32.83	11.77
Q2	359.9	287.1	72.77	25.34
Q3	398.7	294.5	104.21	35.38
Q4	431.0	298.7	132.39	44.33

Index: 1967 = 100.

Table 7.3.
PCMark8 Solution Comparison: Consumer Price Index

	CONPRICE MYSIM	CONPRICE QTRBASE	DIFFERENCE	% DIFFERENCE
1987				
Q1	336.0	333.8	2.20	0.66
Q2	341.9	336.9	4.99	1.48
Q3	347.8	340.1	7.65	2.25
Q4	354.1	343.9	10.28	2.99

Index: 1967 = 100.

ENTER SERIES FOR COMPARISON → #OIL

ENTER FIRST BANK NAME → MYSIM

ENTER SECOND BANK NAME → QTRBASE

ENTER FIRST VERSION QUALIFIER → SOL

ENTER SECOND VERSION QUALIFIER → SOL

After the user supplies the necessary information, scenario (solution) and baseline report tables are generated for each of the data series contained in the earlier list. (Note: The series names used here are not actual mnemonics. Series names have been changed for purposes of exposition.)

First, the GASPRICE data series comparison is generated (see Table 7.2). Gasoline prices rise over 44 percent by the fourth quarter of 1987 because of a similar increase in the refiner cost of crude oil. Heating oil prices would also rise substantially.

Next, consumer price index information is generated (see Table 7.3). Spurred by the soaring oil prices, overall consumer prices rise nearly 3 percent by the end of 1987.

Real disposable income drops $65 billion as the oil price hikes erode real spending power (see Table 7.4).

Table 7.4.
PCMark8 Solution Comparison: Disposable Income

	DISPINC MYSIM	DISPINC QTRBASE	DIFFERENCE	% DIFFERENCE
1987				
Q1	2595.5	2612.9	-17.40	-0.67
Q2	2600.3	2635.4	-35.06	-1.33
Q3	2603.9	2654.6	-50.72	-1.91
Q4	2596.6	2662.1	-65.48	-2.46

Units: Billions of 1982 U.S. dollars.

Table 7.5.
PCMark8 Solution Comparison: Savings Rate

	SAVINGRATE MYSIM	SAVINGRATE QTRBASE	DIFFERENCE	% DIFFERENCE
1987				
Q1	2.8	3.3	-0.44	-13.46
Q2	2.7	3.4	-0.73	-21.19
Q3	2.5	3.4	-0.89	-26.19
Q4	2.1	3.1	-0.99	-32.40

Table 7.6.
PCMark8 Solution Comparison: Consumption

	CONSUMPTION MYSIM	CONSUMPTION QTRBASE	DIFFERENCE	% DIFFERENCE
1987				
Q1	2436.7	2441.7	-4.98	-0.20
Q2	2445.7	2459.3	-13.60	-0.55
Q3	2455.4	2479.0	-23.60	-0.95
Q4	2459.7	2494.1	-34.40	-1.38

Units: Billions of 1982 U.S. dollars.

The rise in prices without an equal rise in wages forces a drop in saving even if consumers decrease spending moderately (see Table 7.5).

Total personal consumption falls by $34.4 billion, or 1.4 percent, a direct result of declining spending power (see Table 7.6).

Real compensation also declines as wage gains, if any, do not keep pace with cost of living increases (see Table 7.7).

Sales of domestically produced cars also fall, the result of disposable income losses and car buyers opting for more fuel efficient imports (see Table 7.8).

Sales of foreign-produced cars also fall, but at roughly a fourth the rate of domestic sales. The number of foreign cars sold in the United States declines, but foreign market share rises, suggesting that some would-be foreign and do-

Table 7.7.
PCMark8 Solution Comparison: Total Compensation

	TOTCOMP MYSIM	TOTCOMP QTRBASE	DIFFERENCE	% DIFFERENCE
1987				
Q1	2203.4	2214.1	-10.74	-0.48
Q2	2201.2	2228.7	-27.42	-1.23
Q3	2199.9	2244.5	-44.54	-1.98
Q4	2202.5	2261.7	-59.14	-2.61

Units: Billions of 1982 U.S. dollars.

Table 7.8.
PCMark8 Solution Comparison: U.S. Automobiles (Cars)

	USCARS MYSIM	USCARS QTRBASE	DIFFERENCE	% DIFFERENCE
1987				
Q1	6.7	6.9	-0.13	-1.92
Q2	6.7	7.0	-0.32	-4.61
Q3	6.9	7.4	-0.50	-6.81
Q4	6.7	7.3	-0.64	-8.69

Units: Millions.

Table 7.9.
PCMark8 Solution Comparison: Foreign Automobiles (Cars)

	FORCARS MYSIM	FORCARS QTRBASE	DIFFERENCE	% DIFFERENCE
1987				
Q1	3.0	3.0	-0.02	-0.66
Q2	3.0	3.1	-0.04	-1.27
Q3	3.1	3.2	-0.05	-1.72
Q4	3.2	3.2	-0.07	-2.25

Units: Millions.

mestic new car buyers delay purchases, and some buyers originally interested in a domestically manufactured car change their mind when faced with steep fuel prices (see Table 7.9).

The increase in energy prices, coupled with a drop in consumption, causes before-tax corporate profits (including capital consumption allowance and inventory adjustments) to plunge almost 10 percent (see Table 7.10).

Total government receipts fall due to losses in corporate taxes and an overall decrease in economic activity (see Table 7.11).

Table 7.10.
PCMark8 Solution Comparison: Profits

	PROFITS MYSIM	PROFITS QTRBASE	DIFFERENCE	% DIFFERENCE
1987				
Q1	287.5	308.1	-20.55	-6.67
Q2	292.3	315.0	-22.69	-7.20
Q3	293.5	322.7	-29.14	-9.03
Q4	302.9	333.9	-31.04	-9.30

Units: Billions of current U.S. dollars.

Table 7.11.
PCMark8 Solution Comparison: Government Receipts

	RECEIPTS MYSIM	RECEIPTS QTRBASE	DIFFERENCE	% DIFFERENCE
1987				
Q1	850.7	859.3	-8.57	-1.00
Q2	855.9	862.5	-6.54	-0.76
Q3	873.2	882.3	-9.15	-1.04
Q4	911.9	920.7	-8.87	-0.96

Units: Billions of current U.S. dollars.

Table 7.12.
PCMark8 Solution Comparison: Federal Deficit

	DEFICIT MYSIM	DEFICIT QTRBASE	DIFFERENCE	% DIFFERENCE
1987				
Q1	-203.1	-194.2	-8.85	4.55
Q2	-193.4	-185.8	-7.64	4.11
Q3	-193.4	-178.2	-15.15	8.50
Q4	-178.0	-159.6	-18.37	11.51

Units: Billions of current U.S. dollars.

The federal budget deficit grows with the decline in receipts and the increases in transfer payments (see Table 7.12).

With the drop in consumption and the rise in interest rates and energy prices, unit labor costs jump over 1 percent (see Table 7.13).

Investment in drilling structures rises by 10 percent as the relative cost of domestic oil extraction plummets (see Table 7.14).

Investment in structures, less drilling, declines by nearly $4 billion, reflecting higher interest rates and the general slowdown in economic activity (see Table 7.15).

Table 7.13.
PCMark8 Solution Comparison: Unit Labor Costs

	UNITLABOR MYSIM	UNITLABOR QTRBASE	DIFFERENCE	% DIFFERENCE
1987				
Q1	172.4	172.2	0.21	0.12
Q2	173.9	173.3	0.64	0.37
Q3	175.5	174.2	1.23	0.71
Q4	177.2	175.2	2.01	1.14

Index: 1977 = 100.

Table 7.14.
PCMark8 Solution Comparison: Spending On Oil Drilling Structures

	OILSTRUC MYSIM	OILSTRUC QTRBASE	DIFFERENCE	% DIFFERENCE
1987				
Q1	19.2	19.1	0.13	0.70
Q2	19.9	19.3	0.59	3.07
Q3	20.8	19.6	1.22	6.24
Q4	22.0	20.0	2.00	10.00

Units: Billions of 1982 U.S. dollars.

Table 7.15.
PCMark8 Solution Comparison: Spending On Other Structures

	STRUCOTH MYSIM	STRUCOTH QTRBASE	DIFFERENCE	% DIFFERENCE
1987				
Q1	106.9	107.1	-0.28	-0.26
Q2	106.3	107.4	-1.04	-0.97
Q3	105.7	107.8	-2.15	-2.00
Q4	105.0	108.6	-3.59	-3.31

Units: Billions of 1982 U.S. dollars.

The prime rate rises for a number of reasons: protection of real interest rates from inflation, the expansion of the deficit, and a general lack of confidence in the economy (see Table 7.16).

Finally, the sum of these effects is a decline in GNP growth of almost 1 percent (see Table 7.17).

Table 7.16.
PCMark8 Solution Comparison: Prime Rate

	PRIME MYSIM	PRIME QTRBASE	DIFFERENCE	% DIFFERENCE
1987				
Q1	7.5	7.5	-0.00	-0.05
Q2	7.4	7.2	0.26	3.59
Q3	8.2	7.5	0.71	9.48
Q4	9.1	7.9	1.18	14.95

Table 7.17.
PCMark8 Solution Comparison: Percentage Growth in GNP

	%GNP MYSIM	%GNP QTRBASE	DIFFERENCE	% DIFFERENCE
1987				
Q1	2.1	2.5	-0.40	-15.55
Q2	2.4	3.2	-0.85	-26.38
Q3	2.7	3.4	-0.71	-20.68
Q4	2.9	3.6	-0.66	-18.38

SUMMARY

Macroeconomic models attempt to identify and quantify historical causal relationships among thousands of economic concepts and to extend those relationships into the future. Some relationships are fairly easy to quantify. For example, changes in the level of consumption expenditures can be accurately predicted by monitoring changes in disposable income. Disposable income changes can be determined by price and labor compensation patterns. Other concepts are not so easily explained by economic relationships. Oil prices, tax rates, and government spending are important inputs to PCMark8 which are not strictly subject to economic interactions. Other events such as strikes, political crises, and natural disasters are random from an econometric point of view. The existence of economic concepts and noneconomic events, which affect macroeconomic activity but are not easily predicted, effectively precludes the generation of a single comprehensive economic forecast. A single forecast may be the most probable outcome, but not the only one by any means. What happens if oil prices fall further, or the Gramm-Rudman-Hollings Act is ruled unconstitutional, or tax reform is not revenue neutral after all? These questions can only be answered through multiple forecasts, with varying assumptions.

The strength of PCMark8 and microcomputer-based econometric models, in general, is their ability to quickly and inexpensively generate and store many econometric forecasts. This broadens the use and audience for statistical modeling. While public and private organizations will always demand a single, most probable forecast, the microcomputer revolution enables the traditional and the novice user to go one step further—to judge the risks associated with various economic scenarios.

APPENDIX: DETAILED SECTOR DESCRIPTIONS

The PCMark8 model can be conceptualized as ten major sections: consumption, investment, government, personal income, prices, financial, profits and capital, employment and demographics, foreign sector, and energy.

Consumption

The consumption sector is broken into three major groups: durables, nondurables, and services. The sum of these is total consumption. The durables sector is dominated by automobile variables such as new and used cars, recreational vehicles and trucks, and tires and parts. There is also a series for furniture and other durables.

The nondurables category contains only three equations: total nondurable consumption, gasoline and heating fuel consumption, and other nondurables.

The service sector also consists of three equations: total services, housing services, and nonhousing services. The equations are generally driven by disposable income, interest rates, prices, and consumer sentiment.

Investment

Investment is broken into two broad categories: residential and nonresidential. The nonresidential category is composed of equations for investment in single family, multi-family, and other residential investment. Additionally there are equations for single and multi-unit housing starts and an identity for total starts.

The nonresidential, or business investment category, is split into two groups: structures, and plant and equipment. There are equations for drilling structures and nondrilling structures and an identity for total structures. Equipment coverage is split among several auto equations and other equipment investment, with total equipment specified as an equation rather than an identity.

Investment is driven by a combination of forces: consumption, inflation, interest rates, user cost of capital, and capacity utilization.

Government

The government sector consists of federal, and state and local categories and subcategories of receipts, expenditures, transfer payments, and tax rates. Federal receipts consist of personal taxes, corporate taxes, indirect business taxes, and social security contributions. Tax revenue is the product of the tax rate and the corresponding tax base. Federal expenditures are divided into defense, nondefense, and farm products purchased by the Commodity Credit Corporation. Defense and nondefense expenditures are also divided between compensation and noncompensation groups. There is also an identity for total compensation. Transfer payments are split between transfers to U.S. citizens and foreigners.

Interest payments are split between domestic payments and foreign payments. There are tax rates for each receipt category except indirect taxes.

The state and local sector mirrors the federal sector except there are no defense purchases, no transfers to foreigners, and no interest payments. An equation for local property tax is included in the sector.

There are identities for total government in each category. The compensation equations are driven by civilian and military employment levels, while receipts are driven by profits and income.

Prices

PCMark8 contains a variety of endogenous and exogenous price variables. There are sectors for producer prices, consumer prices, price deflators, and input costs. There are unit prices for new houses, new cars, and oil. A housing affordability index is also included.

The producer price sector consists of over twenty equations for basic commodities as well as stage of processing categories. Included are indexes for foods, textile products, fuels, electric power, chemicals, lumber, paper products, metal, machinery, furniture, minerals, and transportation equipment. There are stage of processing equations for crude, intermediate and finished goods, and miscellaneous equations for industrial commodities and other commodities. There is also an identity for all commodities.

Because of the many consumption price deflators, the consumer price sector contains much less detail than the producer price sector. The consumer price sector is composed of just nine equations: all items surveyed, food and beverage prices, and several equations for private transportation. Like producer prices, consumer prices are indexes using a base period as a reference point to measure price activity.

There are price deflator equations for most of the GNP components: durables, nondurables, and service consumption; government purchases and compensation; investment in structures and equipment; and imports and exports.

Most producer price equations for commodities and all stage of processing equations are driven by input cost terms. The input cost terms are weighted sums of other producer prices, labor costs, and tax burdens. Consumer price equations are composed of producer price and price deflators. The price deflators for consumption are driven by producer prices and unit labor costs; government and investment deflators are then calculated from weighted consumption deflators. Trade price deflators are determined by aggregate foreign prices, the exchange rate, unit labor costs, and oil prices.

Financial

The financial sector contains equations for reserves and borrowings, interest rates, and monetary aggregates.

The reserve equations measure total, required, excess, and nonborrowed bank reserves. The borrowing equations measure normal borrowing from the Federal Reserve Bank and abnormal borrowing, such as the loans to Continental Illinois Bank.

The interest rates include the federal funds rate, Moody's AAA corporate bond rate, 3-month treasury bills, 20-year treasury bonds, and a host of other mortgage, commercial, and international rates.

The monetary aggregates are total currency, M1, M2, M3, and M1 and M2 velocity.

The federal funds rate directly or indirectly affects almost all interest rates in the model. Through the user cost of capital and mortgage rate equations, the AAA bond rate heavily affects both nonresidential and residential investment. Three-month treasury bills drive the money supply equations, which feed into the reserve sector.

Corporate Profits and Capital

Corporate profits are measured in a number of different ways in PCMark8: adjusted and unadjusted and before- and after-tax profits. Adjusted profits take into account inventory valuation and capital consumption. Profits can be modified by changing the depreciation schedules for equipment and structures or by changing corporate tax rates.

On the capital side there are variables for total capital stock, stock of equipment, and residential and nonresidential structures. Additionally, there are depreciation rates, investment tax credit rates, and cost of capital variables for equipment and structures. To track aggregate economic activity, PCMark8 includes behavioral equations for new orders, shipments, unfilled orders, the value of manufacturing output, and the industrial production index.

Foreign Sector

The foreign sector includes variables for the U.S. exchange rate, foreign GNP and GNP price deflator, balance of payments, and a host of import and export concepts.

Foreign GNP and the GNP price deflator are exogenous to the model but are important inputs to merchandise exports, food exports, and service exports. The price deflator feeds into import series for the same concepts.

The import and export categories include behavioral equations for merchandise, food, other merchandise, and services and identities for total imports and exports and net exports. The import sector also contains behavioral equations for auto imports and petroleum products.

Employment and Demographics

The employment sector consists of a variety of endogenous and exogenous employment and labor force series. There are identities for total employment, government employment, and private sector employment as well as exogenous series for federal employment and state and local employment. Unemployment is driven by changes in real GNP. Employment costs are determined by behavioral equations for compensation and output per man-hour and an identity for unit labor costs.

The labor force component includes behavioral equations for male and female labor force participants ages twenty and over, total labor force participants for sixteen- to nineteen-year-olds, and average weekly hours. Additionally, PCMark8 contains identities for total civilian labor force and total private sector man-hours, and an exogenous assumption for total armed forces.

The demographic inputs to PCMark8 are predominantly exogenous. Population statistics are included for males and females ages twenty and over, sixteen- to nineteen-year-olds, total sixteen and over, total twenty-five to thirty-four, total thirty-five to forty-four, total sixty-five and over, and total U.S. population.

Energy

The energy sector is driven by the exogenous assumption for the price of OPEC oil. This price determines the refiner acquisition cost of oil, which in turn affects producer and consumer prices of refined petroleum products.

Domestic oil demand is determined by a behavioral equation, while domestic oil production is exogenous. The difference between demand and supply helps gauge the level of petroleum imports. Additionally, PCMark8 includes energy prices and deflators for coal, gas fuels, electric power, and all fuels.

Personal Income

The personal income sector is composed of many endogenous income measures. There are behavioral equations for dividend income, farm and nonfarm proprietors' income, and five types of interest income. There are identities for total proprietor income, rental income, nonwage income, taxable income, discretionary income, real and nominal personal income, personal savings, and the personal savings rate.

The behavioral equations are driven by components of nearly every sector of the model. Dividend income is largely determined by before-tax corporate profits. Nonfarm proprietor income is a function of consumer prices, population, labor compensation, AAA bond rates, and six-month commercial paper. Farm income is a function of raw farm product prices, industrial commodities prices, population, and farm subsidies. The interest income measures are driven by public and private interest rates, the federal deficit, population, and the flow of funds concepts.

FUNCTIONAL TOOLS, PLANNING MODELS, AND APPLICATIONS INTEGRATION

Many different types of applications can be integrated in the planning process. These include applications maintained outside of the planning department. Leveraging existing applications increases the range of planning analysis and also provides consistency of reported analysis across departments. This section discusses the design and development of spreadsheet-based applications and traditional planning models. The integration of stand-alone applications is also covered.

The chapters in this section describe microcomputer-based applications built for a hypothetical bicycle frame manufacturing firm. Chapter 8 details the construction of a Lotus 1–2–3 application maintained by the firm's production department. Spreadsheet application developers must realize the importance of design and structure when building spreadsheet applications.

Chapter 9 describes the construction and use of a traditional planning model. The example combines an estimated product-line forecasting equation with a simple financial model. The product-line forecasting equation incorporates macroeconomic variables, including variables output by the PCMark8 model. As discussed in the previous section, the AREMOS system is used to build vendor-supplied models like the PCMark8 model. This system can also be used by in-house planners and other analysts for analysis and applications development. Here, AREMOS is employed in the construction of an internally developed model. AREMOS is used to estimate the example's product-line forecasting equation and to build the final planning model.

An appendix to Chapter 9 discusses user interface formats. Several formats are reviewed in relation to an example planning model developed in this chapter. Query and Template interface formats are introduced.

Chapter 10 discusses the integration of stand-alone computer-based applications to form flexible, modular planning systems. Applications described in previous chapters are interfaced to form both single-tiered and multi-tiered systems. Modular planning systems can incorporate a wide variety of applications, including both internally developed and vended applications. Single-tiered systems employ only firm-level applications, and multi-tiered systems employ macroeconomic, regional, or industry models. An example of a single-tiered system integrates a production department spreadsheet application with a traditional planning model. An example of a multi-tiered system combines a production department spreadsheet application, a traditional planning model, and a macroeconomic model.

It can be difficult to integrate applications controlled by different departments within the organization. There are advantages and disadvantages for all parties concerned. Chapter 10 outlines the advantages and disadvantages of integration and details the concerns of both planners and managers of other departments.

The use of applications for risk analysis studies is a recurring theme stressed in these chapters. The reporting format for example applications is similar to the format presented in the discussion of the PCMark8 model. A common reporting format facilitates applications integration and analysis presentations.

8

A Spreadsheet-Based Functional Tool

DAVID J. GIANTURCO

This chapter presents an example of a functional tool that can be incorporated in the planning process. A functional tool, by definition here, is a computer-based application regularly used by staff or business departments for analysis. This example is a spreadsheet-based costing tool employed by the production department. The tool tracks and analyzes the costs of components used in the manufacture of bicycle frames, measures the costs of each component, and calculates average material cost for a unit of production. Because some bicycle frame components come from foreign manufacturers, exchange rates will partially determine the final cost that the Very Fast Bicycle Frame Company (VFBFC) pays for foreign manufactured components.

The functional tool used by the production department takes the form of a Lotus 1–2–3 spreadsheet program. The production department's main concern is the tracking of quarterly materials costs over a one-year planning period. The tool will be constructed from the ground up.

Before building any spreadsheet, the developer should outline user objectives. A quick way to summarize user needs is to construct example reports. It may seem odd to begin by focusing on output reports, but this approach lessens programming delays. The application developer obtains a good feel for model inputs and dimensions using this approach.

Next, the developer should sketch the proposed spreadsheet—complete with input sections, output sections, and work sections. This will aid in selecting an efficient method of construction for the final spreadsheet tool.

These steps are especially important if the final spreadsheet tool is to be employed by users other than the developer. A careful design helps end-users understand an application and will also help them locate input and output sections. For complex applications, the developer should construct a prototype incorporating the essential elements of the final tool on a limited scale. Such a process helps eliminate design misconceptions and helps clarify data issues. The investment in time and resources invariably saves both in the long run. The developer should make sure the final systems tool is feasible before beginning the research phase of a project. Prototypes should be built early on, as findings may influence a project's research phase. Prototyping also provides a clearer idea of the time needed to complete the final application.

OBJECTIVE

The objective of the VFBFC Component Costing Tool is to report forecast costs for each component used to manufacture a bicycle frame. Information is needed on a quarterly basis over a one-year planning period. These costs are summed to yield a measure of average materials cost per manufactured frame. The tool will be designed so that the user can alter component cost and currency exchange assumptions to produce alternative scenarios.

The tool will contain three output reports: the baseline report, the scenario report, and the delta (scenario minus baseline) report. As a firm plans for the future, it must evaluate alternative scenarios by some relative measure. The baseline report serves as a reference case; it is the firm's best guess of future conditions and is a forecast of the firm's position given the most plausible assumptions concerning future business conditions. The baseline case is sometimes referred to as the most likely case. When an analyst wishes to examine the effects of a change in baseline assumptions, a scenario report is generated. This represents an estimate of the firm's position in absolute terms given new assumptions. Finally, the analyst may need an estimate of the change in the firm's position relative to the baseline case. Here, a delta report provides the needed information.

As noted earlier, before building an application, the developer should draft example output reports. Three reports are required for this application; a scenario report, a baseline report, and a delta report. In this particular case, all three reports will have the same format. A sample scenario report is shown in Illustration 8.1.

The sample scenario report shows final costs for each of ten components (priced in U.S. dollars). Costs appear for all four quarters in the forecast period. Average materials cost also appears for each quarter and is calculated as the sum of the individual component costs for that quarter. In analyzing the report, the application developer notes that the final cost of each component is a function of its price and a relevant currency exchange rate. The application developer must include both component prices and currency exchange rates in the input and work sections of this tool. Because the application incorporates a four-quarter planning horizon, component prices and currency exchange rates must appear for all four quarters of analysis.

The baseline report will have the same format as the scenario report but will

Illustration 8.1
Very Fast Bicycle Frame Company

```
                  SCENARIO AVERAGE MATERIALS COST

 ID#  COMPONENT                    QTR 1    QTR 2    QTR 3    QTR 4
   1  TUBING SET                   50.00    51.00    51.00    52.00
   2  FITTING SET                  14.00    15.00    15.00    15.50
   3  PRIMER                         .10      .10      .10      .10
   4  PAINT                          .50      .50      .50      .50
   5  DECAL SET                     1.65     1.65     1.65     1.65
   6  BRAZING RODS                   .40      .45      .45      .45
   7  STEEL PIN SET                  .10      .10      .15      .16
   8  SHIPPING BOX                   .65      .65      .65      .65
   9  MISCELLANEOUS                  .60      .65      .70      .70
  10  OTHER                          .00      .00      .00      .00

         TOTAL AVERAGE MATERIALS COST =   68.00    70.10    71.20    72.71
         (US DOLLARS)

              (Sample report uses illustrative data)
```

always contain component cost estimates associated with the baseline case. When model assumptions are varied, the scenario report will change but the baseline report will remain the same. Given that the scenario and baseline reports have identical formats, it should not be surprising that the delta report retains this format. This report shows the difference between the scenario report and baseline report entries.

Design Objectives

There is no best design for spreadsheet applications. Each design will have its own advantages and disadvantages. Desirable criteria can be listed, but the application builder must judge which criteria are the most important for the project at hand. Structure is important. An efficient design will speed development and documentation. Model maintenance will be simplified, and users will find the application easier to learn and use. Spreadsheet programs that are data-driven are the easiest to debug and change. Such programs use general code so that modifications are made by adjusting data inputs and not by adjusting the spreadsheet program itself. This point will be stressed in the example.

A term often used in connection with structure is modularity. When an application is modular in design, its component pieces can be envisioned as islands. The parts of the spreadsheet or related macros that move data from module to module can be envisioned as bridges between the islands. Each module has a specific function. Each module accepts specific data inputs to perform its calculations or other work functions and outputs specific data so that other modules can perform their functions. Changes to any module will not affect other modules in the application. The rest of the spreadsheet program will function normally so long as the same input and output data flow to and from the changed module. Modularity is one way to build in flexibility. Modularity is very important for large spreadsheet programs, but flexibility is important for all spreadsheet programs.

Planning models and functional tools share one important characteristic. No matter what job an application is designed to perform, sooner or later someone will use it for a different job. It is important to remember that an application will almost certainly be changed in the future. The builder's design must facilitate change. Preparing and reviewing dummy output reports with managers and end-users before building an application will reduce future changes. However, this will not eliminate all future changes. Managers and end-users have a peculiar tendency of not knowing precisely what they want when they request an application. Organizations change, and tools and models must change with them.

Other important criteria may include development and execution time and the inclusion of a template or menu-driven user interface system. If development time is limited, then large projects should probably not be programmed using a spreadsheet package. Because most popular spreadsheet programs manipulate data on a cell-by-cell basis, programming can be tedious and time consuming. Also, debugging errors can be very difficult. Technological improvements in hardware and software will undoubtedly decrease program execution time. However, large applications must still be constructed and maintained, and other packages or programming languages may be more suitable for large projects. The example application will be small, and execution time will not be a concern.

Providing an enhanced user interface can greatly reduce the time needed for a new user to become acquainted with a spreadsheet application. It is common practice to include a menu interface. (Most spreadsheet applications that employ a menu interface greet the user with menu choices as soon as the spreadsheet file is activated or retrieved.) While the user's first contact with an application will be through a menu interface, the interface is usually among the last parts of the application to be built. Providing a suitable interface can be important in getting a spreadsheet application accepted in an organization. However, construction of a menu system is certainly a secondary consideration in the design stage. An intelligently designed spreadsheet application will lend itself to a suitable interface. For the example at hand, the objective is to develop an efficient, structured design. Suitable menu interface systems will suggest themselves when the completed tool is used to analyze sample problems.

A SKETCH OF THE PROPOSED MODEL

With objectives outlined and sample reports constructed, it's time to sketch a proposed layout. Illustration 8.2 shows nine different boxes or modules. Each box represents one full screen of data (the amount of data available on a monitor at one time). Each box is labeled, numbered, and lettered. The lettering system indicates the primary purpose of each box. "I" indicates that a particular box requires user input; "W" indicates that a box is used for work (that is, performs calculations on data entered in the "I" boxes); "O" indicates that a box rep-

Illustration 8.2
Spreadsheet Sketch, Very Fast Bicycle Frame Company Model

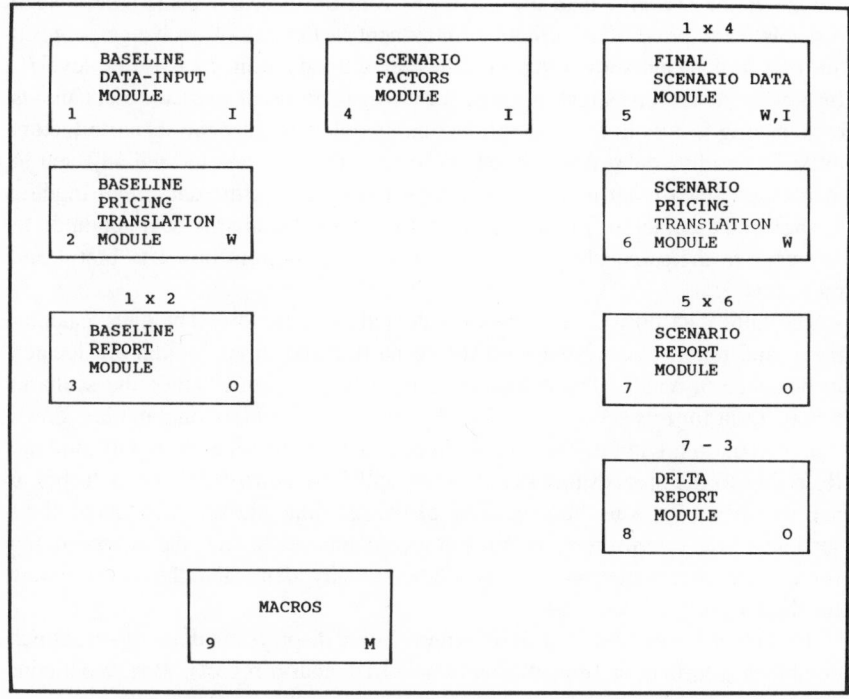

resents an output or report section; and ''M'' indicates the presence of programming macros.

The design is best explained in data flows. Three basic data flows provide the framework for this tool. The first is the baseline data flow, the second is the scenario specification data flow, and the third is the scenario calculations data flow. The geometry of design is important, with each module of the spreadsheet located near related modules.

Each box is numbered to aid in the explanation of the three data flows. All data, calculations, and reports associated with the baseline section of the tool reside in boxes 1, 2, and 3. Note how these modules are located on the left margin of the spreadsheet, one under the other. Information will flow from the baseline data-input module through the baseline pricing translation module, and on to the baseline report module. In reference to the spreadsheet sketch, data flow down from box 1 to box 2 and on to box 3.

The scenario specification data flow encompasses the baseline data-input module, the scenario factors module, and the final scenario data module. These modules are located on the top margin of the spreadsheet. All data and calculations related to scenario specifications are located in boxes 4 and 5. The scenario factors and final scenario data modules are the areas of the spreadsheet where the user will enter data to do what-if investigations. In effect the user will ask, "What if the scenario data are different from the baseline data?" or "What happens if the price of a particular component or the rate of exchange between the U.S. dollar and some other currency should vary from its baseline level?" In most scenario investigations, the user will increase or decrease data inputs by adjusting factors in the scenario factors module. Because the scenario factors multiply baseline data, it is convenient to have these factors located adjacent to the baseline data-input module. Data flow from the baseline data-input module to the scenario factors module and on to the final scenario data module. In reference to the spreadsheet sketch, data flow across from box 1 to box 4 and on to box 5.

The third data flow is the scenario calculations data flow. The data, calculations, and reports associated with the scenario calculations section are located in boxes 5, 6, and 7. The calculations from this section produce the scenario report. Data for this section will flow from the final scenario data module down to the scenario pricing translation module, and on to the scenario report module. Referring to the spreadsheet sketch, data will flow down from box 5 to box 6 and on to box 7. Note the symmetry of the baseline and scenario calculations sections of the spreadsheet. This is not a coincidence. In fact, the programming for the scenario calculations section will be virtually identical to the programming for the baseline section.

Two other boxes appear in the diagram. Box 8 displays the delta report, which combines information from the baseline and scenario reports. Box 9 contains macros and is arbitrarily located in any open area of the spreadsheet.

Macros are collections of keystrokes that are invoked by a single keystroke. The user declares a set of symbols as a macro and invokes them in some simple but special way. Macros can string simple commands or can be used in a true programming sense—that is, to input logic in applications. Based on certain parameters, the spreadsheet will branch off and perform different instructions. In Lotus 1–2–3, macros are also used to build menu interfaces. By selecting the proper menu choice, the user supplies needed information to the program. The user invokes different sets of code by making different selections from the menu.

The baseline, scenario specification, and final scenario calculations sections will be reviewed in detail. Keep in mind the desirability criteria outlined earlier. The goal is to produce a structured, data-driven tool. Modularity was also stressed as a desirable criterion.

The Baseline Data Flow

The baseline section of the application consists of three modules, the baseline data-input module, the baseline pricing translation module, and the baseline report module (see Illustration 8.3). These modules produce a report embodying the analyst's most likely assumption set concerning future conditions.

Illustration 8.3
Baseline Data Flow

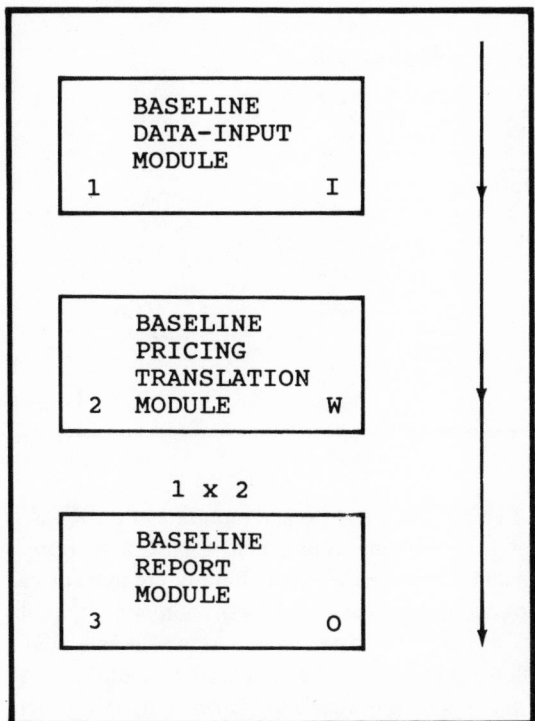

The Baseline Data-Input Module

The baseline data-input module is represented by box 1 in the spreadsheet sketch. The module appears in Illustration 8.4. The entire module is contained in cells A1 to H20. By manipulating the format and width of certain columns, the entire module can appear on screen simultaneously.[1]

There are two data tables in the baseline data-input module: the input prices and foreign exchange tables. No programming (there are no cells with formulas) is needed in this module. The application builder simply labels each of the two tables and completes each table. The input prices table contains information on the components used to manufacture bicycle frames. The foreign exchange table lists foreign currency exchange information. The input prices table includes the following: component ID numbers and names, currency information, country code, and component costs in native currency units. In the foreign exchange table the builder must provide currency conversion labels (US $/foreign currency), country codes, and foreign exchange value information.

Nine components are actually used in the manufacturing process. The tenth

Illustration 8.4
Baseline Data-Input Module

	A	B	C	D	E	F	G	H
1			BASELINE	DATA-INPUT	MODULE			
2	INPUT PRICES:							
3	ID#	COMPONENT	CURRENCY	CODE	QTR 1	QTR 2	QTR 3	QTR 4
4	1	TUBING SET	L. (UK)	3	35.00	35.00	35.00	35.00
5	2	FITTING SET	L. (UK)	3	9.45	9.50	9.60	9.65
6	3	PRIMER	US $	1	0.10	0.10	0.10	0.10
7	4	PAINT	CANADIAN $	2	1.00	1.00	1.00	1.00
8	5	DECAL SET	CANADIAN $	2	2.27	2.27	2.27	2.27
9	6	BRAZING RODS	US $	1	0.40	0.45	0.50	0.55
10	7	STEEL PIN SET	US $	1	0.05	0.05	0.05	0.05
11	8	SHIPPING BOX	CANADIAN $	2	0.88	0.88	0.88	0.88
12	9	MISCELLANEOUS	US $	1	0.60	0.70	0.80	0.90
13	10	OTHER	?	0	0	0	0	0
14								
15	FOREIGN EXCHANGE		(DOLLARS US	/ 1 UNIT	FOREIGN)			
16				CODE	QTR 1	QTR 2	QTR 3	QTR 4
17		US $ / US $		1	$1.00	$1.00	$1.00	$1.00
18		US $ / CANADIAN $		2	$0.73	$0.73	$0.73	$0.73
19		US $ / ENGLISH POUND (L.)		3	$1.45	$1.46	$1.46	$1.47
20		US $ / OTHER		0	$0.00	$0.00	$0.00	$0.00

component is a dummy entry. The dummy component simplifies operations if a new component is added, or if an existing component is purchased from a country not already supplying other components. The dummy component can be manipulated so that the program can be easily updated without code modifications. By design, only data inputs in the baseline data-input module would be changed. The benefits of allowing this tool to be data driven should begin to become apparent. Beside each component is the currency in which the component cost is listed. Next is a country code number. A quick look at the foreign exchange table provides information concerning these codes. In this table a country code of "1" indicates that a particular component is of domestic manufacture, "2" that the component is Canadian in origin, "3" that the component is provided by manufacturers in the United Kingdom, and "0" indicates that a component is not currently purchased or used in the manufacturing process. Only the tenth component (the dummy component) has a 0 country code listing.

This tool calculates projected costs on a quarterly basis over a one-year period. The last four columns of the input prices table show individual baseline component costs for each quarter. Again, these costs are listed in the currency of their respective countries of origin. U.S. manufactured parts are listed in U.S. dollars; components of Canadian manufacture are listed in Canadian dollars; and components of British manufacture are listed in English pounds. Since there is no programming in this module, the application builder would simply move to each cell and enter the appropriate label or numeric data. Again, no formulas need to be entered.

The foreign exchange table shows projected information for currency exchange rates. The table lists the projected U.S. dollar amount needed to purchase one unit of each foreign currency appearing in the input prices table. For example,

Illustration 8.5
Baseline Pricing Translation Module

	A	B	C	D	E	F	G	H
21		BASELINE PRICING TRANSLATION TABLE - EXCHANGE						
22	INPUT PRICES:							
23	ID#	COMPONENT	CURRENCY	CODE	QTR 1	QTR 2	QTR 3	QTR 4
24	1	TUBING SET	L. (UK)	3	1.45	1.46	1.46	1.47
25	2	FITTING SET	L. (UK)	3	1.45	1.46	1.46	1.47
26	3	PRIMER	US $	1	1	1	1	1
27	4	PAINT	CANADIAN $	2	0.73	0.73	0.73	0.73
28	5	DECAL SET	CANADIAN $	2	0.73	0.73	0.73	0.73
29	6	BRAZING RODS	US $	1	1	1	1	1
30	7	STEEL PIN SET	US $	1	1	1	1	1
31	8	SHIPPING BOX	CANADIAN $	2	0.73	0.73	0.73	0.73
32	9	MISCELLANEOUS	US $	1	1	1	1	1
33	10	OTHER	?	0	0	0	0	0

it is projected that in the first quarter of analysis, .73 U.S. dollars (or 73 U.S. cents) are needed to purchase one Canadian dollar. In this same quarter, 1.45 U.S. dollars purchase a single English pound. No formulas are entered in this table. The application builder simply moves to each cell and enters the appropriate labeling or numeric data.

The Baseline Pricing Translation Module

The baseline pricing translation module is represented by box 2 on the spreadsheet diagrams and appears in Illustration 8.5. This is the second module in the baseline section of the application.

The ba ʒline pricing translation module resides in cells A21 to H33 of the spreadsheet. Experienced Lotus 1–2–3 users will know that the number of rows appearing on-screen at one time is twenty. Consequently the second module of the example application will be located precisely one page down from the first module. Using this convention can greatly decrease programming time, as will be illustrated shortly.

The labeling information for the baseline pricing translation module is identical to that of the input prices table in the baseline data-input module. Consequently, each component's ID number, listing, and currency base entries can simply be copied from the input prices table. The quarter (QTR) labels can also be copied. Copying is simplified because label information in the baseline pricing translation module is located exactly one page below the identical label information in the previous module. The page-up and page-down keys can simplify label copying and formula-writing procedures.

The objective is to keep the spreadsheet tool simple, structured, and data driven. By making use of the country code data found in the baseline data-input module, a degree of all these desirable qualities will be obtained. Remember, an objective is to limit the amount of future programming changes spreadsheet tools must undergo. By making applications data driven, changes can be made by altering data. If users must change spreadsheet code, errors become likely.

Illustration 8.6
Using the Choose Function

	A	B	C	D	E	F	G	H
15	FOREIGN EXCHANGE		(US DOLLARS / 1 UNIT FOREIGN)					
16				CODE	QTR 1	QTR 2	QTR 3	QTR 4
17	US $ / US $			1	$1.00	$1.00	$1.00	$1.00
18	US $ / CANADIAN $			2	$0.73	$0.73	$0.73	$0.73
19	US $ / ENGLISH POUND (L.)			3	$1.45	$1.46	$1.46	$1.47
20	US $ / OTHER			0	$0.00	$0.00	$0.00	$0.00
21		PRICING TRANSLATION TABLE - EXCHANGE						
22	INPUT PRICES:							
23	ID# COMPONENT		CURRENCY	CODE	QTR 1	QTR 2	QTR 3	QTR 4
24	1 TUBING SET		L. (UK)	3	1.45	1.46	1.46	1.47

Lotus 1–2–3 offers a function called the Choose function, and the example will make use of this. The baseline pricing translation table will require formula entry for all cells located under the CODE and QTR labels.

To understand the Choose function, examine Illustration 8.6. Both the foreign exchange table (the lower table in the baseline data-input module) and the first component entry in the baseline pricing translation module are shown. This information is contained in cells A15 to H24.

Cells A15 to H20 are from the baseline data-input module and only contain labeling or numeric data. No special functions or formulas were used in any part of this module. Moving to the baseline pricing translation module, examine row 24. This is the row for component 1, tubing set. The ID#, COMPONENT, and CURRENCY columns contain labeling information. The CODE is the same as that listed in the input prices table of the baseline data-input module. The code value is generated by a simple formula expression (cell D24 is set equal to cell D4). The next four cell entries (E24, F24, G24, and H24) must contain currency exchange rates from the country exporting tubing sets. These are generated using the Choose function which is implemented as follows. Cell E24 is set equal to either cell E20, E17, E18, or E19 depending on the value of the country code listing in cell D24. The formula in cell E24 would appear as follows:

@CHOOSE(+ D24, + E20, + E17, + E18, + E19)

The function is read as follows. If the value in cell D24 is 0, set the value of this cell (cell E24) equal to the value in cell E20. If the value of cell D24 is 1, set the value of this cell equal to the value of cell E17. If the value of cell D24 is 2, set the value of this cell equal to the value of cell E18. If the value of cell D24 is 3, set the value of this cell equal to the value of cell E19. The 0, 1, 2, and 3 values are implied by the position of the arguments of the function. In this case, cell D24 is set to 3, indicating that the country of origin for tubing sets is the United Kingdom. The value of cell D24 is 3, the value of cell E24 will be set equal to the value of cell E19. Cell E19 contains the value 1.45, so cell E24 will contain the value 1.45. The value displayed in cell E24 is that of

Illustration 8.7
The Baseline Report Module

	A	B	C	D	E	F	G	H
41			BASELINE AVERAGE MATERIALS COST					
42								
43	ID#	COMPONENT			QTR 1	QTR 2	QTR 3	QTR 4
44	1	TUBING SET			50.75	51.10	51.10	51.45
45	2	FITTING SET			13.70	13.87	14.02	14.19
46	3	PRIMER			0.10	0.10	0.10	0.10
47	4	PAINT			0.73	0.73	0.73	0.73
48	5	DECAL SET			1.66	1.66	1.66	1.66
49	6	BRAZING RODS			0.40	0.45	0.50	0.55
50	7	STEEL PIN SET			0.05	0.05	0.05	0.05
51	8	SHIPPING BOX			0.64	0.64	0.64	0.64
52	9	MISCELLANEOUS			0.60	0.70	0.80	0.90
53	10	OTHER			0.00	0.00	0.00	0.00
54								
55		TOTAL AVERAGE MATERIAL COST =			68.63	69.30	69.60	70.27
56		(US DOLLARS)						

the currency exchange rate of the country of origin for tubing sets (United Kingdom). The exchange rate displayed applies to the first quarter of analysis.

Cell F24 should display the currency exchange rate of English-manufactured tubing sets for the second quarter of analysis. The formula entry for cell F24 would be as follows:

@CHOOSE(+ D24, + F20, + F17, + F18, + F19)

Again, cell D24 (the country code) provides the indicator value. The value of the proper currency exchange rate for the second quarter of analysis is displayed in cell F24. Cells E24 and F24 derive their values from the baseline data-input module's foreign currency exchange table. The baseline pricing translation table shows that relevant cells have the value of the currency exchange rate of the country of origin for each respective bicycle frame component. All English-manufactured components show the U.S. dollar to English pound exchange rate, all components of Canadian manufacture show the U.S. dollar to Canadian dollar exchange rate, and all U.S.-manufactured components show an entry of 1 (one U.S. dollar buys one U.S. dollar). The table shows a 0 listed for the dummy entry, component 10.

The Baseline Report Module

Information from the baseline data-input module and the baseline pricing translation module will be collected and used in the baseline report module (box 3 in the spreadsheet diagrams). The report resides in cell range A41 to H56 and appears in Illustration 8.7.

Construction of this report is straightforward. Necessary labeling information can be copied from either the baseline data-input module or the baseline pricing translation module. Except for column totals, numeric information is the product of a component's price and the exchange rate of the component's country of origin. Cell E44 is simply the product of cells E4 and E24. Cell F44 is the product of cells F4 and F24. This pattern continues so that cell H53 is the product of cells H13 and H33. Note how this pattern speeds programming and debugging. Each cell in the body of the report is the product of the cell twenty rows above it and forty rows above it. A page is twenty rows, so using the page-up key speeds formula entry. Consider the method used to input the appropriate formula in cell E44. After moving to cell E44, the required keystrokes are these:

+ PgUp PgUp * PgUp Return

This formula can be copied to all cells in the range E44 to H53. The bulk of the report is completed. By structuring related modules underneath each other, the application builder increases productivity. Programming is faster and the chance of error is reduced. Further, users will later have little difficulty tracing baseline calculations. All the modules in the baseline section are located using the page-up and page-down keys.

The baseline report is completed by summing the individual component costs for each quarter. Total average materials cost appears in cells E55 through H55.

The completed baseline section occupies cells A1 to H56. If the monitor screen could accommodate fifty-six rows of data at one time, the spreadsheet would appear as in Illustration 8.8.

With this construction, the baseline report will automatically be updated if information in the baseline data-input module is changed. Consider the following example. Assume that U.S./Canadian currency exchange rates have changed since the last update. Assume that the value of the Canadian dollar rises to 90 U.S. cents, and that this new exchange rate is expected to persist for the next four quarters. The baseline data should always incorporate the most current and plausible assumptions concerning component prices and currency exchange rates. The U.S. dollar versus Canadian dollar exchange information is located in cells E18, F18, G18, and H18. After adjusting the value of these cells to .90, the fifty-six rows of the baseline section would appear as in Illustration 8.9.

What has changed? The new baseline pricing transformation table (cells A21 to H33) shows changes for Canadian-manufactured components only. The baseline report shows changes for Canadian-manufactured components and total average materials cost in each quarter.

The Scenario Specification Data Flow

The scenario specification section consists of three modules: the baseline data-input module, the scenario factors module, and the final scenario data module (as shown in Illustration 8.10). The baseline data set embodies assumptions concerning component prices and currency exchange rates. To examine the impacts of changing component prices or currency exchange rates, the user alters

Illustration 8.8
Complete Baseline Section

	A	B	C	D	E	F	G	H
1				BASELINE DATA-INPUT MODULE				
2	INPUT PRICES:							
3	ID#	COMPONENT	CURRENCY	CODE	QTR 1	QTR 2	QTR 3	QTR 4
4	1	TUBING SET	L. (UK)	3	35.00	35.00	35.00	35.00
5	2	FITTING SET	L. (UK)	3	9.45	9.50	9.60	9.65
6	3	PRIMER	US $	1	0.10	0.10	0.10	0.10
7	4	PAINT	CANADIAN $	2	1.00	1.00	1.00	1.00
8	5	DECAL SET	CANADIAN $	2	2.27	2.27	2.27	2.27
9	6	BRAZING RODS	US $	1	0.40	0.45	0.50	0.55
10	7	STEEL PIN SET	US $	1	0.05	0.05	0.05	0.05
11	8	SHIPPING BOX	CANADIAN $	2	0.88	0.88	0.88	0.88
12	9	MISCELLANEOUS	US $	1	0.60	0.70	0.80	0.90
13	10	OTHER	?	0	0	0	0	0
14								
15	FOREIGN EXCHANGE	(DOLLARS US / 1 UNIT FOREIGN)						
16				CODE	QTR 1	QTR 2	QTR 3	QTR 4
17		US $ / US $		1	$1.00	$1.00	$1.00	$1.00
18		US $ / CANADIAN $		2	$0.73	$0.73	$0.73	$0.73
19		US $ / ENGLISH POUND (L.)		3	$1.45	$1.46	$1.46	$1.47
20		US $ / OTHER		0	$0.00	$0.00	$0.00	$0.00
21			BASELINE PRICING TRANSLATION TABLE - EXCHANGE					
22	INPUT PRICES:							
23	ID#	COMPONENT	CURRENCY	CODE	QTR 1	QTR 2	QTR 3	QTR 4
24	1	TUBING SET	L. (UK)	3	1.45	1.46	1.46	1.47
25	2	FITTING SET	L. (UK)	3	1.45	1.46	1.46	1.47
26	3	PRIMER	US $	1	1	1	1	1
27	4	PAINT	CANADIAN $	2	0.73	0.73	0.73	0.73
28	5	DECAL SET	CANADIAN $	2	0.73	0.73	0.73	0.73
29	6	BRAZING RODS	US $	1	1	1	1	1
30	7	STEEL PIN SET	US $	1	1	1	1	1
31	8	SHIPPING BOX	CANADIAN $	2	0.73	0.73	0.73	0.73
32	9	MISCELLANEOUS	US $	1	1	1	1	1
33	10	OTHER	?	0	0	0	0	0
34								
35								
36								
37								
38								
39								
40								
41			BASELINE AVERAGE MATERIALS COST					
42								
43	ID#	COMPONENT			QTR 1	QTR 2	QTR 3	QTR 4
44	1	TUBING SET			50.75	51.10	51.10	51.45
45	2	FITTING SET			13.70	13.87	14.02	14.19
46	3	PRIMER			0.10	0.10	0.10	0.10
47	4	PAINT			0.73	0.73	0.73	0.73
48	5	DECAL SET			1.66	1.66	1.66	1.66
49	6	BRAZING RODS			0.40	0.45	0.50	0.55
50	7	STEEL PIN SET			0.05	0.05	0.05	0.05
51	8	SHIPPING BOX			0.64	0.64	0.64	0.64
52	9	MISCELLANEOUS			0.60	0.70	0.80	0.90
53	10	OTHER			0.00	0.00	0.00	0.00
54								
55		TOTAL AVERAGE MATERIALS COST =			68.63	69.30	69.60	70.27
56		(US DOLLARS)						

Illustration 8.9

Complete Baseline Section Adjusted for New U.S./Canadian Exchange Rate

	A	B	C	D	E	F	G	H
1			BASELINE DATA-INPUT MODULE					
2	INPUT PRICES:							
3	ID#	COMPONENT	CURRENCY	CODE	QTR 1	QTR 2	QTR 3	QTR 4
4	1	TUBING SET	L. (UK)	3	35.00	35.00	35.00	35.00
5	2	FITTING SET	L. (UK)	3	9.45	9.50	9.60	9.65
6	3	PRIMER	US $	1	0.10	0.10	0.10	0.10
7	4	PAINT	CANADIAN $	2	1.00	1.00	1.00	1.00
8	5	DECAL SET	CANADIAN $	2	2.27	2.27	2.27	2.27
9	6	BRAZING RODS	US $	1	0.40	0.45	0.50	0.55
10	7	STEEL PIN SET	US $	1	0.05	0.05	0.05	0.05
11	8	SHIPPING BOX	CANADIAN $	2	0.88	0.88	0.88	0.88
12	9	MISCELLANEOUS	US $	1	0.60	0.70	0.80	0.90
13	10	OTHER	`	?	0	0	0	0
14								
15	FOREIGN EXCHANGE	(DOLLARS US / 1 UNIT FOREIGN)						
16				CODE	QTR 1	QTR 2	QTR 3	QTR 4
17		US $ / US $		1	$1.00	$1.00	$1.00	$1.00
18		US $ / CANADIAN $		2	$0.90	$0.90	$0.90	$0.90
19		US $ / ENGLISH POUND (L.)		3	$1.45	$1.46	$1.46	$1.47
20		US $ / OTHER		0	$0.00	$0.00	$0.00	$0.00
21			BASELINE PRICING TRANSLATION TABLE - EXCHANGE					
22	INPUT PRICES:							
23	ID#	COMPONENT	CURRENCY	CODE	QTR 1	QTR 2	QTR 3	QTR 4
24	1	TUBING SET	L. (UK)	3	1.45	1.46	1.46	1.47
25	2	FITTING SET	L. (UK)	3	1.45	1.46	1.46	1.47
26	3	PRIMER	US $	1	1	1	1	1
27	4	PAINT	CANADIAN $	2	0.9	0.9	0.9	0.9
28	5	DECAL SET	CANADIAN $	2	0.9	0.9	0.9	0.9
29	6	BRAZING RODS	US $	1	1	1	1	1
30	7	STEEL PIN SET	US $	1	1	1	1	1
31	8	SHIPPING BOX	CANADIAN $	2	0.9	0.9	0.9	0.9
32	9	MISCELLANEOUS	US $	1	1	1	1	1
33	10	OTHER	?		0	0	0	0
34								
35								
36								
37								
38								
39								
40								
41			BASELINE AVERAGE MATERIALS COST					
42								
›43	ID#	COMPONENT			QTR 1	QTR 2	QTR 3	QTR 4
44	1	TUBING SET			50.75	51.10	51.10	51.45
45	2	FITTING SET			13.70	13.87	14.02	14.19
46	3	PRIMER			0.10	0.10	0.10	0.10
47	4	PAINT			0.90	0.90	0.90	0.90
48	5	DECAL SET			2.04	2.04	2.04	2.04
49	6	BRAZING RODS			0.40	0.45	0.50	0.55
50	7	STEEL PIN SET			0.05	0.05	0.05	0.05
51	8	SHIPPING BOX			0.79	0.79	0.79	0.79
52	9	MISCELLANEOUS			0.60	0.70	0.80	0.90
53	10	OTHER			0.00	0.00	0.00	0.00
54								
55		TOTAL AVERAGE MATERIALS COST =			69.34	70.01	70.30	70.97
56		(US DOLLARS)						

the assumptions incorporated in the baseline data. The user will make a scenario run of the model.

The application must provide methods for users to input data. In the example, the user can input scenario data in two ways. The user can adjust component prices and currency exchange rates either by altering scenario factors or by

Illustration 8.10
Scenario Specification Data Flow

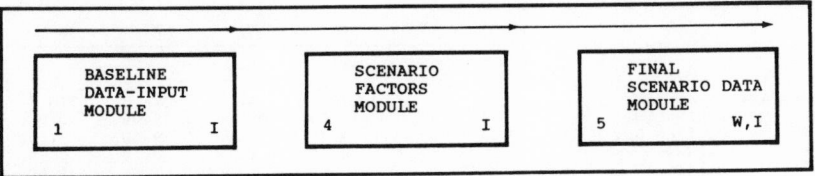

Illustration 8.11
The Scenario Factors Module

	I	J	K	L	M	N	O	P
1					SCENARIO FACTORS			
2	INPUT PRICES:							
3	ID# COMPONENT				QTR 1	QTR 2	QTR 3	QTR 4
4	1 TUBING SET				1	1	1	1
5	2 FITTING SET				1	1	1	1
6	3 PRIMER				1	1	1	1
7	4 PAINT				1	1	1	1
8	5 DECAL SET				1	1	1	1
9	6 BRAZING RODS				1	1	1	1
10	7 STEEL PIN SET				1	1	1	1
11	8 SHIPPING BOX				1	1	1	1
12	9 MISCELLANEOUS				1	1	1	1
13	10 OTHER				1	1	1	1
14								
15	FOREIGN EXCHANGE (DOLLARS US / 1 UNIT FOREIGN)							
16					QTR 1	QTR 2	QTR 3	QTR 4
17	US $ / US $				1	1	1	1
18	US $ / CANADIAN $				1	1	1	1
19	US $ / ENGLISH POUND (L.)				1	1	1	1
20	US $ / OTHER				1	1	1	1

directly inputting scenario data in the final scenario data module. It is also possible to use a combination of these methods.

The baseline data-input module was displayed with the discussion of the baseline data flow section and will not be redisplayed here.

The Scenario Factors Module

The scenario factors module is represented by box 4 on the spreadsheet diagrams (see Illustration 8.11).

The format of the scenario factors module is the same as that of the baseline data-input module, except the CURRENCY and CODE columns are omitted. Not by chance, the location of the scenario factors module (located in cells I1 to P20) is one rightward-margin-key keystroke from the baseline data-input module, from which all labeling information can easily be copied. No formulas are needed to construct this table. Note that all displayed factors in the table are set to one. The cursor is simply moved to the appropriate cells in the table and the number "1" is typed in each cell. Setting all the scenario factors to 1 implies

Illustration 8.12
The Final Scenario Data Module

	Q	R	S	T	U	V	W	X
1				FINAL SCENARIO DATA				
2	INPUT PRICES:							
3	ID# COMPONENT				QTR 1	QTR 2	QTR 3	QTR 4
4	1 TUBING SET				35.00	35.00	35.00	35.00
5	2 FITTING SET				9.45	9.50	9.60	9.65
6	3 PRIMER				0.10	0.10	0.10	0.10
7	4 PAINT				1.00	1.00	1.00	1.00
8	5 DECAL SET				2.27	2.27	2.27	2.27
9	6 BRAZING RODS				0.40	0.45	0.50	0.55
10	7 STEEL PIN SET				0.05	0.05	0.05	0.05
11	8 SHIPPING BOX				0.88	0.88	0.88	0.88
12	9 MISCELLANEOUS				0.60	0.70	0.80	0.90
13	10 OTHER				0.00	0.00	0.00	0.00
14								
15	FOREIGN EXCHANGE	(DOLLARS US / 1 UNIT FOREIGN)						
16					QTR 1	QTR 2	QTR 3	QTR 4
17	US $ / US $				1.00	1.00	1.00	1.00
18	US $ / CANADIAN $				0.73	0.73	0.73	0.73
19	US $ / ENGLISH POUND (L.)				1.45	1.46	1.46	1.47
20	US $ / OTHER				0.00	0.00	0.00	0.00

that no scenario assumptions have been input to the model. The reason for this will soon be apparent.

The Final Scenario Data Module

The final scenario data module is represented by box 5 on the spreadsheet diagrams and appears in Illustration 8.12.

The final scenario data module is located in cells Q1 to X20. The format of this module is the same as that of the scenario factors module located one leftward-margin-key keystroke away, from which all labeling information can easily be copied. Formulas produce the numeric data in the final scenario data module. Each cell is the product of the cell two leftward-margin-key keystrokes away times the cell one leftward-margin-key keystroke away. In simpler terms, each cell is the product of its corresponding baseline value times its corresponding scenario factor.

All numeric data in the final scenario data module (box 5) is identical to the corresponding data entry in the baseline data-input module (box 1). The reason is straightforward. The final scenario data module is the product of the baseline data-input module and the scenario factors module. With all the scenario factors set to 1, the final scenario data set must be equal to the baseline data set.

Getting ahead of the story a bit, the final scenario data module holds the data used to calculate final scenario costs. Final scenario costs will differ from baseline costs if, and only if, the final scenario data set differs from the baseline data set. The easiest way to change the final scenario data is to set the scenario factors to some number other than 1. By adjusting the scenario factors, the final scenario data will differ from entered baseline data.

How would the baseline data-input module, the scenario factors module, and the final scenario data module appear if the price of tubing sets is increased by

10 percent for all four quarters of analysis? This specification is shown in Illustration 8.13.

Note that the cost of tubing sets is different in the baseline data-input module than in the final scenario data module. Tubing sets was the only component that experienced a price change in the scenario specification. No change in exchange rates was specified, and all exchange rates are identical in the two modules.

The Scenario Calculations Data Flow Section

The scenario calculations section consists of three modules: the final scenario data module, the scenario pricing translation module, and the scenario report module. (See Illustration 8.14). This section is easy to construct because of its similarity in design to the baseline data flow section. The final scenario data module is displayed with the discussion of the scenario specifications data flow and will not be redisplayed here.

The Scenario Pricing Translation Module

The baseline pricing translation table identifies the proper country and exchange rate for each input in the baseline data set. A scenario pricing translation table is added to perform the same operations on the final scenario data set and is represented by box 6 in the spreadsheet diagrams (see Illustration 8.15).

The scenario pricing translation module is located just below the final scenario data module in cells Q21 to X33. Programming of this module is simplified by copying an existing piece of the spreadsheet. The baseline pricing translation table (cells A21 to H33) can be copied directly into this cell range. One subsequent adjustment must be made. The code information in the scenario pricing translation table must be set equal to the corresponding cell in the baseline pricing translation table (cell T24 is set equal to cell D24, cell T25 is set equal to cell D25, . . . , and cell T33 is set equal to cell D33).[2] This convention insures that when the country of origin is changed for an input, that information will be conveyed throughout the spreadsheet program. By changing the country of origin in the baseline data-input module (by changing country code data), the proper pricing translations will occur in both the baseline and scenario pricing translation tables. Again, no reprogramming is required. The data drives the model limiting both the need to reprogram and the possibility of error.

The Scenario Report Module

The scenario report module is represented by box 7 in the spreadsheet diagrams. This module is contained in cells Q41 to X60, and is located directly below the scenario pricing translation module. The symmetry of the baseline and scenario parts of the spreadsheet become clear (see Illustration 8.16).

To speed programming, the contents of the baseline report (cells A41 to H56) can be copied to the cells reserved for the scenario report (cells Q41 to X56).

Illustration 8.13
Scenario Specification Data Flow Section, Adjusted for an Increase in a Component Cost

	A	B	C	D	E	F	G	H
1			BASELINE DATA-INPUT MODULE					
2	INPUT PRICES:							
3	ID#	COMPONENT	CURRENCY	CODE	QTR 1	QTR 2	QTR 3	QTR 4
4	1	TUBING SET	L. (UK)	3	35.00	35.00	35.00	35.00
5	2	FITTING SET	L. (UK)	3	9.45	9.50	9.60	9.65
6	3	PRIMER	US $	1	0.10	0.10	0.10	0.10
7	4	PAINT	CANADIAN $	2	1.00	1.00	1.00	1.00
8	5	DECAL SET	CANADIAN $	2	2.27	2.27	2.27	2.27
9	6	BRAZING RODS	US $	1	0.40	0.45	0.50	0.55
10	7	STEEL PIN SET	US $	1	0.05	0.05	0.05	0.05
11	8	SHIPPING BOX	CANADIAN $	2	0.88	0.88	0.88	0.88
12	9	MISCELLANEOUS	US $	1	0.60	0.70	0.80	0.90
13	10	OTHER	?	0	0	0	0	0
14								
15	FOREIGN EXCHANGE	(DOLLARS US / 1 UNIT FOREIGN)						
16				CODE	QTR 1	QTR 2	QTR 3	QTR 4
17		US $ / US $		1	$1.00	$1.00	$1.00	$1.00
18		US $ / CANADIAN $		2	$0.73	$0.73	$0.73	$0.73
19		US $ / ENGLISH POUND (L.)		3	$1.45	$1.46	$1.46	$1.47
20		US $ / OTHER		0	$0.00	$0.00	$0.00	$0.00

	I	J	K	L	M	N	O	P
1					SCENARIO FACTORS			
2	INPUT PRICES:							
3	ID#	COMPONENT			QTR 1	QTR 2	QTR 3	QTR 4
4	1	TUBING SET			1.1	1.1	1.1	1.1
5	2	FITTING SET			1	1	1	1
6	3	PRIMER			1	1	1	1
7	4	PAINT			1	1	1	1
8	5	DECAL SET			1	1	1	1
9	6	BRAZING RODS			1	1	1	1
10	7	STEEL PIN SET			1	1	1	1
11	8	SHIPPING BOX			1	1	1	1
12	9	MISCELLANEOUS			1	1	1	1
13	10	OTHER			1	1	1	1
14								
15	FOREIGN EXCHANGE	(DOLLARS US / 1 UNIT FOREIGN)						
16					QTR 1	QTR 2	QTR 3	QTR 4
17		US $ / US $			1	1	1	1
18		US $ / CANADIAN $			1	1	1	1
19		US $ / ENGLISH POUND (L.)			1	1	1	1
20		US $ / OTHER			1	1	1	1

	Q	R	S	T	U	V	W	X
1					FINAL SCENARIO DATA			
2	INPUT PRICES:							
3	ID#	COMPONENT			QTR 1	QTR 2	QTR 3	QTR 4
4	1	TUBING SET			38.50	38.50	38.50	38.50
5	2	FITTING SET			9.45	9.50	9.60	9.65
6	3	PRIMER			0.10	0.10	0.10	0.10
7	4	PAINT			1.00	1.00	1.00	1.00
8	5	DECAL SET			2.27	2.27	2.27	2.27
9	6	BRAZING RODS			0.40	0.45	0.50	0.55
10	7	STEEL PIN SET			0.05	0.05	0.05	0.05
11	8	SHIPPING BOX			0.88	0.88	0.88	0.88
12	9	MISCELLANEOUS			0.60	0.70	0.80	0.90
13	10	OTHER			0.00	0.00	0.00	0.00
14								
15	FOREIGN EXCHANGE	(DOLLARS US / 1 UNIT FOREIGN)						
16					QTR 1	QTR 2	QTR 3	QTR 4
17		US $ / US $			1.00	1.00	1.00	1.00
18		US $ / CANADIAN $			0.73	0.73	0.73	0.73
19		US $ / ENGLISH POUND (L.)			1.45	1.46	1.46	1.47
20		US $ / OTHER			0.00	0.00	0.00	0.00

Illustration 8.14
Scenario Calculations Data Flow Section

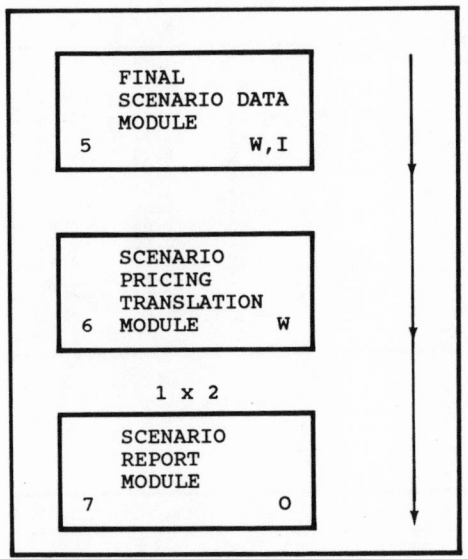

```
┌─────────────────────────────────────────┐
│                                          │
│   ┌──────────────────────────┐           │
│   │   FINAL                  │     │     │
│   │   SCENARIO DATA          │     │     │
│   │   MODULE                 │     │     │
│   │  5              W,I      │     │     │
│   └──────────────────────────┘     │     │
│                                    │     │
│   ┌──────────────────────────┐     │     │
│   │   SCENARIO               │     │     │
│   │   PRICING                │     │     │
│   │   TRANSLATION            │     │     │
│   │  6 MODULE        W       │     ▼     │
│   └──────────────────────────┘           │
│         1 x 2                            │
│   ┌──────────────────────────┐           │
│   │   SCENARIO               │           │
│   │   REPORT                 │           │
│   │   MODULE                 │           │
│   │  7              O        │     ▼     │
│   └──────────────────────────┘           │
│                                          │
└─────────────────────────────────────────┘
```

Illustration 8.15
Scenario Pricing Translation Module

	Q	R	S	T	U	V	W	X
21		SCENARIO PRICING TRANSLATION TABLE – EXCHANGE						
22	INPUT PRICES:							
23	ID#	COMPONENT	CURRENCY	CODE	QTR 1	QTR 2	QTR 3	QTR 4
24	1	TUBING SET	L. (UK)	3	1.45	1.46	1.46	1.47
25	2	FITTING SET	L. (UK)	3	1.45	1.46	1.46	1.47
26	3	PRIMER	US $	1	1	1	1	1
27	4	PAINT	CANADIAN $	2	0.73	0.73	0.73	0.73
28	5	DECAL SET	CANADIAN $	2	0.73	0.73	0.73	0.73
29	6	BRAZING RODS	US $	1	1	1	1	1
30	7	STEEL PIN SET	US $	1	1	1	1	1
31	8	SHIPPING BOX	CANADIAN $	2	0.73	0.73	0.73	0.73
32	9	MISCELLANEOUS	US $	1	1	1	1	1
33	10	OTHER	?	0	0	0	0	0

Only the scenario title must be reentered. Using a symmetric structure reduces programming time and the risk of programming error.

The Delta Report Module

The basic spreadsheet application is complete. All three data flows have been constructed and explained. A useful report called the delta report will also be constructed to identify cost changes associated with scenarios. The delta report appears in Illustration 8.17.

Illustration 8.16
The Scenario Report Module

	Q	R	S	T	U	V	W	X
41			SCENARIO AVERAGE MATERIALS COST					
42								
43	ID#	COMPONENT			QTR 1	QTR 2	QTR 3	QTR 4
44	1	TUBING SET			50.75	51.10	51.10	51.45
45	2	FITTING SET			13.70	13.87	14.02	14.19
46	3	PRIMER			0.10	0.10	0.10	0.10
47	4	PAINT			0.73	0.73	0.73	0.73
48	5	DECAL SET			1.66	1.66	1.66	1.66
49	6	BRAZING RODS			0.40	0.45	0.50	0.55
50	7	STEEL PIN SET			0.05	0.05	0.05	0.05
51	8	SHIPPING BOX			0.64	0.64	0.64	0.64
52	9	MISCELLANEOUS			0.60	0.70	0.80	0.90
53	10	OTHER			0.00	0.00	0.00	0.00
54								
55		TOTAL AVERAGE MATERIALS COST =			68.63	69.30	69.60	70.27
56		(US DOLLARS)						

Illustration 8.17
The Delta Report Module

	Q	R	S	T	U	V	W	X
61			DELTA AVERAGE MATERIALS COST					
62								
63	ID#	COMPONENT			QTR 1	QTR 2	QTR 3	QTR 4
64	1	TUBING SET			0.00	0.00	0.00	0.00
65	2	FITTING SET			0.00	0.00	0.00	0.00
66	3	PRIMER			0.00	0.00	0.00	0.00
67	4	PAINT			0.00	0.00	0.00	0.00
68	5	DECAL SET			0.00	0.00	0.00	0.00
69	6	BRAZING RODS			0.00	0.00	0.00	0.00
70	7	STEEL PIN SET			0.00	0.00	0.00	0.00
71	8	SHIPPING BOX			0.00	0.00	0.00	0.00
72	9	MISCELLANEOUS			0.00	0.00	0.00	0.00
73	10	OTHER			0.00	0.00	0.00	0.00
74								
75	DELTA TOTAL AVERAGE MATERIALS COST =				0.00	0.00	0.00	0.00
76		(US DOLLARS)						

The delta report is located in cells Q61 to X76. This locates the report directly beneath the scenario report. This report will have the same labeling structure as the baseline and scenario reports. Labeling information can be copied from either of these reports. To complete the delta report, the numeric entries must be specified. Each entry is simply the difference between the corresponding entries in the scenario and baseline reports. Because the reports are located exactly one and two pages from each other, entering the needed formulas for the delta report is quite simple. Use is made of the page-up and left-margin keys to enter formulas. To find delta cost for tubing sets in the first quarter of analysis, move to cell U64 and enter the keystrokes:

+ PgUp − PgUp [left margin] [left margin] Return

Illustration 8.18
Specifying an Increase in Tubing Set Costs

	I	J	K	L	M	N	O	P
1				SCENARIO FACTORS				
2	INPUT PRICES:							
3	ID# COMPONENT				QTR 1	QTR 2	QTR 3	QTR 4
4	1 TUBING SET				1.1	1.1	1.1	1.1
5	2 FITTING SET				1	1	1	1
6	3 PRIMER				1	1	1	1
7	4 PAINT				1	1	1	1
8	5 DECAL SET				1	1	1	1
9	6 BRAZING RODS				1	1	1	1
10	7 STEEL PIN SET				1	1	1	1
11	8 SHIPPING BOX				1	1	1	1
12	9 MISCELLANEOUS				1	1	1	1
13	10 OTHER				1	1	1	1
14								
15	FOREIGN EXCHANGE	(DOLLARS US / 1 UNIT FOREIGN)						
16					QTR 1	QTR 2	QTR 3	QTR 4
17	US $ / US $				1	1	1	1
18	US $ / CANADIAN $				1	1	1	1
19	US $ / ENGLISH POUND (L.)				1	1	1	1
20	US $ / OTHER				1	1	1	1

In words, delta tubing set cost in the first quarter of analysis is equal to scenario tubing set cost in the first quarter of analysis minus baseline tubing set cost in the same period.

The report is completed by copying cell U64 to the cell range U64 to X73, and then entering sum formulas in cells U75, V75, W75, and X75.

PERFORMING SCENARIO STUDIES

The spreadsheet tool can now be used to perform analysis. Let's return to an earlier example. Suppose again that the cost of tubing sets is to rise by 10 percent for each of the four quarters of analysis. The user specifies the scenario by changing the tubing set's scenario factors located in the scenario factors module. In the baseline case, all factors are set to 1. This scenario is specified by moving the cursor to cells corresponding to the tubing set for each quarter and typing 1.1 in each. The module appears in Illustration 8.18.

The resultant scenario, baseline, and delta reports appear in Illustration 8.19.

The price of tubing sets is larger in the scenario report than it is in the baseline report. Consequently, total average materials cost is also larger in the scenario case. For example, in the first quarter of analysis, total average materials cost in the scenario is $73.71 and baseline total average materials cost is $68.63. The difference is $5.07, as shown in the delta report.

The only reason the baseline and scenario reports differ is that an assumption from the baseline case was changed. This is a what-if scenario analysis. The assumption in the baseline case was that tubing sets would cost 35 English pounds in all four quarters of analysis. The scenario study posed the question, "What if the price of tubing sets rises 10 percent over baseline estimates (to 38.5 English pounds) for all four quarters of analysis?"

Illustration 8.19

Reports—After a 10 Percent Rise in Tubing Set Prices

	Q	R	S	T	U	V	W	X
41			SCENARIO AVERAGE MATERIALS COST					
42								
43	ID#	COMPONENT			QTR 1	QTR 2	QTR 3	QTR 4
44	1	TUBING SET			55.83	56.21	56.21	56.60
45	2	FITTING SET			13.70	13.87	14.02	14.19
46	3	PRIMER			0.10	0.10	0.10	0.10
47	4	PAINT			0.73	0.73	0.73	0.73
48	5	DECAL SET			1.66	1.66	1.66	1.66
49	6	BRAZING RODS			0.40	0.45	0.50	0.55
50	7	STEEL PIN SET			0.05	0.05	0.05	0.05
51	8	SHIPPING BOX			0.64	0.64	0.64	0.64
52	9	MISCELLANEOUS			0.60	0.70	0.80	0.90
53	10	OTHER			0.00	0.00	0.00	0.00
54								
55		TOTAL AVERAGE MATERIALS COST =			73.71	74.41	74.71	75.41
56		(US DOLLARS)						

	A	B	C	D	E	F	G	H
41			BASELINE AVERAGE MATERIALS COST					
42								
43	ID#	COMPONENT			QTR 1	QTR 2	QTR 3	QTR 4
44	1	TUBING SET			50.75	51.10	51.10	51.45
45	2	FITTING SET			13.70	13.87	14.02	14.19
46	3	PRIMER			0.10	0.10	0.10	0.10
47	4	PAINT			0.73	0.73	0.73	0.73
48	5	DECAL SET			1.66	1.66	1.66	1.66
49	6	BRAZING RODS			0.40	0.45	0.50	0.55
50	7	STEEL PIN SET			0.05	0.05	0.05	0.05
51	8	SHIPPING BOX			0.64	0.64	0.64	0.64
52	9	MISCELLANEOUS			0.60	0.70	0.80	0.90
53	10	OTHER			0.00	0.00	0.00	0.00
54								
55		TOTAL AVERAGE MATERIALS COST =			68.63	69.30	69.60	70.27
56		(US DOLLARS)						

	Q	R	S	T	U	V	W	X
61			DELTA AVERAGE MATERIALS COST					
62								
63	ID#	COMPONENT			QTR 1	QTR 2	QTR 3	QTR 4
64	1	TUBING SET			5.07	5.11	5.11	5.15
65	2	FITTING SET			0.00	0.00	0.00	0.00
66	3	PRIMER			0.00	0.00	0.00	0.00
67	4	PAINT			0.00	0.00	0.00	0.00
68	5	DECAL SET			0.00	0.00	0.00	0.00
69	6	BRAZING RODS			0.00	0.00	0.00	0.00
70	7	STEEL PIN SET			0.00	0.00	0.00	0.00
71	8	SHIPPING BOX			0.00	0.00	0.00	0.00
72	9	MISCELLANEOUS			0.00	0.00	0.00	0.00
73	10	OTHER			0.00	0.00	0.00	0.00
74								
75	DELTA TOTAL AVERAGE MATERIALS COST =				5.07	5.11	5.11	5.14
76		(US DOLLARS)						

Illustration 8.20
Specifying a Change in U.S./Canadian Exchange Rates

	I	J	K	L	M	N	O	P
1				SCENARIO	FACTORS			
2	INPUT PRICES:							
3	ID# COMPONENT				QTR 1	QTR 2	QTR 3	QTR 4
4	1 TUBING SET				1	1	1	1
5	2 FITTING SET				1	1	1	1
6	3 PRIMER				1	1	1	1
7	4 PAINT				1	1	1	1
8	5 DECAL SET				1	1	1	1
9	6 BRAZING RODS				1	1	1	1
10	7 STEEL PIN SET				1	1	1	1
11	8 SHIPPING BOX				1	1	1	1
12	9 MISCELLANEOUS				1	1	1	1
13	10 OTHER				1	1	1	1
14								
15	FOREIGN EXCHANGE (DOLLARS US / 1 UNIT FOREIGN)							
16					QTR 1	QTR 2	QTR 3	QTR 4
17	US $ / US $				1	1	1	1
18	US $ / CANADIAN $				1	1.03	1.06	1.1
19	US $ / ENGLISH POUND (L.)				1	1	1	1
20	US $ / OTHER				1	1	1	1

What would happen if U.S. versus Canadian exchange rates were to deteriorate steadily throughout the four-quarter analysis period? This is a change in baseline assumptions concerning exchange rates. The baseline assumption is that the currency exchange rate will remain at 73 cents throughout the analysis period. Assume that the currency exchange rate deteriorates by 3 percent over the base case in the second quarter, by 6 percent in the third quarter, and 10 percent by the fourth quarter. The user can move to the scenario factors module and input these desired changes. The user would position the cursor at cell N18 and type 1.03. The user would then move the cursor to cells O18 and P18 and enter 1.06 and 1.1 successively. All other factors are returned to 1. The scenario factors module appears in Illustration 8.20.

The resultant scenario and delta reports appear in Illustration 8.21.

The scenario investigates the changes in costs that result from falling U.S. currency exchange rates in relation to the Canadian dollar. In the second quarter of analysis, the scenario specification postulates that it would take 3 percent more U.S. dollars to purchase one Canadian dollar than in the base case for this same quarter. The U.S. dollar continues to decline in value in the third and fourth quarters of analysis.

Only components of Canadian manufacture are affected in the scenario. Paint, decals, and shipping boxes are affected by the change in U.S./Canadian exchange rates. Total average materials cost rises by the sum of the changes in the cost of these three components.

Note that the cost of tubing sets is not affected in this scenario. When the user specifies a scenario, the reference case is the baseline data set, not the output data from the previous scenario. By changing the scenario factor for

Illustration 8.21
Reports—After a Change in U.S./Canadian Exchange Rates

	Q	R	S	T	U	V	W	X
41			SCENARIO AVERAGE MATERIALS COST					
42								
43	ID#	COMPONENT			QTR 1	QTR 2	QTR 3	QTR 4
44	1	TUBING SET			50.75	51.10	51.10	51.45
45	2	FITTING SET			13.70	13.87	14.02	14.19
46	3	PRIMER			0.10	0.10	0.10	0.10
47	4	PAINT			0.73	0.75	0.77	0.80
48	5	DECAL SET			1.66	1.71	1.76	1.82
49	6	BRAZING RODS			0.40	0.45	0.50	0.55
50	7	STEEL PIN SET			0.05	0.05	0.05	0.05
51	8	SHIPPING BOX			0.64	0.66	0.68	0.71
52	9	MISCELLANEOUS			0.60	0.70	0.80	0.90
53	10	OTHER			0.00	0.00	0.00	0.00
54								
55		TOTAL AVERAGE MATERIALS COST =			68.63	69.39	69.78	70.57
56		(US DOLLARS)						

	Q	R	S	T	U	V	W	X
61			DELTA AVERAGE MATERIALS COST					
62								
63	ID#	COMPONENT			QTR 1	QTR 2	QTR 3	QTR 4
64	1	TUBING SET			0.00	0.00	0.00	0.00
65	2	FITTING SET			0.00	0.00	0.00	0.00
66	3	PRIMER			0.00	0.00	0.00	0.00
67	4	PAINT			0.00	0.02	0.04	0.07
68	5	DECAL SET			0.00	0.05	0.10	0.17
69	6	BRAZING RODS			0.00	0.00	0.00	0.00
70	7	STEEL PIN SET			0.00	0.00	0.00	0.00
71	8	SHIPPING BOX			0.00	0.02	0.04	0.06
72	9	MISCELLANEOUS			0.00	0.00	0.00	0.00
73	10	OTHER			0.00	0.00	0.00	0.00
74								
75	DELTA TOTAL AVERAGE MATERIALS COST =				0.00	0.09	0.18	0.30
76		(US DOLLARS)						

tubing sets back to 1, the scenario pricing effects obtained in the previous scenario are eliminated. This characteristic is a major strength of the employed application design.

The two example scenarios will now be combined. The factors entered in the scenario factors module appear in Illustration 8.22.

The resultant scenario and delta reports appear in Illustration 8.23.

The delta costing report offers some valuable information. The only change in total average materials costs in the first quarter results from the cost increase of tubing sets manufactured in Great Britain. This cost increase is sustained throughout the analysis period. Other cost increases begin in the second quarter of analysis and affect the U.S. dollar price of all goods of Canadian manufacture. The scenario specification indicates that cost increases associated with Canadian goods result from altered currency exchange rates and not from direct price increases from Canadian suppliers.

Graphs effectively illustrate reported information. The scenario, baseline, and delta report format lends itself to an interesting graph of activity. Consider the

Illustration 8.22

Specifying a Change in Component Costs and Exchange Rates

	I	J	K	L	M	N	O	P
1				SCENARIO FACTORS				
2	INPUT PRICES:							
3	ID#	COMPONENT			QTR 1	QTR 2	QTR 3	QTR 4
4	1	TUBING SET			1.1	1.1	1.1	1.1
5	2	FITTING SET			1	1	1	1
6	3	PRIMER			1	1	1	1
7	4	PAINT			1	1	1	1
8	5	DECAL SET			1	1	1	1
9	6	BRAZING RODS			1	1	1	1
10	7	STEEL PIN SET			1	1	1	1
11	8	SHIPPING BOX			1	1	1	1
12	9	MISCELLANEOUS			1	1	1	1
13	10	OTHER			1	1	1	1
14								
15	FOREIGN EXCHANGE	(DOLLARS US	/	1 UNIT FOREIGN)				
16					QTR 1	QTR 2	QTR 3	QTR 4
17		US $ /	US $		1	1	1	1
18		US $ /	CANADIAN $		1	1.03	1.06	1.1
19		US $ /	ENGLISH POUND	(L.)	1	1	1	1
20		US $ /	OTHER		1	1	1	1

bar graph in Illustration 8.24. This is a graph of the last scenario's information from the scenario, baseline, and delta reports.

A macro can be written so that a similar graph can be produced after completing new scenarios. A macro is a collection of keystrokes processed at the request of the user. By including the following 1–2–3 macro in the spreadsheet, the user can request a graph similar to the one generated in Illustration 8.24:

'/grgtbxA4..A7~aE55..H55~bU55..X55~clU75..X75~

'otfUNIT MATERIALS COSTS~

'tx(QTRS)~laBASELINE~lbSCENARIO~lcDELTA~qvq

Interpreted:

Line 1: /,Graph,Reset,Graph,Type,Bar,Xrange,A4..A7,RETURN,Arange,E55.. H55,RETURN,Brange,U55..X55,RETURN,Crange,U75..X75,RETURN

Line 2: Options,Titles,First,UNIT MATERIALS COST,RETURN

Line 3: Titles,Xvariable,(QTRS),RETURN,Legend,Avariable,BASELINE, RETURN,Legend,Bvariable,SCENARIO,RETURN,Legend, Cvariable,DELTA,RETURN,Quit,View,Quit

(The symbol / invokes the standard 1–2–3 menu, and the symbol ' must initiate all lines of a 1–2–3 macro.)

Macros can be entered in any open area of the spreadsheet. For reference purposes it is a good idea to collect all macros in one place. In the example application, cell range I101 to P120 is designated as the area in which to place macros. To enter this macro, the application builder would move to cell I103,

Illustration 8.23
Reports—After Changing Both Component Costs and Exchange Rates

	Q	R	S	T	U	V	W	X
41			SCENARIO AVERAGE MATERIALS COST					
42								
43	ID#	COMPONENT			QTR 1	QTR 2	QTR 3	QTR 4
44	1	TUBING SET			55.83	56.21	56.21	56.60
45	2	FITTING SET			13.70	13.87	14.02	14.19
46	3	PRIMER			0.10	0.10	0.10	0.10
47	4	PAINT			0.73	0.75	0.77	0.80
48	5	DECAL SET			1.66	1.71	1.76	1.82
49	6	BRAZING RODS			0.40	0.45	0.50	0.55
50	7	STEEL PIN SET			0.05	0.05	0.05	0.05
51	8	SHIPPING BOX			0.64	0.66	0.68	0.71
52	9	MISCELLANEOUS			0.60	0.70	0.80	0.90
53	10	OTHER			0.00	0.00	0.00	0.00
54								
55		TOTAL AVERAGE MATERIALS COST =			73.71	74.50	74.89	75.71
56		(US DOLLARS)						

	Q	R	S	T	U	V	W	X
61			DELTA AVERAGE MATERIALS COST					
62								
63	ID#	COMPONENT			QTR 1	QTR 2	QTR 3	QTR 4
64	1	TUBING SET			5.07	5.11	5.11	5.15
65	2	FITTING SET			0.00	0.00	0.00	0.00
66	3	PRIMER			0.00	0.00	0.00	0.00
67	4	PAINT			0.00	0.02	0.04	0.07
68	5	DECAL SET			0.00	0.05	0.10	0.17
69	6	BRAZING RODS			0.00	0.00	0.00	0.00
70	7	STEEL PIN SET			0.00	0.00	0.00	0.00
71	8	SHIPPING BOX			0.00	0.02	0.04	0.06
72	9	MISCELLANEOUS			0.00	0.00	0.00	0.00
73	10	OTHER			0.00	0.00	0.00	0.00
74								
75	DELTA TOTAL AVERAGE MATERIALS COST =				5.07	5.20	5.29	5.45
76		(US DOLLARS)						

and would type the entire contents of the first line of the macro in cell I103, type the entire contents of the second line of the macro in cell I104, and type the entire contents of the third line of the macro in cell I105. Before a macro can be invoked, it must be named. The following commands name the macro.

/rnc\gI103

Interpreted: /,Range,Name,Create,\g (a macro named G), I103 (starting in cell I103)).

The user activates the macro by depressing the Alt and G keys simultaneously. This is the standard way to form, name, and invoke 1–2–3 macros.

Note that the generated graphs will not be of much value if requested before scenario specifications are entered. Before a scenario has been run, baseline and scenario costs are equal and delta costs are zero.

SUMMARY

A spreadsheet tool was developed and used to evaluate component costs associated with the manufacture of bicycle frames. The tool developed here is

Illustration 8.24
Unit Materials Costs

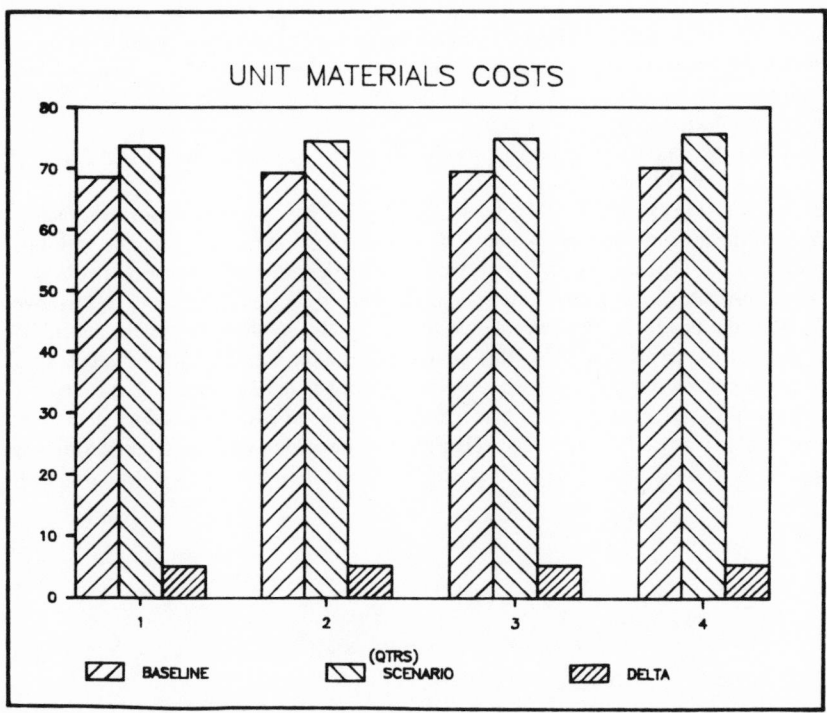

data driven. Changes in the number or origin of components are made by changing data in the data input module. No new formulas or other reprogramming of
the spreadsheet is necessary. This reduces the risk of error and makes the application more flexible in performing analysis.

To input scenario assumptions, the user again has only to change data. The
most common method would be to manipulate scenario factors. By viewing these
factors, it is easy to see just what scenario assumptions are active.

The tool makes use of a scenario, baseline, and delta report format. The
scenario report always reflects the effects of the user's assumption set. The
baseline report embodies the data that are most likely to occur in the forecast
period. It reflects the analyst's best guess about future conditions. The delta
report compares scenario and baseline results. It gives information as to just
how different results will be if the input scenario assumptions actually do come
to pass.

The tool's design takes advantage of logical data flows. Related modules are
located near each other, and module formats minimized programming time and
the chance of programmer error. Such organization will also minimize user
resistance and acceptance time.[3]

NOTES

1. The example spreadsheet uses the following column widths. Columns A, I, Q—4 spaces, columns B, J, R—14 spaces, columns C, K, S—12 spaces, columns D, L, T—6 spaces. All other columns are 9 spaces—the default setting for the Lotus 1-2-3 package.

Columns with $ prefix use a currency format setting. Some other columns use a format fixed at two decimal places.

2. This is accomplished by moving the cursor to cell T24 and typing +D24, moving the cursor to cell T25 and typing +D25, and so on.

3. The scenario examples in this chapter are specified by manipulating scenario factors located in the scenario factors module. There is another way to run scenarios with this application. The final scenario data set is the data set processed in the scenario calculations section. This is true regardless of the way the data set is generated. The user could move directly to the final scenario data module (box 5 on the spreadsheet sketch) and input new data for the scenario. Cells in this module contain formulas. If the user inputs data in these cells, the formula specifications will be replaced by the data entries. The developer should include a short macro that can return the application to its baseline state. The macro would change all scenario factors back to 1 and would re-input all original formulas in the final scenario data module. This will make the tool easier to use and will help eliminate run errors.

9

An AREMOS-Based Planning Model

DAVID J. GIANTURCO

The spreadsheet-based functional tool constructed in Chapter 8 does not use estimation methods such as regression analysis and trend analysis. The production department probably obtained estimates for future component costs and currency exchange rates by asking its suppliers or industry consultants. This information was then used to construct the baseline data set. There was no effort to forecast component prices or currency exchange rates within the spreadsheet tool.

Once the baseline data set is constructed, the tool can investigate the cost implications of various scenarios. For example, what if a particular currency exchange rate should vary from its baseline level by some given percentage? What will be the cost implications for the firm?

The results of such scenario analyses are not forecasts; they simply examine the implications of many possible circumstances, any or none of which may actually come to pass. The only forecast information associated with the application is the baseline data set. It is constructed using the firm's best information concerning future component costs and currency exchange rates.

The planning model presented in this chapter will directly employ regression analysis to forecast sales. The model will forecast sales of bicycle frames from the Very Fast Bicycle Frame Company (VFBFC) and will use this sales forecast to estimate future financial results. The model will be recursive in structure. Specifically, once sales are forecast, it becomes possible to calculate other important measures like revenue, total costs, and profits. These measures are calculated using the sales forecast and other given data. Many econometric and financial forecasting models are simultaneous in structure, meaning that important measures cannot be determined individually. Some or all of the equations of the model are determined together using some simultaneous equation solution algorithm.

In the context used here, planning models are designed for comprehensive corporate planning purposes and differ from functional tools maintained by staff or business departments. Planning models are specifically designed for strategic or organizational planning and are not used in day-to-day operations. They measure the corporate-wide effects resulting from changes in key variables and output report information on sales, revenue, costs, and profits. The model developed here will forecast the sales of VFBFC bicycle frames. Some basic financial information will later be added, but the driving force of the model will center on the sales forecasting equation.

As with the functional tool presented in Chapter 8, the following example is developed in detail. This model offers insight to the design and construction of planning models. Concepts will be of value to those who build planning models or use planning models built by others. The model's design will be simplistic. For instance, sales will be forecast for a single product—bicycle frames. The model will employ very basic financial information. Nevertheless, this example will illustrate the use of regression analysis and systems of equations to solve basic forecasting and financial problems. By employing a sophisticated micro-computer-based econometrics package, AREMOS, the example will offer insight into the use of such systems tools.

The model builder must confront analysis issues and list the analysis objectives. A methodological outline should also be prepared. This is as true for planning models as it is for functional tools. In fact it may be more important because planning models are usually less structured than functional tools, and accuracy checks are more difficult to devise. As discussed in Chapter 8, the model builder should draft sample output reports before designing and coding the various modules. The comments made in chapters 5 and 8 concerning prototypes also apply here.

BUILDING PROTOTYPES

A prototype is a simplified version of a computer-based application. Application developers use prototypes to test their algorithms and systems design in the early stages of an application's development. In this way, many conceptual and practical problems are avoided. Prototypes facilitate communications between application developers and end-users or managers. End-users and managers are able to revise their specifications for an application before the full-scale version is built.

In developing the art of prototyping, try to capture only the most important elements of analysis in the prototype. Use abbreviated data inputs and plausible but concocted data sets. In short, make sure the pieces and data of the envisioned application go together as expected. Invariably they won't, and the subsequent modifications will improve systems design and possibly analysis methodology.

As an example, suppose a proposed tool is to forecast sales of ten products for three years on a quarterly basis. In addition, the costs associated with these sales levels must be projected. The application must automatically generate plots of revenue and costs, and it must display statistics concerning prices and demand. Instead of tracking ten products, track two. Instead of building the model for three years, use four quarters. Use plausible prices and demands for the products, but also use good judgment. Don't waste time gathering exact data inputs. You are testing your systems design, not preparing a report for executive review. If there are ten costing categories, choose two, perhaps one capital and one noncapital. Prepare sample reports and one or two key sample graphs and statistics. Then generate the reports and statistics. This process sounds simple, but data dimensions, programming difficulties, and a host of other issues will surface on the way to completing the successful prototype. The last step is to take the prototype to the end-user or manager and demonstrate its capabilities. Be sure to ask the question "Is this what you want?"

MODEL OBJECTIVE

The objective of the VFBFC sales and financial forecasting model is to produce reports of forecasted sales and financial information. Report information must appear on a quarterly basis over a one-year planning horizon. Sales are forecast based on general economic conditions, product price, and other variables. By using this and other available data, basic financial information is forecast over a four-quarter planning horizon.

For purposes of exposition, assume that the model is built in the middle of 1985. The objective is to forecast sales and other financial measures for the quarterly periods 1985 quarter 3, 1985 quarter 4, 1986 quarter 1, and 1986 quarter 2. Historical data are available from the first quarter of 1978 to the second quarter of 1985.

REPORT SECTION

Like the functional tool constructed in Chapter 8, the model will display scenario, baseline, and delta (scenario minus baseline) report information. The output reports will include estimates for sales (quantity), total revenue, total cost, and profit. The example reports contained in Illustration 9.1 were constructed using Lotus 1–2–3 and show the information needed in the final AREMOS reports.

The sample reports show scenario and baseline sales, revenues, total costs,

Illustration 9.1
Example Reports

```
                              SALES

                    SCENARIO        BASELINE          DELTA
                    --------        --------          -----

    1985Q3
    1985Q4
    1986Q1
    1986Q2


                            REVENUES

                    SCENARIO        BASELINE          DELTA
                    --------        --------          -----

    1985Q3
    1985Q4
    1986Q1
    1986Q2


                          TOTAL COSTS

                    SCENARIO        BASELINE          DELTA
                    --------        --------          -----

    1985Q3
    1985Q4
    1986Q1
    1986Q2


                            PROFITS

                    SCENARIO        BASELINE          DELTA
                    --------        --------          -----

    1985Q3
    1985Q4
    1986Q1
    1986Q2
```

and profits for all four quarters of analysis. Delta (scenario minus baseline) information appears for these report categories as well. As with the functional tool constructed in Chapter 8, the delta report information will simplify the evaluation of alternative scenario results. Note that costs will be reported at a very simple level. In more extensive analysis, costs would be reported at a much lower level. For example, materials costs, labor costs, promotional costs, and fixed costs would appear in addition to total costs. Scenario, baseline, and delta measures would appear for all cost categories.

The baseline information displayed in these reports will always contain estimates associated with the baseline (or business as expected) case. Only the scenario and delta information in the reports will change when various what-if analyses are performed. As with the functional tool constructed in Chapter 8, the baseline report serves as the first reference point to judge scenario results. How do the scenario results compare with the expected business-as-usual case?

DESIGN OBJECTIVES

The model built here is straightforward and consists of what initially appears to be standard computer code. If you have a limited programming background, you may feel as if the microcomputing party is now over. Not so! Of late, advanced packages have become available that are nonprocedural. That means the computer is told what to do, not how to do it. That also means that coding is straightforward and easy to understand and learn. Planners and analysts can now spend far less time struggling with code and far more time planning and analyzing.

AREMOS is a nonprocedural package and can be used in either an interactive or batch mode. In the interactive mode, the user converses with the machine, one command at a time. In batch mode, the user submits a set of code at one time (in one batch) to perform the work desired. Interactive mode is conducive to building forecasting equations. After the analyst has decided on the equations needed, the final planning application usually implements those equations in a command file. A command file is identical in function to a 1–2–3 macro. Several commands are strung together and processed sequentially. The computer does not pause for user input.

Employing nonprocedural systems tools can greatly reduce programming time. They also reduce the frustration that often accompanies the use of languages and packages that are very fussy about how they will accept input. Users need not be trained programmers or know a great deal of computerese to use an application. What is more important here is that analysts and planners don't have to be trained programmers to build an application. This major advance is not specific to microcomputing technology but generalizes to computer technology as a whole. The ability of advanced languages and packages to reduce application development time is a major reason why computing is moving closer and closer to end-users.

The design objective is to produce a simple, straightforward set of code that will initialize a data set, estimate a product forecasting equation, define other equations to form a simple financial model, solve this system of equations, and report desired information. The code will consist of a small number of easily identifiable and alterable program sections. The code must be easy to learn and change.

Before building the general model, a product forecasting equation must be developed. AREMOS will be used in the interactive mode to accomplish this task.

The specifics of developing a user interface for the example planning model are discussed in an appendix to this chapter. The model builder has two choices in this area: Employ a question-and-answer dialogue to prompt the user through the model running process, or provide a template that takes in necessary information before the model is run. A template is a screen of information on which the user indicates what type of scenario to run. The first objective of this chapter is to produce the actual code for the example model. However, suitable interfaces will suggest themselves during the discussion.

Sketch of the Proposed Model

The model sketch as shown in Illustration 9.2 is not significantly affected by the fact that the model is AREMOS-based. The model sketch would be similar if the application were based in any one of several other packages capable of solving systems of equations. The data and logic flows are straightforward. Each box in the diagram represents a program section. These sections often consist of a single statement, and the planning model will be constructed with a limited amount of code.

First, all needed data are brought into the AREMOS environment. This includes data used to estimate the product forecasting equation and also other data needed by the model's financial identities. The data set retrieved in section 1 is referred to as either the original data set or databank file. In section 2 the period of analysis is set. Any newly created data series, fitted equations, and so on will use this period definition. The next step is critical. In section 3 the analyst must specify the product forecasting equation so that future sales (quantity) can be forecast. In the example a single forecasting equation will be developed using regression analysis. However, other methods could be used to form the forecasting equation or equations. In section 4, all the financial identities are specified. These equations are driven by the product forecasting equation estimated in section 3. In section 5 the analyst indicates which of the estimated equations and identities to include in the final model and requests that the system of equations be solved.

Forecasts are generated during the solution process. These forecasts are generated using baseline data and are referred to as baseline forecast estimates. To specify a scenario, the analyst inputs new data (assumptions) in section 6, and

Illustration 9.2
Sketch of the Proposed Model

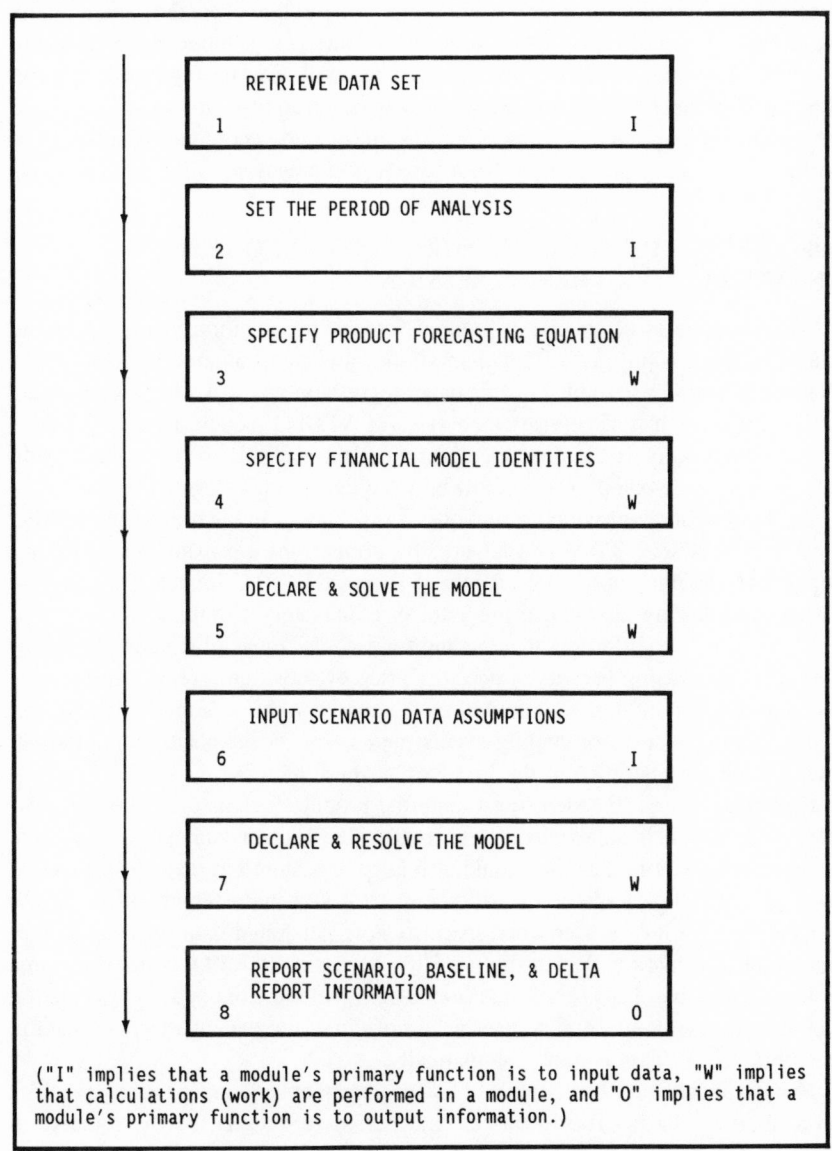

("I" implies that a module's primary function is to input data, "W" implies that calculations (work) are performed in a module, and "O" implies that a module's primary function is to output information.)

then re-solves the model in section 7. The scenario, baseline, and delta forecast information are generated in section 7 and reported in section 8.

Again, the key step in this process is specifying the product forecasting equation in section 3. Before examining the AREMOS code that comprises the planning model, this product forecasting equation must be developed using regression analysis. Regression analysis is covered in detail in Chapter 11, and general background information is not repeated here; however, the salient points are reviewed. AREMOS will be used in the interactive mode to develop the product forecasting equation. The model code will then be reviewed, and the developed product forecasting equation will be inserted at the proper point in the code. The interactive session offers insight in using econometric software to arrive at a suitable specification for a forecasting equation.

SPECIFYING THE PRODUCT FORECASTING EQUATION— AN INTERACTIVE AREMOS SESSION

The objective is to specify a product forecasting equation using regression analysis. Regression analysis explains how movements in one variable affect changes in another variable. In this case, regression analysis identifies the variables that have historically affected sales of VFBFC bicycle frames. VFBFC bicycle frame sales is the dependent variable, the variable to be explained and forecast. A single equation will show how the movements in variables like price or the number of advertising promotions cause changes in the number of VFBFC bicycle frames sold. Price and advertising promotions are examples of the independent variables used to explain and forecast VFBFC bicycle frame sales. These variables are also called predictor or explanatory variables.

Many factors could affect the demand for bicycle frames: the general level of consumer purchasing activity, price, the price of substitute goods, advertising, income, seasonal influences, population, the number of bicycle touring and racing clubs, sports coverage of cycling events, and so on. For expositional purposes, analysis will be restricted to the first four of these factors.

Historical data are needed to estimate the product forecasting equation. AREMOS stores data in databanks. These are files that contain data series, equations, or other information. The user could also keep data stored in text files generated by a spreadsheet package or a word processor. A key characteristic of AREMOS is its employment of a user work space to store generated data series and other important information. When the user first accesses AREMOS, this work area becomes available. Data series read from external files are one type of information stored in the work space. The user need not direct the package to store data in the work space. This is done automatically.

Historical data have been obtained for the dependent and independent variables on a quarterly basis. The historical data period runs from the first quarter of 1978 to the second quarter of 1985. Regression analysis will quantify how changes in the level of consumer spending on durable goods, price, and so on have altered the sales of VFBFC bicycle frames during the historical data period. If these historical relationships are expected to hold in the future, regression analysis becomes a convenient way to forecast sales. Given a reasonable idea of what will happen to consumer spending on durable goods, the price of bicycle frames, the price of gasoline and other variables, a sales forecast for VFBFC bicycle frames can be developed. The forecast period runs from the third quarter of 1985 to the second quarter of 1986.

In this example several variables are needed to develop the product forecasting equation. The following data must be available.

Variable	Variable Name
Number of Bicycle Frames Sold	Q1
Consumer Spending on Durable Goods (billions of dollars)	CED$
Price of Bicycle Frames (dollars)	PRICEBIKE$
Price of Gasoline (dollars per gallon)	PRICEGAS$
A Price Deflator (index, 1982 = 100.0)	PDGNP
Number of Marketing Promotions	PROMO

(Dollars refers to U.S. dollars; a gallon equals 3.7 liters.)

Assume that the needed data are stored in a Lotus 1–2–3 worksheet. To read this data into the AREMOS work space, structure the data in the worksheet as in Table 9.1.

The data contained in the data set come from various places. Historical sales (Q1), promotions (PROMO), and price (PRICEBIKE$) come from records kept by the VFBFC planning department. Estimates for the expected number of promotions and price of bicycle frames during the forecast period come from internal sources at the firm. Note that no estimate appears for future sales levels. This is the variable the forecasting equation will predict. All other data, whether historical or forecast, would probably come from data vendors. The data series stored in the Lotus 1–2–3 worksheet must be read—imported—into the AREMOS environment.

The data in the example appear in the cell range A1 to G35. From within the 1–2–3 environment, the user issues the following 1–2–3 commands to save the data in Table 9.1 in a PRINT (.prn) file called MYDATA.PRN.

/pfMYDATA~rA1..G35~gq

(Translated:
/, Print,File,MYDATA,RETURN,
Range,Al..G35,RETURN,Go,Quit)

(In 1–2–3, the / is used to invoke the package's main menu.)

Exit the 1–2–3 environment by issuing the /qy commands (for Quit, Yes).

The user enters the AREMOS environment by issuing the following two commands:

Table 9.1.
Data Needed to Develop a Product Forecasting Equation

	A	B	C	D	E	F	G
1	"DATE"	"Q1"	"CED$"	"PROMO"	"PDGNP"	"PRICEBIKE$"	"PRICEGAS$"
2	197801	34603	188.88	5	69.90	77.90	0.65
3	197802	33880	207.64	3	71.60	79.70	0.65
4	197803	31127	210.01	4	72.90	81.53	0.65
5	197804	33332	215.79	3	74.40	83.85	0.68
6	197901	36587	215.65	7	76.10	92.43	0.72
7	197902	40087	214.39	7	77.80	99.38	0.82
8	197903	46982	223.89	6	79.40	104.27	0.95
9	197904	47647	221.91	6	81.00	108.53	1.02
10	198001	44987	225.05	5	82.70	119.17	1.18
11	198002	36727	204.86	3	84.60	125.27	1.24
12	198003	37520	218.71	4	86.50	133.24	1.24
13	198004	37088	228.50	5	89.00	137.01	1.23
14	198101	38057	241.14	4	91.30	141.56	1.34
15	198102	40693	235.99	4	92.80	145.98	1.37
16	198103	39468	246.88	5	94.90	156.24	1.35
17	198104	34498	235.50	6	96.70	158.91	1.35
18	198201	33192	245.07	6	98.20	168.00	1.31
19	198202	29073	248.92	4	99.40	170.25	1.24
20	198203	26145	252.80	3	100.80	177.11	1.31
21	198204	26437	263.84	4	101.70	176.63	1.26
22	198301	31162	266.74	7	102.50	173.98	1.17
23	198302	32282	284.46	5	103.30	175.99	1.23
24	198303	34253	295.21	5	104.20	177.83	1.27
25	198304	33425	309.96	6	105.40	179.69	1.23
26	198401	38185	321.20	7	106.60	181.75	1.20
27	198402	36132	331.32	5	107.40	183.36	1.22
28	198403	33915	331.84	6	108.30	187.17	1.19
29	198404	30263	340.37	4	109.20	188.53	1.19
30	198501	31897	347.70	5	110.20	190.04	1.14
31	198502	32013	354.04	4	111.10	191.94	1.22
32	198503	"NA"	373.34	5	111.80	191.59	1.22
33	198504	"NA"	362.02	5	112.80	192.45	1.19
34	198601	"NA"	360.81	6	113.50	193.79	1.19
35	198602	"NA"	373.88	6	114.00	195.27	1.17

CD \AREMOS	(Change the current directory to the AREMOS directory.)
AREMOS	(Call AREMOS.)

The user is now in the AREMOS environment, and is greeted with a message indicating entry to the environment.

AREMOS Version X.X (C) Copyright The WEFA Group, 1987

C:>

At the prompt, the user types the following commands:

SET FREQUENCY QUARTERLY ;
SET PERIOD 78Q1 86Q2 ;
SET IMPORT FORMAT PRN ;
IMPORT MYDATA.PRN ;

The SET command invokes user options concerning the computing environment. The first SET command establishes that quarterly data will be used in all related work. Annual, monthly, daily, and other frequency data can also be used. The second SET command establishes that the working time period is the first quarter of 1978 to the second quarter of 1986. The third SET command indicates that any imported files will be print files (also known as ASCII, text, or flat files). AREMOS also accepts data interchange format files. The IMPORT command brings the data stored in the MYDATA.PRN file into the AREMOS work space. The Q1, CED$, PROMO, and remaining variables are now read into the work space. If the user chooses, these variables (now referred to as data series) can be saved in a permanent AREMOS databank file. The data series have exactly the same name given to them in the 1–2–3 print file MYDATA.PRN. (Data can also be sent back to 1–2–3 for other work using AREMOS's export command. These facilities make it easy to use different packages for different purposes, optimizing analyst productivity.)

THE AREMOS USER WORK SPACE

AREMOS employs a user work space to store data series, equation specifications, and other information. Data series contained in print (.PRN) files generated using Lotus 1–2–3, a word processor, or other means are read into the work space and referenced in AREMOS commands. After data series are brought into the work space, they can be saved in a permanent AREMOS data file called a databank. Data series stored in a databank file can be retrieved during future AREMOS sessions. Consider the following example. Two data series, series X and series Y, are stored in a print file called XY.PRN. The user has just entered the AREMOS environment, and has an empty work space (see Illustration 9.3).

At this point the user issues an IMPORT command from within the AREMOS environment. The data series stored in the XY.PRN file are copied into the user work space and can be referenced in subsequent AREMOS commands. The data series retain their original names (see Illustration 9.4).

The data in the work space can be saved in a permanent AREMOS databank file. In effect, this is a photograph of the user work space. The

Illustration 9.3
The Work Space is Empty

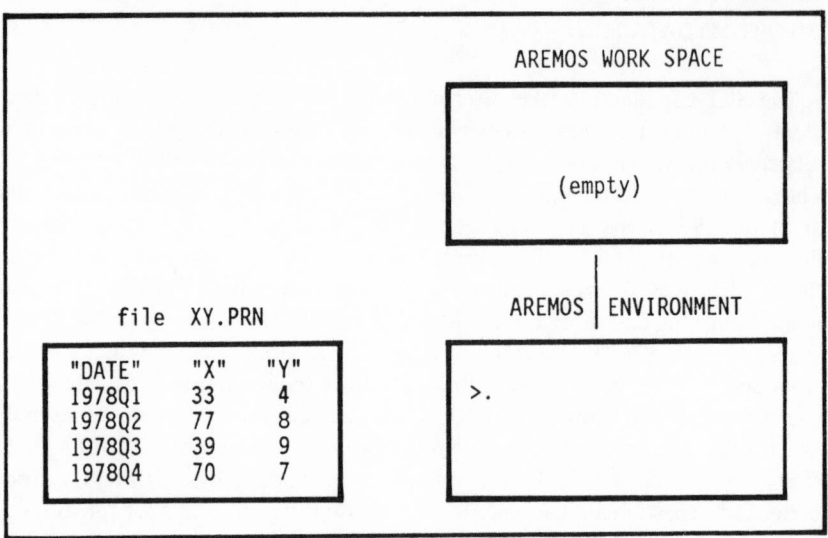

Illustration 9.4
Data Enters the Work Space

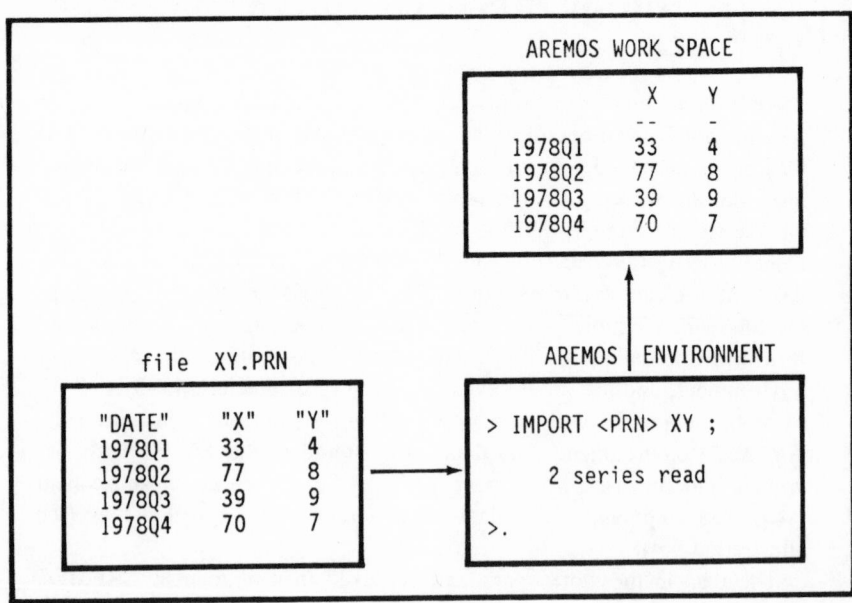

databank file is created by issuing a BACKUP command from within the AREMOS environment. For example, issuing the command:

BACKUP WORK: XY;

creates a databank file called XY.BNK. Data from this file can be retrieved during future AREMOS sessions. This eliminates the need to import data from the XY.PRN file in the future.

An equation is specified to explain sales of bicycle frames. The first attempt at explaining VFBFC bicycle frame sales uses real consumer spending on durables, the price of bicycle frames (relative to the general rise in prices), and the price of gasoline (relative to the general rise in prices) as explanatory variables. The AREMOS input for specifying this equation is:

SET PERIOD 78Q1 85Q2 ;

EQUATION Q1 = (CED$/PDGNP), (PRICEBIKE$/PDGNP), (PRICEGAS$/PDGNP) ;

FIT ;

The first command sets the period of analysis. The historical patterns for the first quarter of 1978 through the second quarter of 1985 will be reviewed. The second command specifies a regression equation with quantity explained by the level of consumer spending on durable goods divided by an index of inflation; the price of bicycle frames divided by an index of inflation; and the price of gasoline divided by an index of inflation. The third command instructs AREMOS to fit the equation (calculate the regression results). These results will appear on the user's screen. Before reviewing these results, the equation specification is examined more closely.

Consumer expenditures on durables serves as an explanatory variable for bicycle frame sales. Why? Bicycles are durable goods, and the general level of spending on durable goods should indicate public interest in durable goods in general. The employed measure of consumer expenditures on durable goods is adjusted for inflation. Why? Because we are interested in both the level of expenditures and the level of expenditures adjusted for the general rise in prices. For example, if expenditures and prices are rising 10 percent a year, a consumer outlay of 10 percent more this year over last year implies a static situation. In effect, no more goods would be bought this year than last year. However, the number of dollars by which purchases are measured would have increased. These inflationary phenomena cloud the picture of consumer willingness to spend on durable goods. Consider, if inflation rises 10 percent this year and consumer spending on durables rises 12 percent, consumers are spending approximately

Illustration 9.5
The First Product Forecasting Equation Specification

```
Q1
QUARTERLY data for 30 periods from 1978Q1 to 1985Q2

q1

   =     17580.1 * (ced$/pdgnp) - 21742.1 * (pricebike$/pdgnp)
        ( 4.5195)                ( 6.5516)

        + 3508300 * (pricegas$/pdgnp) - 21850.2
        ( 6.4972)                       ( 1.5585)


Sum Sq    2.603E8    Std Err    3164.60    LHS Mean  35388.6
R Sq      0.6708     R Bar Sq   0.6328     F  3, 26  17.657
D.W.( 1)  1.1026     D.W.( 4)   2.4281
```

2 percent more on durables this year over last year. It is the movement of 2 percent, not 12 percent, that matters.

Why are the price terms on the right-hand side of the equation (PRICEBIKE\$ and PRICEGAS\$) divided by the inflation index? The price of VFBFC bicycle frames and gasoline are deflated by a measure of the change in prices because what matters to consumers is the cost of an item relative to other goods and services they can purchase. If the price of bicycle frames rises 5 percent this year but the average price rise of other consumer goods and services rises 10 percent, bicycle frames are relatively cheaper this year. This is true even though the nominal price of bicycle frames has risen by 5 percent. In short, it is the relative cost of bicycle frames and gasoline vis-à-vis other available consumer goods and services that is of interest.

The AREMOS output from these commands appears in Illustration 9.5. The middle section of the display lists the fitted regression equation. The variables are listed along with their corresponding numeric coefficients. For example, the coefficient for the (CED\$/PDGNP) variable is 17580.1. The lower section of the display shows the support statistics of the fitted regression equation. These are used to interpret the quality of the equation and indicate whether or not the equation is trustworthy for forecasting purposes.

How are the coefficients of the equation interpreted? The coefficient for the (CED\$/PDGNP) variable indicates that increasing (CED\$/PDGNP) by one unit would increase bicycle frame sales by 17,580.1 units. Similar interpretations apply to the other explanatory variables. Note the signs on the pricing variables. As expected, the sign for the price of bicycles is negative, and the sign for the price of gasoline is positive. The higher the price of bicycle frames, the fewer bicycle frames people buy (everything else equal). The adage, "price goes up, quantity demanded goes down" is appropriate. Why should increases in the price of a gallon of gasoline cause an increase in bicycle frame sales? Bicycles serve as a form of transportation and recreation. Gasoline is an input to alternative means of transportation and recreation. As the price of this input rises, consumers substitute away from transportation and recreation that involve purchasing gasoline. They decide to purchase bicycles instead.

T-statistics appear beneath each coefficient. The regression results indicate that all three explanatory variables have an impact on sales. Each t-statistic is well above 2 (or below -2). A rule of thumb sets 2 as the t-statistic value indicating that a particular independent variable is important in explaining the dependent variable. If a variable sports a t-statistic between -2 and 2, the variable is said to be insignificant. There is not enough statistical evidence to believe that the coefficient is different from zero. Consequently, a variable with a low t-statistic is often dropped from the equation, and the equation is re-fit (recalculated). Only the significant variables are included when the equation is re-fit. It is customary to include a constant term in regression equations, regardless of its t-statistic. The constant is an intercept term and is easy to conceptualize in a two variable world. If:

$$X = 3Y + 5$$

X and Y are variables, 3 is the slope (analogous to coefficients in the fitted regression equation), and 5 is the intercept, the starting point for the line.

The R Sq (R-Square or R^2) statistic is a measure of how well the explanatory variables as a group explain movements in the dependent variable. The maximum value for the R-Square statistic is 1. The closer this measure is to 1, the better the explanatory power of the fitted equation. The .6708 value for this statistic can be interpreted as follows. Approximately 67 percent of the variation in sales is being explained by the variation in the three explanatory variables and the constant term.

The VFBFC emphasizes promotional campaigns to sell bicycle frames. Promotions should positively affect sales. Inserting the number of marketing promotions (PROMO) in the equation might make the equation more desirable. The new equation is specified and fit by issuing the following AREMOS commands:

ADD PROMO ;

FIT;

The new variable PROMO is added to the set of explanatory variables and the equation is re-fit. The results appear in Illustration 9.6.

The results indicate that the number of promotions is an important explanatory variable which positively affects sales. Its t-statistic is well above 2. The positive sign on the variable is as expected. The greater the number of promotions, the more frames the firm sells. The coefficient for the PROMO variable is 2031.88.

Illustration 9.6
The Second Product Forecasting Equation Specification

```
Q1
QUARTERLY data for 30 periods from 1978Q1 to 1985Q2

q1

  =     17704.4 * (ced$/pdgnp) - 23684.8 * (pricebike$/pdgnp)
      ( 8.1845)                   (12.7155)

      + 3780212 * (pricegas$/pdgnp) + 2031.88 * promo - 32495.4
        (12.5028)                     ( 7.6863)           ( 4.1038)


  Sum Sq    7.742E7    Std Err    1759.80    LHS Mean   35388.6
  R Sq      0.9021     R Bar Sq   0.8864     F  4, 25   57.593
  D.W.( 1)  1.8666     D.W.( 4)   1.7060
```

If the number of promotions increases by 1, the firm will sell 2,031.88 more bicycle frames. The overall fit of the equation has improved, the R-Square statistic rising to .9021.

Another criterion for judging an equation is its ability to track the actual series over the historical period. Whenever an equation is fit, AREMOS automatically develops a predicted series and stores the series in the user work space. These predicted results are derived by plugging in the historical data values for the set of explanatory variables and calculating expected sales. In this case, the automatically generated predicted data series is Q1.PREDICT. Actual sales can be compared with those predicted by the equation. A graph of these two series may prove useful in judging the worth of the product forecasting equation. The AREMOS command used to generate the appropriate graph is:

GRAPH Q1, Q1.PREDICT ;

The generated graph appears in Illustration 9.7.

The graph shows that the predicted series (Q1.PREDICT) rarely matches the actual series (Q1) exactly. This finding will be true in general. No regression equation incorporates all the variables that at one time or another impact demand. Consequently, equations rarely predict actual values without error.

Other, more sophisticated analyses are available for judging the forecasting capabilities of regression equations. Post sample forecast statistics are generally regarded as the most rigorous tests available. Regression equations are generated over some shortened historical period and then are used to predict known values for the series. In the example, the selected regression equation is calculated (or fit) over the period first quarter 1978 to second quarter 1985. Once an equation is selected (in this case, the second example forecasting equation), the analyst

Illustration 9.7
Quantity and Predicted Quantity

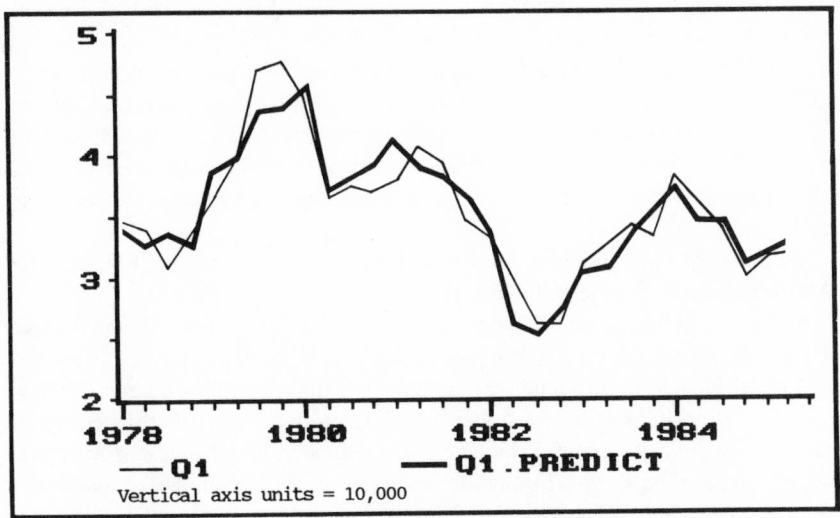

Vertical axis units = 10,000

can perform a post sample test. The period of equation estimation is shortened and runs from the first quarter 1978 to first quarter 1985. The known values of the explanatory variables are plugged into this equation for the second quarter of 1985. Next, predicted sales are calculated for the second quarter, and the predicted results are compared to the actual (known) value for 1985 second quarter sales. (For a further discussion of these methods, see Chapter 11.)

AREMOS has been used to investigate alternative product forecasting equations. The second investigated equation was selected. Its predicted series for sales was graphed against the actual series for sales for the historical period first quarter 1978 to second quarter 1985. The first AREMOS session is complete. Issuing a STOP command will end the AREMOS session and remove the user from the AREMOS environment.

STOP;

THE PLANNING MODEL

The second product forecasting equation drafted earlier is the key driving equation in the AREMOS-based planning model. The financial components of the model will be simple. The firm considers these four cost areas to be important: fixed costs, promotional costs, materials costs, and labor costs. Fixed costs are a data input covering general overhead, executive salaries, and so on. Promotional costs are the number of marketing promotions undertaken in the quarter times the average cost of marketing promotions in that quarter. Materials costs are average materials cost (cost per unit) times the number of units (frames) sold. Labor costs are the number of hours needed to manufacture a bicycle frame times the wage rate times the number of frames sold. Total cost will be the sum of these four cost categories.

The planning model does not incorporate inventory storage costs, lags between production and sales, depreciation, taxes, and a host of other factors. Further, the model includes only one type of laborer and one average wage. Omitting and simplifying factors helps unclutter the analysis. Each of these considerations will lengthen a model but will not affect the employed methods or analysis design.

The code for the AREMOS model, to be presented shortly, will be an AREMOS translation for the following model.

Use historical information from the first quarter of 1978 to the second quarter of 1985 to derive a forecasting equation for bicycle frame sales. Forecast the quantity of bicycle frames sold for the next four quarters (third quarter 1985 to second quarter 1986) using consumer spending on durable goods divided by an index of inflation; the price of bicycle frames divided by an index of inflation; the price of gasoline divided by an index of inflation; and the number of marketing promotions as the explanatory variables. After that, predict total revenue by multiplying expected price by the sales forecast for each future quarter. Calculate labor costs as the wage rate multiplied by the number of labor hours needed to complete a single frame multiplied by the projected number of frames sold. Calculate promotional costs as the number of expected marketing promotions for each future quarter times the expected average cost of marketing promotions for that quarter. Calculate materials costs as the projected materials cost per frame times the projected number of frames sold. Calculate total cost as the sum of labor, promotions, materials, and fixed costs. Calculate profit as total revenue minus total cost.

It's convenient if all the data series needed to run the planning model are in one data file (databank). It's assumed that all the needed data series are available from the first quarter of 1978 on. The data series used to estimate the product-line forecasting equation must be in the databank. The description of the planning model just offered indicates that other data series are needed as well. These include a series for total revenue, profit, and several cost series. The following list shows the names of the data series needed by the model.

Data series needed by the product forecasting equation

Q1	Quantity of Bicycle Frames Sold (sales)
PDGNP	A price deflator
CED$	Consumer Expenditures on Durables
PRICEBIKE$	Price of Bicycle Frames
PRICEGAS$	Price of Gasoline (gallon)

PROMO   Number of Marketing Promotions

Other data series needed

TOTALREV   Total Revenue = PRICEBIKE\$ * Q1

WAGE   Wage rate for bicycle frame builders

HPB   Labor hours needed to build one bicycle frame (hours per bike)

LABORCOST   Labor Costs = (WAGE * HPB) * Q1

APROMOCOST   Average Cost of Marketing Promotions

PROMOCOST   Promotional Costs = PROMO * APROMOCOST

AMATERLCOST   Average Material Costs

MATERLCOST   Materials Costs = AMATERLCOST * Q1

FIXEDCOST   Fixed Costs

TOTALCOST   Total Cost = LABORCOST + PROMOCOST +
                    MATERLCOST + FIXEDCOST

PROFIT   Profit = TOTALREV − TOTALCOST

The data needed in the databank appear in Table 9.2. The data series used in the estimation of the product-line forecasting equation have already been displayed and are not shown again here.

Note that the data series in the upper portion run through the second quarter of 1985. This table holds the financial identity data series. One of the objectives of the planning model will be to extend these data series through the second quarter of 1986. The data in the second table are needed through the second quarter of 1986. These data must be available through the forecast period for the model to run. These points will become clearer as the model is described and applied.

As discussed earlier, the data series needed to run the AREMOS planning model could exist in many different types of files. They could exist in a spreadsheet file like a Lotus 1–2–3 worksheet file. They could be stored in a text file created by a word processor or Lotus 1–2–3. (An earlier example showed how to create a print file using Lotus 1–2–3 and then how to import needed information into AREMOS.) Alternatively, data series can be created in AREMOS and stored in an AREMOS databank. The most common case is having the data series stored as a print file, however generated. Presuming this to be the case, a short AREMOS session will bring all the data series into a single AREMOS databank. The planning model will later call this databank.

The first set of data series presented in this chapter relate to the product-line forecasting equation developed earlier. The next set of data series presented relate to the financial section for the described AREMOS planning model. It is quite possible that these two sets of data series would originally exist in different print files. A short AREMOS session will import the data series from these two files and save the data series in a single AREMOS databank. This single databank

Table 9.2
Planning Model Data

DATE	TOTALREV	LABORCOST	MATERLCOST	PROMOCOST	TOTALCOST	PROFIT
197801	2695574	1445929	1487531	356490	3757880	-1062306
197802	2700236	1450148	1491872	219096	3647236	-947000
197803	2537784	1356503	1395532	297432	3549497	-1011713
197804	2794888	1482485	1525139	227664	3751368	-956480
197901	3381737	1664437	1712326	543354	4464388	-1082651
197902	3983846	1864400	1918043	555492	4900395	-916549
197903	4898813	2230016	2294178	485928	5589702	-690889
197904	5171129	2307154	2373535	495720	5773109	-601980
198001	5361101	2224070	2288061	421770	5553791	-192691
198002	4600791	1857427	1910869	258876	4667392	-66601
198003	4999165	1940148	1995970	352920	4949588	49577
198004	5081427	1973237	2030012	453900	5144449	-63023
198101	5387349	2077119	2136882	372504	5303414	83935
198102	5940364	2257479	2322431	378624	5691494	248871
198103	6166481	2239068	2303491	483990	5781979	384502
198104	5482078	1994235	2051613	591804	5412342	69736
198201	5576256	1948502	2004564	600984	5344790	231466
198202	4949678	1727556	1777262	405552	4713950	235729
198203	4630541	1575452	1620781	308448	4323241	307301
198204	4669568	1607271	1653515	414936	4503912	165656
198301	5421565	1909436	1964375	731850	5442411	-20846
198302	5681310	1993502	2050859	526830	5416502	264808
198303	6091211	2133645	2195035	531420	5715040	376171
198304	6006139	2106046	2166642	645048	5785516	220623
198401	6940124	2433357	2503370	761124	6578472	361653
198402	6625164	2319809	2386555	547740	6143284	481880
198403	6347871	2195716	2258892	662796	6016214	331657
198404	5705484	1975561	2032403	445536	5361940	343544
198501	6061706	2101297	2161755	562020	5744212	317494
198502	6144576	2126162	2187336	453288	5695556	449020

DATE	AMATERLCOST	APROMOCOST	FIXEDCOST	HPB	WAGE
197801	42.99	71298	467930	7	5.97
197802	44.03	73032	486120	7	6.11
197803	44.83	74358	500030	7	6.23
197804	45.76	75888	516080	7	6.35
197901	46.80	77622	544270	7	6.50
197902	47.85	79356	562460	7	6.64
197903	48.83	80988	579580	7	6.78
197904	49.81	82620	596700	7	6.92
198001	50.86	84354	619890	7	7.06
198002	52.03	86292	640220	7	7.22
198003	53.20	88230	660550	7	7.39
198004	54.74	90780	687300	7	7.60
198101	56.15	93126	716910	7	7.80
198102	57.07	94656	732960	7	7.93
198103	58.36	96798	755430	7	8.10
198104	59.47	98634	774690	7	8.26
198201	60.39	100164	790740	7	8.39
198202	61.13	101388	803580	7	8.49
198203	61.99	102816	818560	7	8.61
198204	62.55	103734	828190	7	8.69
198301	63.04	104550	836750	7	8.75
198302	63.53	105366	845310	7	8.82
198303	64.08	106284	854940	7	8.90
198304	64.82	107508	867780	7	9.00
198401	65.56	108732	880620	7	9.10
198402	66.05	109548	889180	7	9.17
198403	66.60	110466	898810	7	9.25
198404	67.16	111384	908440	7	9.33
198501	67.77	112404	919140	7	9.41
198502	68.33	113322	928770	7	9.49
198503	68.76	114671	994556	7	9.54
198504	69.07	115600	1008088	7	9.63
198601	69.55	120941	1028992	7	9.74
198602	70.08	122042	1052143	7	9.84

will then contain all the data series needed by the AREMOS planning model. Data from this databank file can be called whenever there is a need for any of the data series stored in it.

The data series needed for the product-line forecasting equation were originally stored in a Lotus 1–2–3 worksheet. The method for creating a print file containing these data series was described earlier. The generated print file was MY-DATA.PRN. Presuming that the second set of data series are stored in print file FINANCE.PRN, the following commands can be used to generate the needed AREMOS databank:

```
CD \AREMOS

AREMOS

SET FREQUENCY QUARTERLY ;

SET PERIOD 78Q1 86Q2 ;

SET FILE IMPORT PRN ;

IMPORT MYDATA.PRN ;

IMPORT FINANCE.PRN ;

BACKUP WORK: BIKEDATA ;

STOP ;
```

The first two commands are executed while the user is in the operating system (some version of the Disk Operating System). The first command changes the current directory to the AREMOS directory. The second command is used to enter the AREMOS environment. The rest of the commands are AREMOS commands. The three SET commands establish user options. The first SET command indicates that the user will be using quarterly data. The second SET command establishes the active time period, from the first quarter of 1978 to the second quarter of 1986. The third SET command indicates that any files to be read into AREMOS will be print (.prn) files. The IMPORT commands sequentially reads the two needed print files into the AREMOS environment. The first IMPORT command reads in the file called MYDATA.PRN—the file containing the data series needed by the product-line forecasting equation. The second IMPORT command reads a file called FINANCE.PRN—the file containing the data series needed by the financial section of the planning model. All the data series read into the AREMOS environment now reside in the user work space. (Remember that this work space is automatically provided by AR-EMOS and stores new data series, equation specifications, and other information.) The BACKUP command instructs AREMOS to save all the information contained in the user work space in a file (databank) by a different name. In this case, the information in the user work space is stored in a databank file called BIKEDATA.BNK. The BNK file extension is automatically appended to the file

name BIKEDATA and stands for databank. Now BIKEDATA.BNK exists as
an AREMOS databank and contains all the data series needed by the AREMOS
planning model.

The code for the AREMOS planning model is presented next. Program section
numbers appear at the left of each logical program section but are not part of
the actual AREMOS code.

Code for the VFBFC AREMOS Planning Model[1]

(BASELINE MODEL SECTIONS)

1 OPEN BIKEDATA ;

2 SET PERIOD 78Q1   85Q2 ;

3 EQUATION Q1 = (CED$/PDGNP), (PRICEBIKE$/PDGNP),
   (PRICEGAS$/ PDGNP), PROMO ;
   FIT ;

4 SET EQUATION CONSTANT NO ;
   EQUATION TOTALREV = PRICEBIKE$ * Q1 ;
   EQUATION LABORCOST = (HPB * Q1) * WAGE ;
   EQUATION PROMOCOST = PROMO * APROMOCOST ;
   EQUATION MATERLCOST = (Q1 * AMATERLCOST) ;
   EQUATION TOTALCOST = MATERLCOST + LABORCOST + PROMOCOST
   + FIXEDCOST ;
   EQUATION PROFIT = TOTALREV − TOTALCOST ;

5 MODEL BIKE1 = Q1, TOTALREV, LABORCOST, PROMOCOST,
   MATERL COST, TOTALCOST, PROFIT ;

6 SET PER 85Q3 86Q2 ;
   SET SOLVE SOLUTION BASELINE ;
   SOLVE ;

(NOTE: This code could be generated with any word processing package, the EDLIN
    editor (that comes standard with DOS), or the AREMOS editor.)

Section 1 of the program makes the data stored in the BIKEDATA databank
available for analysis. Section 2 designates the period of analysis, which runs
from the first quarter of 1978 to the second quarter of 1985. In section 3 the
product forecasting equation statements are applied. The statements are identical
to the statements entered during the interactive session of AREMOS when can-
didate product forecasting equations were investigated. The equation explains

sales by the level of consumer spending on durable goods, the number of marketing promotions, and so on. Section 4 specifies the model's financial identities. Identities define total revenue, labor cost, promotional cost, materials cost, total cost, and profit. Note how it is indicated that these equations are identities. AREMOS is instructed not to include a regression constant in identity equations (SET EQUATION CONSTANT NO), and AREMOS is not directed to FIT the equations in section 4. Identities differ from fitted equations. They are algebraic definitions, and there is no desire to regress one variable on another. In the following identity,

REVENUE = (PRICE * QUANTITY)

the objective is NOT to obtain a fit of revenue as a function of price and quantity. A simple fact is being stated—revenue equals price times quantity. Now REVENUE is an algebraic shorthand for the mathematical expression (PRICE * QUANTITY).

Section 5 is used to indicate which equations are included in the simultaneous equation model. Note that in this example all the specified equations are included in the simultaneous equation model, one fitted equation and six identities. In general this is not true. The model builder may attempt several different sets of equations and examine alternative simultaneous equation model results. The possibility exists that an analyst will examine several models during a single AREMOS session and won't need all the specified equations in any particular simultaneous equation model. Consequently, it is necessary to declare desired equations when a model is specified. Note that the name given to the simultaneous equation model is BIKE1. AREMOS saves this name and specification in the user work space, and the BIKE1 simultaneous equation model can be referred to as BIKE1 in the future.

The first statement in section 6 sets the forecast (or solution) period. The forecast horizon spans the third quarter of 1985 to the second quarter of 1986. The second statement in section 6 names generated variables. This statement informs AREMOS that when it SOLVES the simultaneous equation model, that the SOLUTION values for the forecast period should have the extension BASELINE. (Solution name is just one of many solve options in AREMOS. The user can adjust other options including those that affect the employed simultaneous solution algorithm.)

Program sections 1 through 6 make up the baseline division of the planning model. The review of these sections is complete, and they can be used to generate the business-as-usual forecast for the VFBFC. When the SOLVE command is issued at the end of program section 6, AREMOS solves the system of simultaneous equations and provides forecast estimates for quantity (sales), total revenue, labor cost, materials cost, promotional cost, total cost, and profit for each of the four quarters in the forecast period. The SET SOLVE SOLUTION BASELINE command was used to name these predicted series, and each series has its own name with the extension BASELINE. For example, forecasted quantities are called Q1.BASELINE; forecasted total revenues are called TOTAL-REV.BASELINE; forecasted materials costs are called MATERL-COST.BASELINE. If some other label (other than BASELINE) were used in the SET SOLVE SOLUTION statement, these series would take on that other extension. These series exist only in the forecast period. AREMOS stores these data series in the user work space just as it stored certain predicted series when the product forecasting equation was estimated earlier.

After the baseline model sections (sections 1–6) are processed, the baseline data series can be printed or graphed. The baseline data series represent the firm's best guess concerning future conditions. The model that generated these series used as input the firm's most trustworthy forecasting equation and best estimates of future bicycle frame prices, gasoline prices, worker wage rates, average materials costs, and a host of other similar information. Indeed, it may be the sole point of many studies to produce these baseline estimates. In this example, a scenario (what-if) study is also investigated. Both the baseline and scenario results are reported after the scenario study is specified and run.

The scenario study will examine the profitability effects of rising materials prices. What if the firm's best guess about future average materials prices proves to be incorrect, with these costs rising 2 percent above baseline values? The code needed to investigate the profitability risks associated with such a scenario appear next.

(SCENARIO MODEL SECTIONS)

7 SET SOLVE SOLUTION SCENARIO ;
   COPY BIKEDATA: AMATERLCOST ;
   SERIES AMATERLCOST = AMATERLCOST * 1.02 ;
   SOLVE ;

8 PRINT "SALES" Q1.SCENARIO "SCENARIO", Q1.BASELINE "BASELINE",
   (Q1.SCENARIO − Q1.BASELINE) "DELTA" ;

   PRINT "REVENUE" TOTALREV.SCENARIO "SCENARIO",
   TOTALREV.BASELINE "BASELINE",
   (TOTALREV.SCENARIO − TOTALREV.BASELINE) "DELTA" ;

   PRINT "TOTAL COST" TOTALCOST.SCENARIO "SCENARIO",
   TOTALCOST.BASELINE "BASELINE",
   (TOTALCOST.SCENARIO − TOTALCOST.BASELINE) "DELTA" ;

   PRINT "PROFIT" PROFIT.SCENARIO "SCENARIO,"
   PROFIT.BASELINE "BASELINE",
   (PROFIT.SCENARIO − PROFIT.BASELINE) "DELTA" ;

Another SET SOLVE SOLUTION statement appears as the first command of section 7. The SOLVE command tells AREMOS to use the extension SCENARIO for the new series it will generate when the simultaneous equation model is re-solved. These series will be stored in the user work space and can be compared with the BASELINE series created and stored earlier. For example, TOTALCOST.SCENARIO can be compared with TOTALCOST.BASELINE.

Note how AREMOS utilizes the user work space in the next line of code. The second command in section 7 copies the variable AMATERLCOST (average materials cost) from the original databank (BIKEDATA) to the work space. The third command of section 7 instructs AREMOS to increase the value of the variable AMATERLCOST by 2 percent over baseline levels for all quarters in the forecast period. Which version of the AMATERLCOST data series will be increased by 2 percent: the version in the BIKEDATA databank file or the version stored in the user work space? The rule here is that AREMOS always searches the user work space first for data series. If the data series does not reside there, AREMOS will search databank files for the data series. Here the BIKEDATA databank file is searched for data series not found in the work space. This rule implies that the AMATERLCOST data series version stored in the user work area is the one affected by the 2 percent increase. The AMATERLCOST series stored in the BIKEDATA databank is ignored.

Note the safety of this operation. The value of the AMATERLCOST data series stored in the user work space can be increased without changing the value of the AMATERLCOST data series stored in the permanent databank. This insures the integrity of the original data file. Data changes made in the user work space don't affect data stored in databank files, even if certain data series have the same name in both places.

The fourth command in section 7 instructs AREMOS to re-solve the simultaneous equation model. What will happen? AREMOS begins looking for the data series needed to solve the simultaneous equation system and forecast series through the second quarter of 1986. The first place AREMOS looks for data is the user work space. One of the variables needed to re-solve the model and forecast results is AMATERLCOST. The data series exists in two places: the work space and the BIKEDATA databank. Which version will be used to solve the model? The previous rule applies again. Since AREMOS searches the work space first and finds a version of the AMATERLCOST data series there, it will use this version of the AMATERLCOST data series. AREMOS will ignore the AMATERLCOST data series stored in the BIKEDATA databank.

The operations just explained are all that is needed to input the scenario assumptions in the planning model. After copying the AMATERLCOST variable from the BIKEDATA databank to the work space, the value of the AMATERLCOST variable in the work space is increased. This task was not performed in the baseline solution of the model. In the baseline solution, AREMOS used the value of the AMATERLCOST variable originally found in the BIKEDATA databank. Consequently, the two simultaneous equation model solutions will differ only in their treatment of average materials cost. The second solution (the SCENARIO solution) will have 2 percent higher average materials cost than did the first solution (the BASELINE solution).

Section 8 of the model is dedicated to displaying the results of the two model solutions. AREMOS uses the following convention. Any information found in single or double quotes is a user-defined label for displaying data. Let's examine the first command of section 8.

PRINT "SALES" Q1.SCENARIO "SCENARIO", Q1.BASELINE "BASELINE",
    (Q1.SCENARIO − Q1.BASELINE) "DELTA" ;

The command word PRINT appears first. SALES is an optional title for the overall report. Q1.SCENARIO is a data series generated during the second (the SCENARIO) solution of the model. An optional title for this data series, called SCENARIO, is specified. Without the inclusion of the SCENARIO label, the Q1.SCENARIO data series would be entitled Q1.SCENARIO, not SCENARIO. The Q1.BASELINE data series is generated from the first (the BASELINE) solution of the model and given an appropriate title—BASELINE. Last, a display of the Q1.SCENARIO data series minus the Q1.BASELINE data series is requested. The display of this data series has the appropriate name of DELTA. Again, without the optional title, AREMOS would generate a data series display that would be labeled (Q1.SCENARIO − Q1.BASELINE). The explanation generalizes to displaying information for TOTAL COSTS, REVENUES, and PROFITS.

The philosophy advanced here is a good one. Reports can be enhanced by use of report headings and alternative data series display names. However, work can also be completed in a hurry by using default display labels. This is most convenient if the analyst is not fussy about the looks of displayed data. It is also reassuring and encouraging for new users to have easy means of obtaining output while learning a new systems tool. Worthwhile output can be obtained by replacing the first print command by the following one:

PRINT Q1.SCENARIO, Q1.BASELINE, (Q1.SCENARIO − Q1.BASELINE) ;

Now that the model's code has been reviewed, how would AREMOS be instructed to process it? The OBEY statement processes AREMOS code. Assuming that the code is contained in file VFBFC.CMD (Very Fast Bicycle Frame Company, Command File), the following AREMOS command is entered.

OBEY VFBFC.CMD ;

This command processes the VFBFC.CMD file all at once, without pausing for user input. If desired, each command could be entered individually in an interactive framework. Reports generated using the displayed set of code appear in Illustration 9.8.

The comparative results from the two model solutions show changes in costs and profits, but no changes in quantity or revenue. Why? The only data series that varied between the BASELINE and SCENARIO model solutions was average materials costs, the AMATERLCOST variable. This variable does not appear in the product (sales) forecasting equation. Because the variables affecting the sales of bicycle frames didn't change, sales didn't change and revenue didn't change. Only the cost side of the model is affected in the SCENARIO solution. In each of the quarters of the forecast period, profit fell by exactly the amount that costs increased.

The code needed to examine a different scenario will now be examined. This code will be supplemental to the model code displayed before. What if consumer spending on durables (variable CED$) were to rise by 2 percent over baseline levels for all forecast quarters of analysis? This variable does appear in the product forecasting equation. Consequently, sales, revenue, costs, and profit will change in this new scenario. In the last run of the model, the AMATERLCOST variable was copied from the BIKEDATA databank file into the user work space. If this variable is not deleted from the work space before the new scenario is run, then these increased average materials costs will persist in new scenario studies. Assume that, in the following study, the goal is to examine the impacts of increased spending on durables independently of increased average materials costs. That is, average materials costs are not to vary from their baseline level. The AMATERLCOST variable must be deleted from the user work space before specifying the new scenario. This is done with the delete command:

DELETE AMATERLCOST ;

The AMATERLCOST series is deleted from the work space, but none of the other variables in the work space is affected. The code needed to examine the new scenario is as follows:

```
A  SET SOLVE SOLUTION SCENARIO2 ;
   COPY BIKEDATA: CED$ ;
   SERIES CED$ = CED$ * 1.02 ;
   SOLVE ;

B  PRINT 'SALES' Q1.SCENARIO2 "SCENARIO2", Q1.BASELINE "BASELINE",
   (Q1.SCENARIO2 - Q1.BASELINE) "DELTA" ;

   PRINT "REVENUE" TOTALREV.SCENARIO2 "SCENARIO2",
   TOTALREV.BASELINE "BASELINE",
   (TOTALREV.SCENARIO2 - TOTALREV.BASELINE) "DELTA" ;
```

Illustration 9.8
Reports—After Increasing Average Material Costs

SALES

	SCENARIO	BASELINE	DELTA
1985			
Q3	37448	37448	00
Q4	33955	33955	00
1986			
Q1	35172	35172	00
Q2	35987	35987	00

REVENUE

	SCENARIO	BASELINE	DELTA
1985			
Q3	7174634	7174634	00
Q4	6534676	6534676	00
1986			
Q1	6815890	6815890	00
Q2	7027244	7027244	00

TOTAL COST

	SCENARIO	BASELINE	DELTA
1985			
Q3	6695091	6643593	51498
Q4	6267198	6220292	46906
1986			
Q1	6647736	6598812	48924
Q2	6835633	6785193	50440

PROFIT

	SCENARIO	BASELINE	DELTA
1985			
Q3	479543	531041	-51498
Q4	267478	314384	-46906
1986			
Q1	168154	217078	-48924
Q2	191611	242051	-50440

```
PRINT "TOTAL COST" TOTALCOST.SCENARIO2 "SCENARIO2",
  TOTALCOST.BASELINE "BASELINE",
  (TOTALCOST.SCENARIO2 − TOTALCOST.BASELINE) "DELTA" ;

PRINT "PROFIT" PROFIT.SCENARIO2 "SCENARIO2",
  PROFIT.BASELINE "BASELINE",
  (PROFIT.SCENARIO2 − PROFIT.BASELINE) "DELTA" ;
```

The code for this extension to the original planning model is divided into program sections A and B. Section A is virtually identical to section 7 of the original model. The SET SOLVE SOLUTION statement instructs AREMOS to use the extension "SCENARIO2" for new series generated and stored in the work space when the model is resolved. The next command in section A copies a version of the CED$ data series from the original databank file (BIKE-DATA.BNK) to the user work space. If AREMOS performs any subsequent actions that involve the CED$ data series, it will search the work space, find a version of the data series there, use that series, and ignore the version of the CED$ data series stored in the BIKEDATA.BNK databank file. The third command in section A increases the value of the CED$ data series stored in the user work space. This new scenario will incorporate consumer spending on durables that is 2 percent greater than the baseline level for all quarters in the forecast period. The fourth and final command in section A will re-solve the model. New data series will be generated and stored in the user work space. These new series will bear the extension SCENARIO2. Among the newly generated series stored in the user work space will be Q1.SCENARIO2, REVENUE.SCENARIO2, TOTALCOST.SCENARIO2, and PROFIT.SCENARIO2.

Section B is dedicated to producing a display of the new scenario study results. The baseline values generated earlier are also displayed, giving a reference case to judge the results of the new study.

Assuming that the commands for the extended portion of the planning model are contained in a command file called VFBFC2.CMD, the following OBEY command would execute these commands.

```
OBEY VFBFC2.CMD ;
```

How do these new solution results compare with the baseline case? The results appear in Illustration 9.9.

Since the level of consumer spending on durables (variable CED$) is changed, sales of bicycle frames will also change. In this case sales will rise. Consumers are spending more on durables, including bicycles and bicycle frames, than expected in the baseline case. Higher sales will result in higher revenues (assuming no change in prices), as reflected in the revenue report. SCENARIO2 revenues are higher than BASELINE revenues. Because sales are increasing,

Illustration 9.9
Reports—After Increasing Consumer Spending on Durables

	SALES		
	SCENARIO2	BASELINE	DELTA
1985			
Q3	38630	37448	1182
Q4	35092	33955	1136
1986			
Q1	36297	35172	1126
Q2	37149	35987	1161

	REVENUE		
	SCENARIO2	BASELINE	DELTA
1985			
Q3	7401174	7174634	226541
Q4	6753377	6534676	218702
1986			
Q1	7034024	6815890	218135
Q2	7254008	7027244	226764

	TOTAL COST		
	SCENARIO2	BASELINE	DELTA
1985			
Q3	6856983	6643593	213390
Q4	6423864	6220292	203572
1986			
Q1	6804334	6598812	205522
Q2	6998632	6785193	213439

	PROFIT		
	SCENARIO2	BASELINE	DELTA
1985			
Q3	544191	531041	13151
Q4	329513	314384	15130
1986			
Q1	229691	217078	12613
Q2	255376	242051	13325

Illustration 9.10
Profits

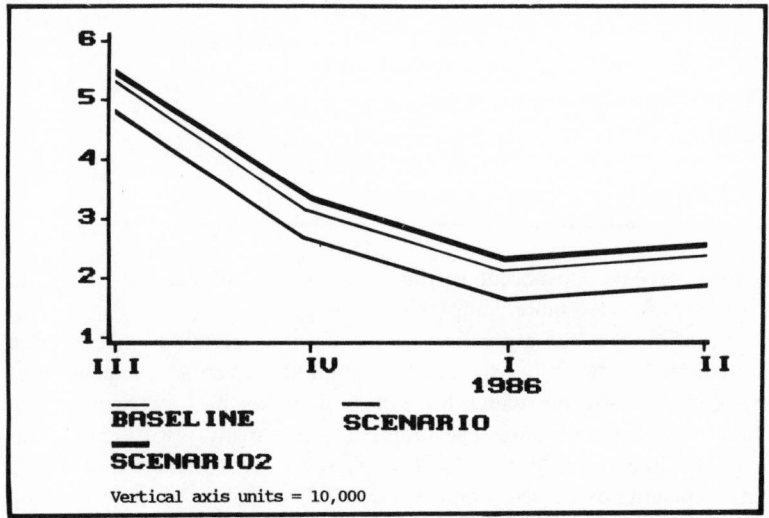

Vertical axis units = 10,000

production must also increase. (Remember that this simple model does not include an inventories equation. All new sales are met by new production.) Rising production implies that more labor must be employed and more frame components must be purchased to manufacture bicycle frames. Total costs will rise. The TOTALCOST.SCENARIO2 data series is greater than the TOTALCOST.BASELINE data series in all the forecast periods. Finally, all this ac tivity changes profit levels. In this study, revenues are increasing faster than costs, and profits rise. PROFIT.SCENARIO2 will be greater than PROFIT.BASELINE.

The data series from the BASELINE, SCENARIO, and SCENARIO2 solutions of the planning model are available for graphing and printing. How does profitability compare in the three studies? A graph of profitability (shown in Illustration 9.10) is generated using the following statement:

GRAPH PROFIT.BASELINE "BASELINE", PROFIT.SCENARIO "SCENARIO",

  PROFIT.SCENARIO2 "SCENARIO2" ;

MODEL REVIEW

Consider the model that was developed to analyze the baseline case and two scenario studies. There were several simplifying assumptions—for example, the VFBFC markets only one product, and some costs normally associated with a

Illustration 9.11
Recursive and Simultaneous Equation Systems

RECURSIVE	SIMULTANEOUS
$Y1 = 2 X$	$Y1 = Y2 - 4 X$
$Y2 = Y1 + X$	$Y2 = 4 Y1 + X - 51$
$Y3 = 4 Y2 + Y1 + X$	

manufacturing process are absent in the analysis. The reader can expect to perform analyses that are more complex than these.

While not apparent in the regression work presented, certain problems often occur that can at first be disheartening. For example, advertising expenditures are often negatively correlated with sales. This is not to say that higher advertising expenditures caused lower sales. The problem is that many firms increase advertising expenditures during periods of weak sales. To conclude that higher advertising expenditures caused a demand shortfall would be similar to saying that the number of doctors always increases when illness is rife, therefore doctors cause illness! By similar arguments, price is often positively correlated with demand. Firms increase prices when demand is rising. However, to conclude that rising demand is encouraged by rising prices is a difficult hypothesis. In such situations, quantity demanded would probably be even higher had prices remained constant. Sometimes one invokes a price expectations model, where the change in current prices is an indicator to future price increases. The "get in before the price increase" argument is applied.

The upshot of all of this is to be careful in your interpretations and to do your best to obtain sensible coefficients. Try numerous sensible specifications, and do not quit too early if the signs of coefficients seem counter to expectations. Be on guard against individuals that attempt to explain strange coefficient relationships. By trying hard enough, any set of numbers can be logically explained. Let good judgment and common sense be your guide.

It was mentioned earlier that the planning model is recursive in structure and not simultaneous. The product forecasting equation is the driving force in the model. Once sales have been forecast, the rest of the model's equations are determined. A recursive system is defined as a system of equations where all equations can be solved with previously available information. Simultaneous equation systems offer no ordering that precludes at least two equations in the equation set being determined together. Consider the hypothetical cases in Illustration 9.11.

The planning model is similar to the recursive equation system shown in Illustration 9.11, where unique values for Y1, Y2, and Y3 can be obtained once a value for X is given. Here, X is equivalent to the Q1 (quantity or sales) variable in the planning model. The Y equations are similar to all the planning model's financial identities. Once Q1 was forecast in the planning model, unique values for all the financial identities could be obtained. Since the price of bicycle frames was given for the forecast quarters, predicted revenue was obtained by multiplying price by predicted quantity. Similarly, labor costs were calculated as the wage rate multiplied by the number of hours needed to complete a bicycle frame multiplied by the number of completed bicycle frames (that is, quantity). Wages were given for all forecast periods. The number of labor hours needed to complete a bicycle frame was also given information. The only unknown was quantity. Once quantity was forecast, the calculation of predicted labor costs became trivial.

The methodology continues from here. In a simultaneous model system, there is no such convenient ordering of equations. Consider the simultaneous model in Illustration 9.11. If X is set equal to 10, can the values of Y1 and Y2 be determined without solving the equation system by some method (probably simple equation substitution)? No! Some solution method must be invoked to obtain algebraic expressions that make use of the knowledge that X equals 10. Once a value for one of the variables (usually X) is given, the simultaneous example becomes a case of two equations with two unknowns. Given a value for X, simple equation substitution will provide values for Y1 and Y2. Most applied problems are not quite so convenient and will have more equations than unknowns. More complex mathematical methods must be used to solve the system of equations.

Simultaneity can occur in either the economic or financial sections of a model. Both cases are illustrated in the following examples. The bicycle market is highly competitive, and many firms participate in the industry. No one firm has enough market share to significantly influence prevailing prices, and firms are price takers. This simplifies the problem considerably. The implications of such a market structure are that output can be described as a function of price. No one firm's output appreciably affects market prices. Model modifications would be needed if the VFBFC's output were large enough to affect market prices or if the firm had a monopoly on the market and could set price. An equation would be added to the model to describe quantity effects on price. Consider, in the example, quantity is a function of price and other variables. These relationships are described in the product forecasting equation. Quantity is explained by a number of variables, including the price of bicycle frames (PRICEBIKE$). However, if the firm's sales have an effect on the price it receives for bicycle frames—the prevailing market price—then an equation describing price as a function of quantity is also needed! In effect:

Q1 = function (PRICEBIKE$, and possibly other variables)

And simultaneously

PRICEBIKE$ = function (Q1, and possibly other variables)

The previously recursive model becomes simultaneous. The AREMOS code needed to incorporate the example is straightforward. Assume that a PRICE-BIKE$ (price) regression equation were included along with the Q1 (quantity or sales) regression equation in the model. A PRICEBIKE$ variable declaration would be added in the model definition statement. Section 5 of the planning model made use of the model declaration statement:

MODEL BIKE1 = Q1, TOTALREV, LABORCOST, PROMOCOST, MATERLCOST, TOTALCOST, PROFIT ;

After including the PRICEBIKE$ equation declaration, the new statement would appear as follows:

MODEL BIKE1 = Q1, TOTALREV, LABORCOST, PROMOCOST, MATERLCOST, TOTALCOST, PROFIT, PRICEBIKE$;

The new equation would be added to the equation system. The method of solving systems of equations presented here is used for either recursive or simultaneous systems. The example contained a recursive model, and more efficient means could have been presented to solve this model. However, presentation of the general method should give the reader insight into handling more complex models.

There is another important example requiring a simultaneous equation model. The case specifies sales as a function of advertising expenditures, advertising expenditures as a function of profits, and profits as a function of sales. The reader should see why this case requires a simultaneous model. The problem shows three equations in three unknowns. No convenient ordering of the equations precludes the need for a simultaneous solution algorithm to solve the system.

The largest simultaneous models that a planner might use are probably macroeconomic or regional models. These models involve hundreds of simultaneous equations. AREMOS can solve such systems on a microcomputer, and do so in a matter of ten or fifteen seconds per forecast period.

Many complex financial models use simultaneous equation systems. The classic problem for financial analysis is calculating final profits when company officers' salaries are tied to profitability. For example:

REVENUE = PRICE * QUANTITY

TOTAL COST = OFFICERS' PROFIT BONUS + ALL OTHER COSTS

OFFICERS' PROFIT BONUS = function (PROFIT)

PROFIT = REVENUE − TOTAL COST

In this example, profits are tied to costs, and costs are tied to profits. The system must be solved by simultaneous equation methods. The planner would supply data for all other costs, price, quantity, and an equation for calculating officer bonuses as some function of profits. As with the planning model presented earlier, the model's equations would be declared in a model statement. The model would then be solved and its results reported. The model could be solved for one period or an indefinite number of periods.

SUMMARY

The previous chapter centered on functional tools. This chapter was dedicated to planning models. The differences between planning models and functional tools have been discussed. Functional tools are employed by staff or business departments for narrow and specific tasks. Planning models are used for comprehensive planning analysis. Most planning models evaluate interactions among diverse parts of a business. They analyze how changes in any area—prices, costs, regulation, and so on—affect the firm in general.

Common themes appear in discussions of planning models and functional tools, including the SCENARIO, BASELINE, and DELTA reporting format. This reporting format is conducive to comparing the results of any scenario vis-à-vis the baseline case. The baseline case offers a common ground by which to judge different scenarios.

The next chapter will discuss combining diverse planning models and functional tools to form modular planning systems and should prove interesting for those who wish to form multi-application planning systems.

NOTE

1. For expositional purposes, this model includes a FIT command for the included product-line forecasting equation. This is not a general practice. It is wiser to estimate product-line forecasting equations outside of the planning model and include the equation in the model without reestimation. The equation is estimated in the previous step (drafting the product-line forecasting equation) and can be saved in a databank just as data series can be saved. The equation can be retrieved and used from the databank when the planning model is run.

APPENDIX: Planning Models and User Interfaces

The discussion of spreadsheet-based functional tools in Chapter 8 stressed the desirability of a modular, data-driven design. There are many advantages to such a design: ease of learning, reduced model maintenance needs, and a reduction in errors caused by incorrectly altered code or embedded data. Because these issues were not addressed in building the AREMOS-based planning model, some notes are included here.

For small planning models, such as the one developed in this chapter, defining program modules is difficult. Modules are best described by function, and track data and logic flows in a run of a model. All the basic parts of the example model—the product-line forecasting equation, the financial identities, and the model solutions—essentially used the same set of data. Larger planning models are notorious for calling endless subroutines and data files. In such situations the analyst should make every effort to incorporate a modular design and include integrity checks on inputted and outputted data.

In addition to this lack of modularity, the model was not completely data driven. In fact, the user might be required to edit the command file (the file holding the program code) to change the input databank file name, forecast period, and scenario assumptions. The model is data driven only to the extent that any data set containing the needed variables (data series) could use the program code. Therefore, data input and model updates would be structured and straightforward. However, the need to edit model code for new runs of a model is an important pitfall that should be avoided. Frequently modified code develops consistency difficulties. As more people use a particular model, the probability of difficulties increases. By providing an appropriate user interface, the model builder can reduce or eliminate the user's need to edit program files. The larger the application, the more care the application developer must take in designing the user interface.

The comments made here are general. The AREMOS-based planning model developed in this chapter is used in examples, but the comments are not specific to AREMOS. No AREMOS programming notes are included.

Any of the following three methods, reduce or eliminate the need for users to independently edit an application's command file. The three methods are Argument Passing, Query, and Input Template. In the Argument Passing Method, the user includes a few extra key words in the call to the command file. These key words are passed to their proper places in the code and denote data input files or other information. In the Query method, the user must answer a series of questions before the model is run. For example, the user is asked the name of the data or print file holding the baseline data set, the forecast period, and so on. In the Template method the user completes a screen requesting the same kind of information.

A review of the program code might be useful. The program extension housing sections A and B of the original command file are not included:

Code for the VFBFC AREMOS Planning Model

1 OPEN BIKEDATA ;

2 SET PERIOD 78Q1 85Q2 ;

3 EQUATION Q1 = (CED$/PDGNP), (PRICEBIKE$/PDGNP),
   (PRICEGAS$/PDGNP), PROMO ;
   FIT ;

4 SET EQUATION CONSTANT NO ;

  EQUATION TOTALREV = PRICEBIKE$ * Q1 ;

  EQUATION LABORCOST = (HPB * Q1) * WAGE ;

  EQUATION PROMOCOST = PROMO * APROMOCOST ;

  EQUATION MATERLCOST = (Q1 * AMATERLCOST) ;

  EQUATION TOTALCOST = MATERLCOST + LABORCOST +
    PROMOCOST + FIXEDCOST ;

  EQUATION PROFIT = TOTALREV − TOTALCOST ;

5 MODEL BIKE1 = Q1, TOTALREV, LABORCOST, PROMOCOST,
  MATERLCOST, TOTALCOST, PROFIT ;

6 SET PER 85Q3 86Q2 ;

  SET SOLVE SOLUTION BASELINE ;

  SOLVE ;

7 SET SOLVE SOLUTION SCENARIO ;

  COPY BIKEDATA:AMATERLCOST ;

  SERIES AMATERLCOST = AMATERLCOST * 1.02 ;

  SOLVE ;

8 PRINT "SALES" Q1.SCENARIO "SCENARIO",
  Q1.BASELINE "BASELINE",
  (Q1.SCENARIO − Q1.BASELINE) "DELTA" ;

  PRINT "REVENUE" TOTALREV.SCENARIO "SCENARIO",
  TOTALREV.BASELINE "BASELINE",
  (TOTALREV.SCENARIO − TOTALREV.BASELINE) "DELTA" ;

  PRINT "TOTAL COST" TOTALCOST.SCENARIO "SCENARIO",
  TOTALCOST.BASELINE "BASELINE",
  (TOTALCOST.SCENARIO − TOTALCOST.BASELINE) "DELTA" ;

  PRINT "PROFIT" PROFIT.SCENARIO "SCENARIO",
  PROFIT.BASELINE "BASELINE",
  (PROFIT.SCENARIO − PROFIT.BASELINE) "DELTA" ;

The items that may change on successive model runs include the input databank file, the historical analysis period, the forecast (solution) period, scenario data labels, and scenario data assumptions. The Argument Passing, Query, and Template methods can be used to change model information.

ARGUMENT PASSING METHOD

Passing arguments to a program is a fundamental concept in computing. Envision the set of code as follows:

1 OPEN Argument-1 ;

2 SET PERIOD 78Q1 Argument-2 ;

3 EQUATION Q1 = (CED$/PDGNP), (PRICEBIKE$/PDGNP),
  (PRICEGAS$/PDGNP), PROMO ;
  FIT ;

4 SET EQUATION CONSTANT NO ;
  EQUATION TOTALREV = PRICEBIKE$ * Q1 ;
  EQUATION LABORCOST = (HPB * Q1) * WAGE ;
  EQUATION PROMOCOST = PROMO * APROMOCOST ;
  EQUATION MATERLCOST = (Q1 * AMATERLCOST) ;
  EQUATION TOTALCOST = MATERLCOST + LABORCOST +
  PROMOCOST + FIXEDCOST ;
  EQUATION PROFIT = TOTALREV − TOTALCOST ;

5 MODEL BIKE1 = Q1, TOTALREV, LABORCOST, PROMOCOST,
  MATERLCOST, TOTALCOST, PROFIT ;

6 SET PER Argument-3 Argument-4 ;
  SET SOLVE SOLUTION BASELINE ;
  SOLVE ;

7 SET SOLVE SOLUTION SCENARIO ;
  COPY BIKEDATA:AMATERLCOST ;
  SERIES AMATERLCOST = AMATERLCOST * 1.02 ;
  SOLVE ;

8 PRINT "SALES" Q1.SCENARIO "SCENARIO", Q1.BASELINE "BASELINE",
  (Q1.SCENARIO − Q1.BASELINE) "DELTA" ;

  PRINT "REVENUE" TOTALREV.SCENARIO "SCENARIO",
  TOTALREV.BASELINE "BASELINE",
   (TOTALREV.SCENARIO − TOTALREV.BASELINE) "DELTA" ;

  PRINT "TOTAL COST" TOTALCOST.SCENARIO "SCENARIO",
  TOTALCOST.BASELINE "BASELINE",
   (TOTALCOST.SCENARIO − TOTALCOST.BASELINE) "DELTA" ;

```
PRINT "PROFIT" PROFIT.SCENARIO "SCENARIO",
   PROFIT.BASELINE "BASELINE",
   (PROFIT.SCENARIO − PROFIT.BASELINE) "DELTA" ;
```

Arguments substitute for key inputs in the program code, and the program call is modified. The OBEY command previously called the VFBFC.CMD program file:

```
OBEY VFBFC.CMD ;
```

Arguments will now appear with the OBEY command:

```
OBEY VFBFC.CMD BIKEDATA 85Q2 85Q3 86Q2 ;
```

Now when AREMOS processes the VFBFC.CMD file, it will substitute BIKE-DATA for ARGUMENT-1, 85Q2 for ARGUMENT-2, 85Q3 for ARGUMENT-3, and 86Q2 for ARGUMENT-4. Arguments substitute for any inputs that change on successive runs of a model. Note again that these comments are general. Every software package or language that allows this type of programming handles arguments in a slightly different fashion. *The second set of code presented is not syntactically correct AREMOS code.* The code is used to present the concept of employing arguments to replace program elements that would otherwise be edited each time a model is run.

The reader should keep the following thoughts in mind. The method employed here is simplistic in its use of arguments. Programmers use arguments in many tasks, and these tasks often involve more complex uses of arguments than the example presented here.

Note that the use of an argument is implied by its position in the argument string found in the calling routine. (Here, the calling routine is the OBEY statement.) This implies that the user knows the position order of the needed arguments. If the user gets confused and forgets that the first argument calls the data input file (BIKEDATA in the example), an error will result. Assume that the first argument is forgotten in the previous example. Then "85Q2" becomes the first argument in the string. The first command attempts the input of a data file and uses the first argument as the name of that file. This program will search for data file 85Q2, and of course this will not exist. The worst case occurs when the user enters the wrong argument, but the argument is valid. For example, assume that instead of BIKEDATA being entered for the first argument, the user enters BIKEOLD, last quarter's data file. If BIKEOLD exists and is a valid set of data, the program will run and give results. The user may not recognize the error, and work will be lost. It should also be clear that the more arguments a program needs, the more confusion results.

The use of arguments is probably not the best way to interface a model that others will use. Clever arrangements can lessen the difficulties posed by the method. The method can eliminate the need to edit program code. For some applications this method will represent the quickest way to avoid requiring changes to program code by the user. The method is especially useful if the number of elements that might change is small.

QUERY METHOD

The Query method is perhaps the best available. The user is prompted for all the data needed to make a new run of the model. The user may even be presented with a set of choices by each prompt. By front-ending a model with a Query interface, the model builder forces the user to supply needed information in the proper order. This limits the chance of data input error.

When a query routine front-ends an application, the user's request to run the model does not automatically pass code on for processing. Instead, the user's request invokes a question-and-answer routine. For example, the user might be confronted by the following.

>Welcome to the VFBFC Planning Model. Please supply the information requested.

> What is the name of the databank file you wish to use?

>

Here the user would type in "BIKEDATA" and would be prompted for the appropriate time periods over which to run the model. The model developer could build in checks to be sure that the entered data are appropriate.

In a slightly more sophisticated query, the model builder would request that a choice be made among several possible inputs. Scenario assumptions are input in section 7 of the program code. The model is set to increase the AMATERL-COST data series by 2 percent (a factor of 1.02). What if the user wanted to change a different variable, increase or decrease the scenario variable by a different factor, or both? The user would be required to edit the program file, input the new variable name and factor, and then run the model. To avoid requiring the user to edit the file, a query system could prompt the user in the following way:

> What variable will be changed in this scenario?

AMATERLCOST, WAGE, PROMO, . . .

The user then selects one of the variables. To increase the AMATERLCOST variable by 2 percent, the user would select the AMATERLCOST variable in the previous query. Next the user is asked for the factor of increase (or decrease):

> Do you wish to increase or decrease this variable?

DECREASE, INCREASE

The user selects INCREASE.

> By how much do you wish to INCREASE the AMATERLCOST variable?

.5%, 1%, 1.5%, 2%, 2.5%, 3%, 5%, OTHER

The user selects 2%.

> Do you wish to change any other baseline assumptions?

YES, NO

The user selects NO, and the model is now sent off to be processed. The model builder could pass these selections on as arguments to the model, or would find some other method of substituting these selections in the code. AREMOS and other systems offer facilities for this type of query routine. Other possibilities abound. For example, a spreadsheet package like Lotus 1–2–3 could be employed to build the query file. The previous format could be used, and the output from the query session could be a print file containing data or AREMOS code. A simple 1–2–3 menu selection routine could substitute very nicely for simpler query routines. A 1–2–3 macro would generate a print file of data or AREMOS code to be processed in the AREMOS environment.

The Query method offers an effective interface and reduces errors. However, such systems can be time-consuming and frustrating to build. They require much thought, because all types of runs and logical data changes must be prompted for. Query systems can also generate hefty amounts of code. Building these systems requires some knowledge of programming concepts. For simpler model structures, a spreadsheet menu interface may offer a suitable option.

TEMPLATE METHOD

The Template method offers an efficient means of gathering information. The user is confronted with lists of information and indicates selections by entering a number or other indicator next to desired choices. Consider the following example template where the user makes data file and scenario variable choices:

Data File Information: Select 1

_____ BIKEOLD (Use not suggested past July 1, 1985)

_____ BIKEDATA (Use not suggested past October 1, 1985)

Scenario Variable (s): Indicate selections by replacing 1 in the left-hand column with desired factor of change.

___ 1 ___ AMATERLCOST (Average Material Cost)

___ 1 ___ WAGE (Hourly Wage)

___ 1 ___ PROMO (Number of Marketing Promotions)

For the example planning model, the completed template would appear as follows:

Data File Information: Select 1

_____ BIKEOLD (Use not suggested past July 1, 1985)

___ 1 ___ BIKEDATA (Use not suggested past October 1, 1985)

Scenario Variable (s): Indicate selections by replacing 1 in the left-hand column with desired factor of change.

___ 1.02 ___ AMATERLCOST (Average Material Cost)

___ 1 ___ WAGE (Hourly Wage)

___ 1 ___ PROMO (Number of Marketing Promotions)

Template systems can be built in a variety of ways. For simple applications, a spreadsheet interface might be employed. Note how easy it is to suggest to users which choices to make or avoid. Messages can be conveniently placed next to each choice.

10

Modular Planning Systems

DAVID J. GIANTURCO

A modular planning system is formed by the direct integration of two or more stand-alone computer-based applications. Component applications can be functional tools, planning models, or other models developed by outside vendors. For example, macroeconomic or industry models can be components of modular planning systems. Modular planning systems can be single-tiered or multi-tiered. Single-tiered systems employ firm-level applications only, but multi-tiered systems necessarily employ industry, regional, or macroeconomic models.

Why would a planner wish to integrate separate computer-based applications? There are several reasons. First, most planning models are comprehensive and investigate the corporate-wide effects of varying business conditions, proposed corporate strategies, competitor actions, or changing regulatory environments. They include pricing sections, investment sections, expense sections, and the like. Specialized applications are maintained by various staff and business departments within the firm. These applications have a narrow scope and consequently are more accurate and detailed than the organization's planning models. When this level of accuracy and detail are needed, the planning department may wish to avail itself of these applications.

The Very Fast Bicycle Frame Company (VFBFC) component costing tool constructed in Chapter 8 is a stand-alone computer-based application controlled by the production department. This application can be used for planning. Materials costs are included in the VFBFC AREMOS-based planning model constructed in Chapter 9 but are not treated in great detail. For example, the planning model can't directly investigate cost changes resulting from varying currency exchange rates because exchange rates are not included as a variable in the planning model. Scenario specifications can't directly investigate the cost effects associated with movements in particular exchange rates unless they appear in the model. The 1–2–3 component costing tool evaluates the cost effects resulting from varying currency exchange rates. An interface between the component costing tool and the planning model extends planning model analysis to include currency exchange scenario studies. A single-tiered planning system is formed by interfacing the Lotus 1–2–3 component costing tool and the AREMOS-based planning model.

The second reason to integrate applications is the analysis of the firm-level effects resulting from changes in industry or macroeconomic conditions. By interfacing a firm's planning model and the PCMark8 macroeconomic model, the planner can evaluate the effects of general economic conditions on the firm's revenues, costs, and profits. For example, changes in government spending can affect sales of the firm's product. Changes in sales affect revenues, production costs, and so on. A multi-tiered planning system is formed by interfacing the PCMark8 model with a firm's planning model.

The third major motivation for interfacing applications addresses political concerns. For example, the planning department may feel that its planning model handles the effects of price changes on product sales very nicely. The planning department may not want to ask the marketing department for estimates of pricing effects. However, proceeding without the approval of the marketing department may cause problems for the planning department. Therefore, the planning department may decide to interface its planning model with the marketing department's pricing model. This will minimize friction and will also insure continuity of results reported by the two departments.

Some definitions may be helpful. Two computer applications are *interfaced* if at least one of the applications produces data that can be used as input in the other application. The exchange of data between applications is usually automated. Data pass from one application to another with little or no human intervention.

Modular means that each computer-based application included in a planning system can stand alone. For example, both the 1–2–3 component costing tool and the AREMOS-based planning model are stand-alone applications. They can be run independently, with each producing meaningful analysis for some general class of problem studied by the firm. This also implies that if either of the applications is changed, there will be no effect on the other application so long as the data elements shared by the two applications do not change.

SINGLE-TIERED MODULAR PLANNING SYSTEMS

Single-tiered modular planning systems are formed by integrating two or more firm-level computer-based applications. The most common single-tiered systems interface a planning model with one or more specific costing (including tax) or pricing applications. There are many advantages to interfacing a planning model with other applications. The planner achieves greater flexibility in the scenarios that can be investigated, obtains more precise baseline and scenario estimates

Illustration 10.1
A Single-Tiered Planning System

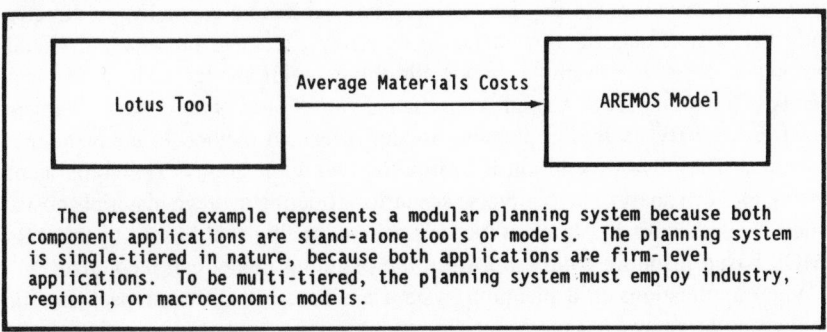

| Lotus Tool | Average Materials Costs → | AREMOS Model |

The presented example represents a modular planning system because both component applications are stand-alone tools or models. The planning system is single-tiered in nature, because both applications are firm-level applications. To be multi-tiered, the planning system must employ industry, regional, or macroeconomic models.

than can be generated using the planning model alone, and insures consistency between information reported by the planning department and other departments.

The first example interfaces the 1–2–3 component costing tool developed in Chapter 8 and the AREMOS-based planning model developed in Chapter 9. By interfacing these two applications, the planning department will achieve greater flexibility in performing scenario studies. The planning department will also obtain increased consistency with the production department's reported results.

The 1–2–3 component costing tool and the AREMOS-based planning model share a common data series: average materials costs. The actual data values found in the two versions of this data series may differ because the production department will need more precise data with which to work than will the planning department.

By interfacing the planning model with the production department's component costing tool, the planning model can analyze a greater variety of scenarios. Scenarios investigating the change in production costs associated with fluctuating currency exchange rates or changes in individual component costs can be evaluated. Further, the planning model's output reports will be consistent with results reported by the production department's component costing tool. In this example, the interfaced applications will share only one data series. In actual cases, applications can share tens or hundreds of data series. Nevertheless, the example offers a convenient framework for thinking about applications integration (see Illustration 10.1)

The 1–2–3 component costing tool is designed to analyze only component costs, and the application performs that function well. The component costing application yields new average materials costs when currency exchange rates or individual component prices (tubing sets or decals, for example) change. This information appears on the last line of the component costing tool's baseline and scenario reports. The AREMOS-based planning model uses average materials costs (variable AMATERLCOST) as a direct data input. The data series AMATERLCOST can be manipulated during scenario studies. However, this arrangement has limited flexibility. The user can increase or decrease the AMA-TERLCOST data series in the planning model by some percentage or can directly input new data values for the data series. The user has no capability to directly study the cost effects of movements in currency exchange rates or individual component costs. For example, how could the planning model evaluate the cost effects of changing U.S./Canadian exchange rates? How would these changes affect profits? By itself, the planning model offers no method to analyze such scenarios. The obvious solution is to link the two applications. The component costing tool can analyze more diverse scenarios affecting average materials costs. When needed, output data from the component costing tool is sent to the AR-EMOS-based planning model in a form the planning model can recognize.

When applications in a planning system are based in different packages or languages, the analyst has many options for automating the applications interface. The simplest and most general method is to exchange information through a print file (also referred to as a text, flat, or ASCII file).

To complete the interface process, the developer performs the following tasks. The 1–2–3 component costing tool is modified to include a short macro that will output two small print (.prn) files. The first of these print files contains average materials costs from the baseline output report, and the second contains average materials costs from the scenario output report. The print files must contain these two respective pieces of data for all four quarters of the forecast period. The data contained in these print files must be in a format that the AREMOS-based planning model can read.

The AREMOS-based planning model is modified to include two new lines of code. These two lines of code will read data output from the 1–2–3 component costing tool. It's imperative that both the baseline and scenario average materials cost information be passed from the component costing tool to the planning model. There is no guarantee that the production department and the planning department are using the same baseline data values for average materials costs in their respective applications. By incorporating the production department's baseline data for materials costs, it's certain that the two applications will have consistent baseline cost data. There are reasons why the two sets of baseline data would differ. The production department employs up-to-the-minute data in its baseline data set, but the planning department would not require such precision.

The first step in constructing the interface system involves the 1–2–3 component costing tool. After entering the 1–2–3 environment and retrieving the worksheet file holding the component costing tool, the baseline report should be displayed. The following commands will display the baseline report:

F5 A41~   (Goto, A41, Return)

The baseline report appears as in Illustration 10.2.
The needed data from the baseline report are in cells E55 to H55. This data

Illustration 10.2
The Baseline Report

	A	B	C	D	E	F	G	H
41		BASELINE AVERAGE MATERIALS COST						
42								
43	ID#	COMPONENT			QTR 1	QTR 2	QTR 3	QTR 4
44	1	TUBING SET			50.75	51.10	51.10	51.45
45	2	FITTING SET			13.70	13.87	14.02	14.19
46	3	PRIMER			0.10	0.10	0.10	0.10
47	4	PAINT			0.73	0.73	0.73	0.73
48	5	DECAL SET			1.66	1.66	1.66	1.66
49	6	BRAZING RODS			0.40	0.45	0.50	0.55
50	7	STEEL PIN SET			0.05	0.05	0.05	0.05
51	8	SHIPPING BOX			0.64	0.64	0.64	0.64
52	9	MISCELLANEOUS			0.60	0.70	0.80	0.90
53	10	OTHER			0.00	0.00	0.00	0.00
54								
55		TOTAL AVERAGE MATERIALS COST =			68.63	69.30	69.60	70.27
56		(U.S. DOLLARS)						

must be prepared in such a way that AREMOS can read it. To do this, the following commands must be entered in the appropriate cells.

In cell B61, type "DATE".

In cell B62 type Space (spacebar) 198503.

In cell B63, type Space 198504.

In cell B64, type Space 198601.

In cell B65, type Space 198602.

In cell D61, type "AMATERLCOST".

In cell D62, type the formula +E55.

In cell D63, type the formula +F55.

In cell D64, type the formula +G55.

In cell D65, type the formula +H55.

In cell F61, type BASELINE.

Cells A61 through H65 appear in Illustration 10.3.

Perform the same operation for the scenario report by modifying cells R61 through X61.

In cell R61, type Space "DATE".

In cell R62, type Space 198503.

In cell R63, type Space 198504, and so on through cell R65.

Illustration 10.3
Adding a Model Interface—Step 1

	A	B	C	D	E	F	G	H
61		"DATE"		"AMATERLCOST"		BASELINE		
62		198503		68.63				
63		198504		69.30				
64		198601		69.60				
65		198602		70.27				

Illustration 10.4
Adding a Model Interface—Step 2

	Q	R	S	T	U	V	W	X
61		"DATE"		"AMATERLCOST"		SCENARIO		
62		198503		68.63				
63		198504		69.30				
64		198601		69.60				
65		198602		70.27				

In cell T61, type "AMATERLCOST".

In cell T62, type the formula +U55.

In cell T63, type the formula +V55, and so on through cell T65.

In cell V61, type SCENARIO.

Cells Q61 through X65 appear in Illustration 10.4.

A macro must be created to output the baseline information in cells B61 through D65 and the scenario information in cells R61 through T65. Both sets of information will be output as print (.prn) files. Note that the structure of the output information will be in a form that AREMOS can read.

Macros for the component costing tool were arbitrarily placed in cells I101 to P120. The following key strokes are entered in cell I110.

'/PFBASE~RRB61..D65~GQ

Interpreted: Print, File, BASE, Return, Replace (previous file by the name of BASE.PRN[1]), Range, B61..D65, Return, Go, Quit. (The symbol / invokes the 1–2–3 main menu, and the symbol ' must initiate any cell in a 1–2–3 macro.)

Continue the macro in cell I111.

'/PFSCENARIO~RRR61..T65~GQ

Interpreted: Print, File, SCENARIO, Return, Replace (previous file by the name of SCENARIO.PRN[2]), Range, R61..T65, Return, Go, Quit.

The macro must now be named. The following commands give a one letter name to the macro. Here the macro is given the name "Z". After this macro is named, the macro is invoked by simultaneously pressing the Alt and Z keys.

/RNC\Z~ I110..I111

Interpreted: Range, Name, Create, Z (a macro named Z), Return, located in cells I110 to I111.

Save the file and type /qy (for Quit, Yes) commands to exit the 1–2–3 environment.

The next step in building the bridge between the 1–2–3 component costing tool and the AREMOS-based planning model is to modify the planning model's code. Two lines of code will be used to read the BASE.PRN and the SCENARIO.PRN files generated by the 1–2–3 component costing tool macro.

Code for the AREMOS-based planning model follows. The program section numbers included at left are not part of the code and are shown for expositional purposes. Sections 1 through 6 represent the baseline sections of the model. Sections 7 and 8 represent the scenario section.

Code for the VFBFC AREMOS Planning Model

```
1 OPEN BIKEDATA ;

2 SET PERIOD 78Q1 85Q2 ;

3 EQUATION Q1 = (CED$/PDGNP), (PRICEBIKE$/PDGNP),
     (PRICEGAS$/PDGNP), PROMO ;
   FIT ;

4 SET EQUATION CONSTANT NO ;
   EQUATION TOTALREV = PRICEBIKE$ * Q1 ;
   EQUATION LABORCOST = (HPB * Q1) * WAGE ;
   EQUATION PROMOCOST = PROMO * APROMOCOST ;
   EQUATION MATERLCOST = (Q1 * AMATERLCOST) ;
   EQUATION TOTALCOST = MATERLCOST + LABORCOST +
     PROMOCOST + FIXEDCOST ;
   EQUATION PROFIT = TOTALREV − TOTALCOST ;

5 MODEL BIKE1 = Q1, TOTALREV, LABORCOST, PROMOCOST,
   MATERLCOST, TOTALCOST, PROFIT ;
```

```
6 SET PER 85Q3 86Q2 ;
  SET SOLVE SOLUTION BASELINE ;
  SOLVE ;

7 SET SOLVE SOLUTION SCENARIO ;
  COPY BIKEDATA:AMATERLCOST ;
  SERIES AMATERLCOST = AMATERLCOST * 1.02 ;
  SOLVE;

8 PRINT "SALES" Q1.SCENARIO "SCENARIO", Q1.BASELINE "BASELINE",
    (Q1.SCENARIO - Q1.BASELINE) "DELTA" ;

  PRINT "REVENUE" TOTALREV.SCENARIO "SCENARIO",
    TOTALREV.BASELINE "BASELINE",
    (TOTALREV.SCENARIO - TOTALREV.BASELINE) "DELTA" ;

  PRINT "TOTAL COST" TOTALCOST.SCENARIO "SCENARIO",
    TOTALCOST.BASELINE "BASELINE",
    (TOTALCOST.SCENARIO - TOTALCOST.BASELINE) "DELTA" ;

  PRINT "PROFIT" PROFIT.SCENARIO "SCENARIO",
    PROFIT.BASELINE "BASELINE",
    (PROFIT.SCENARIO - PROFIT.BASELINE) "DELTA" ;
```

It was noted earlier that the production department's version of average materials costs might differ from the planning department's version. Reasonable estimates would suffice for the planning department, but the production department must constantly revise their estimate of average materials costs. The component costing tool would be updated each time a component price changed (say for tubing sets, decals, or paint) or any time relevant currency exchange rates changed (U.S./Canadian or U.S./United Kingdom). To insure that the planning model uses baseline data consistent with the production department's baseline estimates, the planning model is modified to read baseline data for the AMATERLCOST variable as listed on the component costing tool's baseline report. The data will be read just before the model solution is run—that is, in section 6. The modified baseline section of the planning model appears as follows:

Modified Code for the Baseline Section of the Planning Model

```
1 OPEN BIKEDATA ;

2 SET PERIOD 78Q1 85Q2 ;

3 EQUATION Q1 = (CED$/PDGNP), (PRICEBIKE$/PDGNP),
    (PRICEGAS$/PDGNP), PROMO ;
  FIT ;
```

4 SET EQUATION CONSTANT NO ;

   EQUATION TOTALREV = PRICEBIKE\$ * Q1 ;

   EQUATION LABORCOST = (HPB * Q1) * WAGE ;

   EQUATION PROMOCOST = PROMO * APROMOCOST ;

   EQUATION MATERLCOST = (Q1 * AMATERLCOST) ;

   EQUATION TOTALCOST = MATERLCOST + LABORCOST +
      PROMOCOST + FIXEDCOST ;

   EQUATION PROFIT = TOTALREV - TOTALCOST ;

5 MODEL BIKE1 = Q1, TOTALREV, LABORCOST, PROMOCOST,
      MATERLCOST, TOTALCOST, PROFIT ;

6 SET PER 85Q3 86Q2 ;

   IMPORT C:\123\BASE.PRN ;

   SET SOLVE SOLUTION BASELINE ;

   SOLVE ;

Closer analysis is warranted. Just before the baseline solution is run, the contents of the baseline data file BASE.PRN generated by the component costing tool are read (imported) into the AREMOS user work space. (This file is assumed to exist in the 123 directory on the C drive.) This file contains only one data series, AMATERLCOST. The planning department's version of this data series already exists in file BIKEDATA.BNK. The process of importing the BASE.PRN file implies that a version of the AMATERLCOST data series (the production department's version of that data series) will now be placed in the user work space before the baseline section of the planning model is solved. When the baseline section of the model is solved, the AMATERLCOST data series stored in the BIKEDATA.BNK databank file will be ignored. As always, AREMOS will search the user work space for a needed data series first. It will then search accessed (opened) databank files if no version of the data series is found in the work space. By this method, the planning department's planning model will use the same baseline average materials cost estimates as the production department's.

When the component costing tool is run, a report of scenario average materials costs appears on that application's scenario report. This scenario information is incorporated in the AREMOS-based planning model by importing reported average materials costs just before the planning model's scenario solution is run. This step will be performed in section 7 of the planning model code. The third line in section 7 will be changed. The objective of interfacing these two applications is to incorporate the scenario average materials costs produced by the component costing tool directly into the planning model. Scenarios will be specified in the component costing tool, and the information will then be passed to the planning model. Sections 7 and 8 of the planning model are specified as follows:

Modified Code for the Scenario Section of the Planning Model

```
7  SET SOLVE SOLUTION SCENARIO ;
   COPY BIKEDATA:AMATERLCOST ;
   IMPORT C:\123\SCENARIO.PRN ;
   SOLVE ;

8  PRINT "SALES" Q1.SCENARIO "SCENARIO", Q1.BASELINE "BASELINE",
   (Q1.SCENARIO - Q1.BASELINE) "DELTA" ;

   PRINT "REVENUE" TOTALREV.SCENARIO "SCENARIO",
   TOTALREV.BASELINE "BASELINE",
   (TOTALREV.SCENARIO - TOTALREV.BASELINE) "DELTA" ;

   PRINT "TOTAL COST" TOTALCOST.SCENARIO "SCENARIO",
   TOTALCOST.BASELINE "BASELINE",
   (TOTALCOST.SCENARIO - TOTALCOST.BASELINE) "DELTA" ;

   PRINT "PROFIT" PROFIT.SCENARIO "SCENARIO",
   PROFIT.BASELINE "BASELINE",
   (PROFIT.SCENARIO - PROFIT.BASELINE) "DELTA" ;
```

When the SCENARIO.PRN file is imported, a new version of the AMA-TERLCOST variable will read into the user work space. This will be the version of the AMATERLCOST data series that will be used in all subsequent calculations and operations. (This scenario version of the AMATERLCOST data series will over-write the baseline version of this data series previously read into the AREMOS user work space.) Again, AREMOS checks the user work space first for needed data series. AREMOS will only look to opened databank files for data series that do not appear in the work space. The new solution undertaken in the scenario section of the planning model incorporates scenario average materials costs exactly as these costs appear on the component costing tool's scenario report.

The interface has been completed. When running the component costing tool, the user has the option to run the Z macro that creates the BASE.PRN and SCENARIO.PRN print files. The data series in these files can then be incorporated in the AREMOS-based planning model.

The component costing tool evaluates effects on average materials costs when individual component prices change or when there are movements in currency exchange rates. The final example in Chapter 8 analyzed scenario and baseline results when both a component cost (tubing sets) and a foreign exchange rate (U.S. dollar/Canadian dollar) were altered. This example will be revisited to

Illustration 10.5
The Scenario Factors Module—Baseline Case

	I	J	K	L	M	N	O	P
1				SCENARIO FACTORS				
2	INPUT PRICES:							
3	ID# COMPONENT				QTR 1	QTR 2	QTR 3	QTR 4
4	1 TUBING SET				1	1	1	1
5	2 FITTING SET				1	1	1	1
6	3 PRIMER				1	1	1	1
7	4 PAINT				1	1	1	1
8	5 DECAL SET				1	1	1	1
9	6 BRAZING RODS				1	1	1	1
10	7 STEEL PIN SET				1	1	1	1
11	8 SHIPPING BOX				1	1	1	1
12	9 MISCELLANEOUS				1	1	1	1
13	10 OTHER				1	1	1	1
14								
15	FOREIGN EXCHANGE (U.S. DOLLARS / 1 UNIT FOREIGN)							
16					QTR 1	QTR 2	QTR 3	QTR 4
17	US $ / US $				1	1	1	1
18	US $ / CANADIAN $				1	1	1	1
19	US $ / ENGLISH POUND (L.)				1	1	1	1
20	US $ / OTHER				1	1	1	1

illustrate how the application interface process works. Recall from Chapter 8 that scenarios are usually specified by manipulating scenario change factors located in the scenario factors module. In the baseline case, all these factors are 1, and the module appears as in Illustration 10.5.

The final example from Chapter 8 specified an increase in the price of tubing sets by 10 percent over baseline levels for all four quarters of analysis. The scenario also called for the Canadian dollar to appreciate in value vis-à-vis the U.S. dollar. The percentage of increase was 0 in the first quarter, 3 percent in the second quarter, 6 percent in the third quarter, and 10 percent in the fourth quarter. These assumptions are entered in the scenario factors module as shown in Illustration 10.6.

The scenario is specified and run. The resultant scenario and baseline reports appear in Illustration 10.7.

The spreadsheet contains data in a form that AREMOS can read. Baseline data are displayed in cells B61 through D65, and scenario data are displayed in cells R61 through T65. These parts of the spreadsheet appear in Illustration 10.8.

The Z macro was created to output data in cells B61 through D65 to a print file called BASE.PRN and to output data in cells R61 through T65 to a print file called SCENARIO.PRN. To activate this macro, the user simultaneously presses the Alt and Z keys. The BASE.PRN and SCENARIO.PRN print files are created and will exist in the default directory. (For most users, this will be the 1–2–3 directory.)

To exit the 1–2–3 environment, the user types:

/qy   (Quit, Yes)

Illustration 10.6
The Scenario Factors Module—A Scenario Specification

	I	J	K	L	M	N	O	P
1					SCENARIO FACTORS			
2	INPUT PRICES:							
3	ID#	COMPONENT			QTR 1	QTR 2	QTR 3	QTR 4
4	1	TUBING SET			1.1	1.1	1.1	1.1
5	2	FITTING SET			1	1	1	1
6	3	PRIMER			1	1	1	1
7	4	PAINT			1	1	1	1
8	5	DECAL SET			1	1	1	1
9	6	BRAZING RODS			1	1	1	1
10	7	STEEL PIN SET			1	1	1	1
11	8	SHIPPING BOX			1	1	1	1
12	9	MISCELLANEOUS			1	1	1	1
13	10	OTHER			1	1	1	1
14								
15	FOREIGN EXCHANGE	(U.S. DOLLARS / 1 UNIT FOREIGN)						
16					QTR 1	QTR 2	QTR 3	QTR 4
17		US $ / US $			1	1	1	1
18		US $ / CANADIAN $			1	1.03	1.06	1.1
19		US $ / ENGLISH POUND (L.)			1	1	1	1
20		US $ / OTHER			1	1	1	1

All that remains now is to run the AREMOS-based planning model. When the model is run, the BASE.PRN and SCENARIO.PRN print files will be read into the AREMOS user work space as needed. To run the AREMOS-based planning model, the user issues the following commands:

CD \AREMOS

AREMOS OBEY VFBFC.CMD

The first command makes the AREMOS directory the current directory. The second command accesses the AREMOS environment and then runs the planning model (contained in the VFBFC.CMD command file). If the access and OBEY commands are combined, the AREMOS program will run as soon as the AREMOS environment is accessed. After the model is run, its reports will appear on screen. Reported results will incorporate information from the 1–2–3 component costing tool. The resultant reports appear in Illustration 10.9.

The reports show increasing costs and decreasing profits. In this particular scenario, no variables affecting demand are changed and price has not changed. Consequently only the total cost and profit reports will show changes in the delta categories. Profit will fall by the exact amount costs rise.

Baseline costs are different in this version of the planning model compared with the version of the model presented in Chapter 9. The version presented here uses baseline average materials costs directly as reported by the production department. These were slightly different from the baseline average materials

Illustration 10.7
Costing Tool Reports After Scenario Is Run

	Q	R	S	T	U	V	W	X
41			SCENARIO AVERAGE MATERIALS COST					
42								
43	ID#	COMPONENT			QTR 1	QTR 2	QTR 3	QTR 4
44	1	TUBING SET			55.83	56.21	56.21	56.60
45	2	FITTING SET			13.70	13.87	14.02	14.19
46	3	PRIMER			0.10	0.10	0.10	0.10
47	4	PAINT			0.73	0.75	0.77	0.80
48	5	DECAL SET			1.66	1.71	1.76	1.82
49	6	BRAZING RODS			0.40	0.45	0.50	0.55
50	7	STEEL PIN SET			0.05	0.05	0.05	0.05
51	8	SHIPPING BOX			0.64	0.66	0.68	0.71
52	9	MISCELLANEOUS			0.60	0.70	0.80	0.90
53	10	OTHER			0.00	0.00	0.00	0.00
54								
55		TOTAL AVERAGE MATERIALS COST =			73.71	74.50	74.89	75.71
56		(U.S. DOLLARS)						

	A	B	C	D	E	F	G	H
41			BASELINE AVERAGE MATERIALS COST					
42								
43	ID#	COMPONENT			QTR 1	QTR 2	QTR 3	QTR 4
44	1	TUBING SET			50.75	51.10	51.10	51.45
45	2	FITTING SET			13.70	13.87	14.02	14.19
46	3	PRIMER			0.10	0.10	0.10	0.10
47	4	PAINT			0.73	0.73	0.73	0.73
48	5	DECAL SET			1.66	1.66	1.66	1.66
49	6	BRAZING RODS			0.40	0.45	0.50	0.55
50	7	STEEL PIN SET			0.05	0.05	0.05	0.05
51	8	SHIPPING BOX			0.64	0.64	0.64	0.64
52	9	MISCELLANEOUS			0.60	0.70	0.80	0.90
53	10	OTHER			0.00	0.00	0.00	0.00
54								
55		TOTAL AVERAGE MATERIAL COST =			68.63	69.30	69.60	70.27
56		(U.S. DOLLARS)						

cost data used by the planning department. Consistency of reported results is one advantage gained by interfacing applications.

The planning model has been made more flexible by its interface with the component costing tool. The user can now directly investigate cost scenarios not adequately addressed by the planning model alone. In the example, a scenario directly investigating changes in currency exchange rates and individual component prices is investigated. While not done here, the user could change other variables in the planning model at the same time that new cost information is imported from the component costing tool. In fact, many interesting scenarios

Illustration 10.8
The Costing Tool Model Interface Section—After Scenario Is Run

	A	B	C	D	E	F	G	H
61		"DATE"		"AMATERLCOST"		BASELINE		
62		198503		68.63				
63		198504		69.30				
64		198601		69.60				
65		198602		70.27				

	Q	R	S	T	U	V	W	X
61		"DATE"		"AMATERLCOST"		SCENARIO		
62		198503		73.71				
63		198504		74.50				
64		198601		74.89				
65		198602		75.71				

could be devised in this way. The method used to interface these two applications is just one of many possible methods.

Interesting cases arise when applications share data. Whole sections of a model may be circumvented. Consider the case discussed in Illustration 10.10.

Illustration 10.9
Planning Model Reports—After Incorporating Costing Tool Scenario Results

SALES

	SCENARIO	BASELINE	DELTA
1985			
Q3	37448	37448	00
Q4	33955	33955	00
1986			
Q1	35172	35172	00
Q2	35987	35987	00

REVENUE

	SCENARIO	BASELINE	DELTA
1985			
Q3	7174634	7174634	00
Q4	6534676	6534676	00
1986			
Q1	6815890	6815890	00
Q2	7027244	7027244	00

TOTAL COST

	SCENARIO	BASELINE	DELTA
1985			
Q3	6828960	6638725	190235
Q4	6404669	6228102	176567
1986			
Q1	6786628	6600571	186058
Q2	6987802	6792031	195771

PROFIT

	SCENARIO	BASELINE	DELTA
1985			
Q3	345674	535909	-190235
Q4	130007	306574	-176567
1986			
Q1	29262	215319	-186058
Q2	39442	235213	-195771

Illustration 10.10
Circumventing Sections of a Planning Model

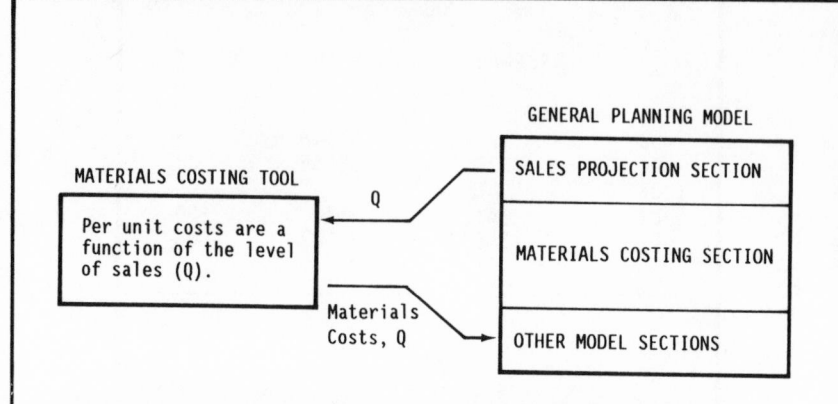

GENERAL PLANNING MODEL

MATERIALS COSTING TOOL

Q

SALES PROJECTION SECTION

Per unit costs are a
function of the level
of sales (Q).

MATERIALS COSTING SECTION

Materials
Costs, Q

OTHER MODEL SECTIONS

Many possible data paths can exist between interfaced applications in
single-tiered systems. For example, many costing models need sales
projections to run, because costs will vary according to the level of sales.
A manufacturer may receive discounts on product components according to the
volume of components purchased. In such cases a general planning model's
demand section can project future sales, this sales forecast can drive a
materials costing application, and the materials costing application outputs
a dollar value of costs based on projected units sold. This information is
then fed back to the relevant section of the general planning model. The
planning model's own materials costing section is essentially circumvented,
and will not have an effect on report information.

ADVANCED TOPIC: USING A DOS BAT PROGRAM TO INTERFACE TWO APPLICATIONS

Readers with advanced DOS and spreadsheet knowledge might find the
following information useful. The interface for the AREMOS-based planning model and the 1–2–3 component costing tool could be improved by
use of a BAT program. This program serves as a simple DOS batch
executive. Using this simple program executive requires the user to rename
the worksheet file containing the 1–2–3 component costing tool to

AUTO123.WK1 (or AUTO123.WKS for users of Lotus 1–2–3 Version 1A).

First, rename the worksheet file containing the component costing tool to AUTO123.WK1. Next, create the following BAT program in file BIKE.BAT. (It's assumed that the user's Lotus 1–2–3 files are stored in directory 123.)

File BIKE.BAT

```
C:
CD \123
123
CD \AREMOS
AREMOS OBEY VFBFC.CMD
```

The BIKE.BAT utility is invoked simply by typing BIKE. The first command insures that the C drive is the current drive (assumes that you run AREMOS and 1–2–3 from a hard disk designated as the C drive). The second command changes the current directory to the 123 directory. The third command accesses 1–2–3. Since a file named AUTO123.WK1 exists, this file will automatically be retrieved when 1–2–3 is accessed. The user then specifies a scenario run of the component costing tool. After activating the Z macro, the necessary BASE.PRN and SCENARIO.PRN print files will exist in the 123 directory. Now, when the user exists the 1–2–3 environment (by issuing the /, Quit, Yes commands), control of operations will return to the BIKE.BAT program at line 4. The directions in line 4 are followed without pause for user input. Line 4 designates AREMOS as the current directory. Line 5 accesses the AREMOS environment and automatically activates the planning model (contained in the VFBFC.CMD command file). It is possible to include the OBEY statement with the AREMOS access command precisely for this reason. Using a BAT program in this way automates steps the user would otherwise execute. Clever use of such utilities can help reduce errors and simplify end-user operations.

The concept of using BAT programs to automate application interfaces is not unique to Lotus 1–2–3 and AREMOS. Most packages will lend themselves to such interfaces. The example passes data in only one direction, but data can also be passed back and forth between applications. BAT programs can run applications outside of the 1–2–3 environment and then automatically return needed data to the 1–2–3 environment. BAT programs, spreadsheet macros, and specialized packages (or programs written in high-level languages) can be combined to create flexible and powerful applications systems with sophisticated automated interfaces.

MULTI-TIERED MODULAR PLANNING SYSTEMS

Multi-tiered planning systems share some similarities with single-tiered systems. First, a multi-tiered system consists of two or more stand-alone applications. The interface between member applications is achieved by the exchange of data series. Like well-designed single-tiered planning systems, multi-tiered planning systems are modular.

There are also many differences between single-tiered and multi-tiered systems. By definition, the multi-tiered system includes industry, regional, or macroeconomic models. Possible configurations for multi-tiered systems are more varied than those for single-tiered systems. Most multi-tiered systems are hierarchical, with a macroeconomic model driving a firm-level model. However, configurations can be more complex. Macroeconomic models can drive industry models, which then drive firm-level models, and so on. Consider also that single-tiered planning systems might be subsumed by a multi-tiered system. The single-tiered example interfaced a 1–2–3 component costing tool and an AREMOS-based planning model. This single-tiered system could be part of a multi-tiered system. A macroeconomic model would drive variables in the planning model's product forecasting equation.

This section will not include a detailed working example of a multi-tiered planning system but will outline such a system. This system employs the PCMark8 macroeconomic model, the 1–2–3 component costing tool, and the AREMOS-based planning model. The discussion in the previous section concerned the development of a single-tiered planning system. The application interface between the 1–2–3 component costing tool and the AREMOS-based planning model was possible because the two applications shared a common data series—average materials costs. Just as the planning model shares a common data series with the component costing tool, it may also share common data series with industry, regional, or macroeconomic models. If so, an interface to any of these models is possible.

Consider the product-line forecasting equation developed in Chapter 9, the driving equation in the planning model:

Q1 = (CED$/PDGNP), (PRICEBIKE$/PDGNP), (PRICEGAS$/PDGNP), PROMO;

Again, the quantity of bicycle frames sold is a function of the level of consumer spending on durable goods, the price of bicycle frames, the price of gasoline, and the number of marketing promotions undertaken by the firm. Expenditure and price variables are relative to the general rise in prices.

Macroeconomic models report data series for several of the variables in this equation. Consumer spending on durable goods, the price of gasoline, and a general inflation index are all output by the PCMark8 model. Similar variables are also output by other macroeconomic models offered by other vendors and

Illustration 10.11
A Hierarchical Planning System

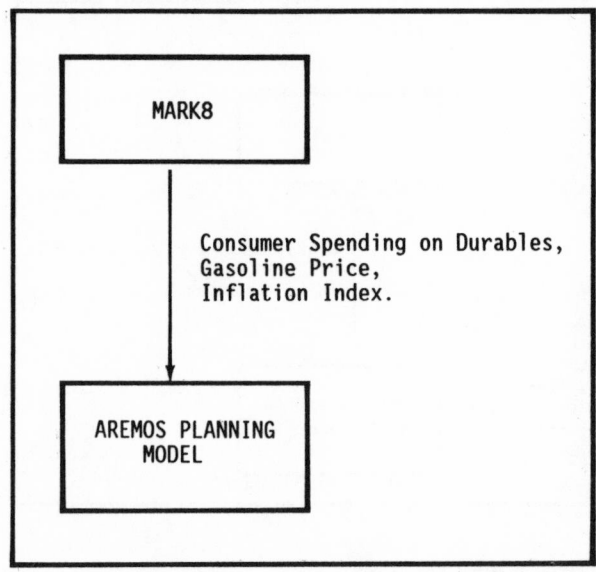

are included in macroeconomic models for other countries. Similar to the way
the 1–2–3 component costing tool was linked to the AREMOS-based planning
model, the PCMark8 model can be linked to the planning model. By linking the
PCMark8 model and the AREMOS-based planning model, a hierarchical planning system is formed (see Illustration 10.11).

The PCMark8 model is covered in detail in Chapter 7, and its capabilities
will not be reviewed here. A wealth of scenarios involving macroeconomic
variables can be examined with the model. These include changing energy prices
and new fiscal or monetary policy implementations. Insofar as these scenarios
affect consumer spending on durables, the price of gasoline, and inflation, the
effects of PCMark8 model scenarios can be incorporated in the AREMOS-based
planning model. Changes in these variables affect the number of VFBFC bicycle
frames sold and will consequently impact production, costs, and profits. Like
the firm-level planning model, the PCMark8 model is AREMOS-based; the
interface between the PCMark8 model and the firm-level planning model will
be simplified. The main point is that, by sharing common data series, scenarios
that could not be directly examined using the firm-level planning model alone
can now be performed.

The hierarchical interface between the PCMark8 model and the firm-level
planning model does not preclude interfacing the planning model and the 1–2–3
component costing tool (see Illustration 10.12).

Illustration 10.12
Multi-Tiered Planning System Subsuming a Single-Tiered Planning System

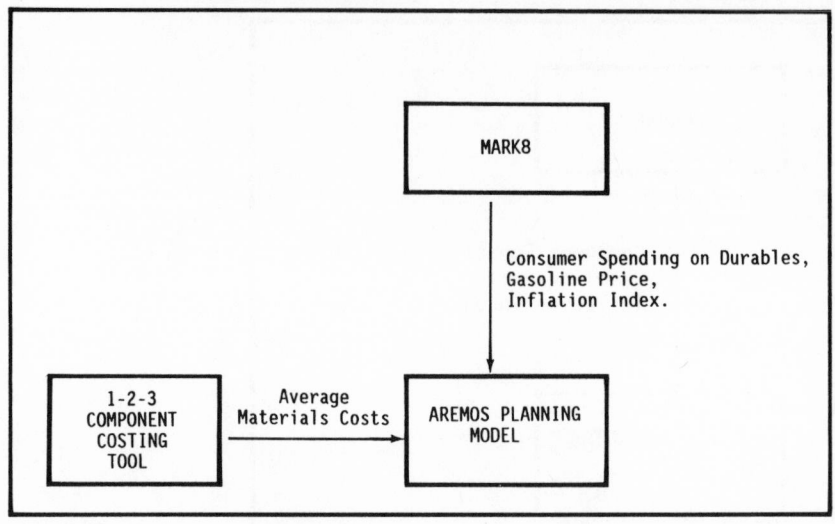

ORGANIZATIONAL CONSIDERATIONS

The discussion of modular planning systems logically leads to a discussion of the organizational considerations of forming such systems. The following comments are general and not exclusive to the microcomputing environment. They are relevant whenever computer-based applications or data are shared by different groups within a firm or other organization.

If the analyst controls the applications needed to form a planning system, the only concerns in interfacing member applications are technical. The analyst need not address organizational considerations such as "Who owns and controls an application?" or "Who is ultimately responsible for updating certain data?" Organizational concerns are also less important in smaller firms, where managers are less territorial about data and applications. However, analysts working for large corporations confront organizational issues when they wish to use another department's data or applications for corporate planning. Several factors must be considered by both the planner and the staff or department manager.

By using data or applications from another department, the planner obtains the following technical and organizational benefits:

- The planner obtains greater flexibility in the scenarios that can be investigated.

- The planner uses data consistent with that used by the responsible staff or department.

- The planner is not responsible for errors in staff or department applications. It may be incumbent on the planning department, however, to report errors or irregularities in staff or department applications or data.

- The planner can afford to be less concerned with the computing characteristics of borrowed applications. If planning models are interfaced with applications coming from other departments, the planner's main responsibility will concern the design and support of a standardized application interface.
- Application maintenance, documentation, and support concerning borrowed applications will not be the responsibility of the planning department. The computing and support expenses for borrowed applications will be the responsibility of the responsible staff or department.

By allowing their applications and data to be used by planning groups, staff and department management obtain the following organizational benefits:

- The responsible staff or department will have the final say on data inputs and employed applications algorithms.
- By achieving consistency with information reported by the planning group, the responsible department eliminates the need to explain data discrepancies.
- By leveraging applications, the value of existing staff and department applications becomes greater. The more widespread the use of a department's applications and data, the more authority and control that department can assert over analyses.

By using staff or department data or applications, the planner incurs the following technical and organizational liabilities:

- The planning department may face difficulties in obtaining current data or model versions. Organizational planning will not be a major priority with staff and departments; this will cause delays and other difficulties for planning groups.
- At some point the planning department may become dependent on other departments for data or application updates. This limitation in autonomy can be especially frustrating during critical planning periods.
- Staff or departments may hand-off erroneous data or flawed applications. Also, data communications and other problems can develop during the hand-off process. Any such difficulties will degrade planning department output information and/or cause delays in reporting information.

By allowing their applications and data to be used by planning groups, staff and department management incur the following technical and organizational liabilities:

- Department models and methods are exposed to scrutiny by outside individuals, namely, planners. Ad hoc methods, model errors, and so on will be recognized by planners and other outside individuals. This will be especially risky in large corporations where several models are competing for dominance in operational and planning environments.
- Planning department personnel may not be properly trained in the use of borrowed applications and may generate error-filled outputs. This may tarnish the reputation of the department that lent the application.

- Planning group personnel might take the liberty to change staff or department models or data. The planning group might not make upper-management aware of these changes.
- Planning-related activities will increase the workload borne by staff and line department personnel. Additional expenses for new staff may be incurred.

To overcome some of the difficulties associated with interdepartmental data and applications exchange, staff and department managers may opt for a middle-of-the-road solution. They may allow the use of their data by planning departments and will also perform requested runs of their applications for planning departments. By cooperating with the planning department but denying the planning department direct use of applications, staff and department managers retain complete control of their department applications. Reports can be carefully checked before going to the planning department, and model updates will be immediately instituted in the planning process as they are implemented in staff and department operations. This keeps all users current and avoids the use of different model versions by different departments.

SUMMARY

Methods for combining stand-alone computer-based applications into single- or multi-tiered modular planning systems have been discussed. Single-tiered systems employ firm-level applications only, while multi-tiered planning systems necessarily employ industry or macroeconomic models. Member applications are interfaced through the exchange of common data series. By leveraging existing applications to form modular planning systems, the value of each member application is increased. Each application retains its value as a stand-alone tool or model but also increases the flexibility and/or accuracy of the other applications in the modular planning system. While most or all member applications would be expected to reside on microcomputers, it is possible that some member applications reside on mainframes or minicomputers.

In large corporations, exchanging data and interfacing applications may entail organizational considerations. The direct interface of applications may be precluded by technical or political considerations. Nevertheless, the concept of leveraging independent applications remains valid and should be encouraged even if direct application interface is not allowed. In this way, planners can investigate a greater variety of scenarios and can insure greater data consistency between planning and staff or department reports. This will also encourage other departments to use sensible, quantifiable, and defendable analysis methods.

NOTES

1. This command assumes that a previous version of the BASE.PRN file exists in the current directory.

2. This command assumes that a previous version of the SCENARIO.PRN file exists in the current directory.

MODELING, FORECASTING, AND ECONOMETRIC METHODS

Many of the examples in this book have econometric foundations and include information on forecasting. This final section serves as a general reference for these topics. In addition, Chapter 11 compares the three forms of forecasting: time series, consensus, and econometric. Econometric methods are then reviewed. This chapter covers a variety of topics including the estimation of both single equation and multi-equation models and the use of time-series and cross-section data in econometric analysis.

Many planners use econometric models provided by other individuals within their organization or by outside consultants. This chapter offers these individuals background on the construction of forecasting models and will help them evaluate models developed by others. Information is also included on the relationship of forecasting and risk analysis studies. This chapter can serve as an excellent primer in econometric methods for persons with limited background or as a review of important concepts for those with more training.

Econometric Modeling and Forecasting

JAMES TSITANIDIS

This chapter serves as a primer on econometric methods for uninitiated readers or as a general review for those with more training. The chapter introduces important concepts, including the interpretation of results and support statistics for estimated equations (or systems of equations). The level of analysis will be kept simple and as nonmathematical as possible. Since this is intended as a general review of the econometric modeling and forecasting process, much of the intricate and esoteric information will be omitted. Where appropriate, the reader will be referred to an econometric textbook for more detail.

The chapter will begin by defining various forecasting techniques and providing an example of each. Some simple support statistics will be introduced. Next, the chapter will focus on econometric modeling and forecasting by using a single equation—two variable model—and expanding it into a more elaborate multivariate model. Additional statistics will be reported and explained. Some of the major statistical problems associated with estimation techniques will be explored as well. Finally, the chapter will conclude with multi-equation models.

FORECASTING ALTERNATIVES

There are three alternative approaches to forecasting: (1) time-series, (2) consensus, and (3) econometric forecasting.

Time-Series Forecasting

Time-series forecasting is the application of mathematical models for the purpose of tracking historical data. No assumptions are made concerning the underlying reasons or causes for the shape of the data series over time. Therefore,

Table 11.1.
Sales Data

	1980	1981	1982	1983	1984	1985	1986
Jan	2,582	2,839	3,034	3,287	3,578	4,121	4,456
Feb	2,621	2,876	3,029	3,342	3,650	4,233	4,436
Mar	2,690	2,881	3,045	3,336	3,664	4,439	4,699
Apr	2,635	2,967	3,066	3,427	3,643	4,167	
May	2,676	2,944	3,077	3,413	3,838	4,326	
Jun	2,714	2,939	3,046	3,503	3,792	4,329	
Jul	2,834	3,014	3,094	3,472	3,899	4,423	
Aug	2,789	3,031	3,053	3,511	3,845	4,351	
Sept	2,768	2,995	3,071	3,618	4,007	4,406	
Oct	2,785	2,998	3,186	3,554	4,092	4,357	
Nov	2,886	3,012	3,167	3,641	3,937	4,485	
Dec	2,842	3,031	3,230	3,607	4,008	4,445	

Units: Sales in hundreds of thousands of Widgetstan dollars (Widgedollars).

a time series is a set of chronologically ordered points of raw data; an example would be the monthly sales figures of a product over several years. Time-series analysis helps identify trends[1] and patterns that repeat in the data. These patterns are usually related to changes in economic conditions—namely, expansions and contractions (business cycles).

To illustrate the theoretical underpinnings of time-series forecasting and to introduce the reader to the various statistics associated with forecasting models, consider the following example.

A variable y(t) represents blue jeans sales in the fictitious country of Widgetstan. Sales are tracked over a certain period of time (t) and are measured in units of local currency (see Table 11.1). Assume also that these sales figures have fluctuated up and down partly in response to changes in the prices of blue jeans as well as the prices of substitutes, personal income, consumer fashion tastes, and so on. Some fluctuations, however, may be due to factors that are not explainable such as unexpected seasonal variations in consumer spending, changes in consumer preferences, unexpected import/export quotas, and so on. Therefore, it may be impossible to depict the movement of the sales variable y(t) through the use of a formal model simply because needed data are not available.

The researcher wishes to determine whether there is an overall trend in the sales variable which, because it has dominated the past behavior of the series, might dominate its future behavior. If such a behavioral pattern can be identified, the researcher can attempt to construct a model for the time series. This model does not offer a structural explanation for the series being modeled in terms of other variables but does replicate past trends and uses them to predict future movements for the modeled series.

In the simple example of blue jean sales in Widgetstan, assume the data consist of monthly sales figures of jeans for the time period January 1980 to March

1986. Assume also that the researcher has failed to acquire reliable data on any other variables that would allow estimating (and testing the validity of) a formal economic model. As an alternative, time-series analysis can be used to estimate a simple model[2] of the general form:

$$SALES_t = a_0 + a_1 \, TIME \tag{1}$$

Where: TIME = time period equal to 0 in the base period (January 1980), equal to 1 for February 1980, and increasing by 1 for every subsequent observation.

Regression analysis[3] produces the following results:

$$SALES_t = 2463.1 + 26.70 \, TIME \tag{2}$$
$$ (84.9) \quad (39.5)$$

$$R^2 = .995$$

The numbers 2463.1 and 26.70 in the estimated equation (2) are the coefficients of the regression. They measure the effect of a particular right-hand-side (independent or explanatory) variable on the left-hand-side (dependent or explained) variable of the equation. This information is useful when performing sensitivity analysis, which provides information on the effect of a change of an explanatory variable on the dependent variable. Here, the coefficient of TIME (26.70) shows that a change in the TIME variable by one unit (a month) will lead to an increase in the sales of blue jeans in Widgetstan by 26.70 current (hundreds of thousands) Widgedollars.[4]

In a two-variable case such as this, the coefficient of the right-hand-side variable is also known as the slope parameter. In a more general multivariate case, the coefficients of the right-hand-side variables are also referred to as impact multipliers. Impact multipliers demonstrate the impact on the dependent variable as a result of a one unit change in an explanatory variable.

The term a_0 in equation (1) which has been estimated to be 2,463.1 is called the constant term. The constant term demonstrates the value of sales when all the explanatory variables are equal to zero. In TIME = 0 (January 1980), the sales of blue jeans in Widgetstan are estimated at 2,463.1 (in hundreds of thousands of Widgedollars).

The reported R-Square, known as the coefficient of determination and occasionally as the measure of goodness-of-fit, measures the variation in the dependent variable that is explained by the right-hand-side variables of the estimated equation. Therefore, the closer the fitted values[5] are to the actual data values of the dependent variable, the closer the R-Square is to the perfect value of one. Illustration 11.1a shows that an R-Square of one depicts a perfect fit. This can only occur when all the data points lie on the estimated regression line. Illustration 11.1b depicts the opposite situation; the R-Square is very close to zero, and the estimated regression equation does not explain any variation in the dependent variable.

Illustration 11.1
R² and Goodness of Fit

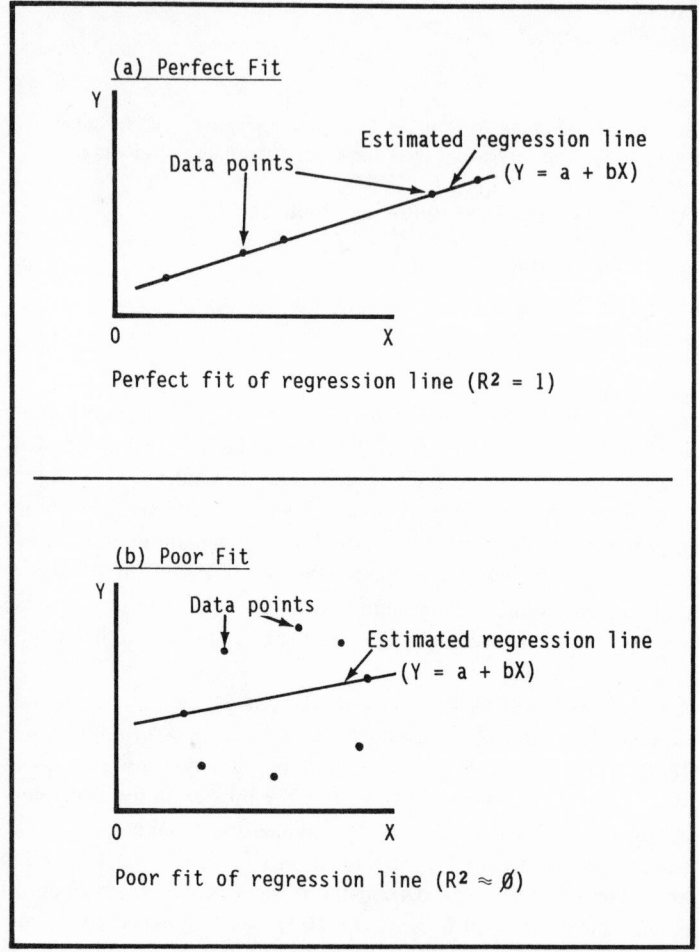

In the estimated model (2), an R-Square of .995 indicates that a time trend variable (TIME) explains 99.5 percent of the variation in the SALES of blue jeans in Widgetstan over the sample time period.

The numbers in parentheses below the estimated coefficients are the corresponding t-statistics and are used to determine whether the coefficients of (2) are statistically significant. A t-statistic can be used in a statistical test for the hypothesis that a coefficient has a particular value. The t-statistic to test if a coefficient is zero (that is, if the variable does not belong in the regression) is the ratio of the coefficient value to its standard error (see the appendix for mathematical formulation).

As a rule of thumb, if the magnitude of the t-statistic exceeds the value of 2 and the degrees of freedom[6] are at least 8, there is a 95 percent probability that the observed coefficient is not zero. In this case, the corresponding variable should be included in the estimated model, and the coefficient is considered to be statistically significant. In the example of equation (2), this would mean:

1. There is a 95 percent probability of a direct relationship between time and the sales of blue jeans in Widgetstan as depicted in the general form of equation (1),

2. The estimated coefficient is statistically different from zero,

3. The estimated coefficient is correctly included as an independent variable.

Instead of t-statistics, standard error values are sometimes displayed in parentheses below the estimated coefficients. These are also used to "test" the statistical significance of the estimated coefficients and will be explained in the context of an econometric forecasting model later in this chapter.

Equation (2) can now be used to forecast sales in the future. The forecasted sales figure for April 1986 (which is time period $t = 76$) would be:

$SALES_{t=76} = 2463.1 + (26.7 \times 76)$
$= 4,492.3$ (in hundreds of thousands of local currency)

Similarly, by substituting time period equal 77 and 78 for May and June 1986, respectively, the sales figures are calculated as $SALES_{t=77} = 4,519$ and $SALES_{t=78} = 4,545.7$.

So far, a simple example of a time-series forecasting model has been provided along with an explanation of some of the associated statistics. The time-series model provided is only one of a larger group of various time-series models such as autoregressive, quadratic and logarithmic trend models, and moving average/ exponential smoothing models.

Consensus Forecasting

Consensus forecasting is the least scientifically structured of the three types of forecasting. However, it is often the only available alternative when there are no reliable data.

Consensus forecasting is performed every time executives of a firm meet to analyze the current status quo and give their (often educated) opinions about the future of the market and/or their product. The final consensus forecast is often a function of the power wielded by the individuals involved in the decision-making process. A marketing director may query subordinates concerning their sales expectations for a product being introduced in a new market. However, the director is apt to weigh his or her personal expectations more heavily than those of subordinates when producing a final forecast.

In a simpler example, envision a scenario whereby three of the top executives of the local blue jeans manufacturing company are interested in forecasting the future sales of blue jeans in Widgetstan. Executives give their predicted figures for April 1986 based on their personal set of expectations, beliefs, and voodoo economics. Assume, for example, that the three figures quoted are 4,290, 4,370, and 4,500 hundreds of thousands of Widgedollars. The three executives, not knowing which figure to use, unanimously decide to use an average (4,387.65 hundreds of thousands of Widgedollars) as their forecast. This is their consensus forecast.

Econometric Forecasting

Econometric forecasting techniques presuppose the formulation of a model based on economic theory and the collection and use of corresponding data. Although the estimated model is valid over the data sample period, given certain assumptions the model can also be used to forecast the future values of the dependent variable.

In the event data availability is not a problem and a formal economic model can be formulated and estimated, an econometric forecast can be derived. Assume a model of the following general form:

$$SALES_t = a_0 + a_1 INC_t + a_2 PRICE_t + e_t \qquad (2)'$$

Where: $SALES_t$ = sales of blue jeans in Widgedollars
  INC_t = average income in the major urban centers in time period t (where the majority of the consumers of blue jeans are located).
  $PRICE_t$ = the price of the commodity in time period t
  a_0 = the constant term.
  a_1 = the coefficient of the average income variable.
  a_2 = the coefficient of the price variable.
  e_t = the error term.

Estimating this model yields the following results:

$$SALES_t = 1.85 + .0635 INC_t - .0053 PRICE_t + e_t \qquad (2)''$$

This equation provides the basis for econometric forecasting. For example, given the data values for the INC_t and $PRICE_t$ variables at period t, sales can be predicted for period t. But this estimated equation also gives information on the independent effects of income and price on the sale of blue jeans in Widgetstan during the estimation period. The coefficients for these variables quantify these effects and can be used for sensitivity analysis. For example, the model can be used to predict sales for varying levels of income or price. Therefore, if average income increases by one unit of Widgedollars, the sale of blue jeans will increase by .0635 Widgedollars. Alternatively, it can be stated that 6.35 percent of any increase in average income goes toward the purchase of blue jeans in Widgetstan.

Illustration 11.2
A Comparison of Alternative Forecasting Techniques

	ADVANTAGES	DISADVANTAGES
	less expensive than econometric forecasting	when in error, source of error not easily identifiable
	less subjective than consensus forecasting	does not lend itself to complete sensitivity analysis
TIME SERIES FORECASTING	can be more accurate than consensus forecasting	estimation of forecasting model based on the assumption that forces affecting the series in
	minimal amount of data required	the past continue to dictate the shape of the series in the future
CONSENSUS FORECASTING	least time consuming of the three techniques	does not lend itself to any type of sensitivity and/or formal theoretical analysis
	no formal data collection necessary	
	no need to specify an economic model	
	lends itself to formal sensitivity analysis and analysis of what-if scenarios	most expensive of the three methods
ECONOMETRIC FORECASTING	cause of errors can be traced	most time consuming of the three techniques
	lends itself to post-sample testing of forecasting accuracy and reliability	data requirements can be difficult to fulfill
		must specify economic models; forecasts are as reliable as the specified models

Similarly, sensitivity analysis can be performed regarding the effect of the remaining right-hand-side variables on the SALES$_t$ variable. The sensitivity analysis is valid only for the time period over which the equation has been estimated. The validity of the post-sample qualitative statements ultimately depend on how accurately the estimated equation forecasts the SALES figures in the post-sample time period.

Illustration 11.2 summarizes the advantages and disadvantages of the three alternative forecasting techniques.

Having briefly analyzed the three types of forecasting, we now key on the main objective of this chapter, econometric forecasting.

Econometric forecasting presupposes an appropriate set of economic variables and methodological steps. In particular, economic relationships must be defined using economic theory. For example, economic theory dictates that the demand for particular goods depends on (among other variables) the real income consumers command in the marketplace, the price of substitute goods, the price of complement goods, and so on. The next step is to transform these economic relationships into a mathematical model in general functional form, for example:

$$D = f(Y, P_o, P_s, P_c)$$

Where: D = quantity demanded for the good.

$\quad\quad Y$ = consumer (real) income.

$\quad\quad P_o$ = price of good.

$\quad\quad P_s$ = price of a substitute good.

$\quad\quad P_c$ = price of a complement good.

Next, a specific functional form must be created. For example:

$$D = a_o + a_1 Y + a_2 P_o + a_3 P_s + a_4 P_c \tag{3}$$

Once the mathematical form has been specified, data must be collected for the variables included in the equation. At this stage, the first applied difficulties may occur; data on some variables may simply not be available. Variable modification and/or the use of proxy variables (variables that approximate the originally specified variables in a specific and systematic manner) may be necessary.[7]

Once the data have been collected, the equation is estimated via a chosen econometric technique (ordinary least squares, two stage least squares, maximum likelihood). This stage provides the researcher with numerical estimates of the coefficients in the specified mathematical model.

Having arrived at the empirical form of the mathematical model, the verification step (i.e., the determination of statistical significance) follows. One way to verify a model is to examine the algebraic signs of the estimated coefficients to see whether they conform with theoretical economic expectations. For example, in equation (3), the estimated coefficient a_1 is expected to have a positive sign since the demand for a product is generally positively influenced by consumer real income, and coefficient a_2 is expected to have a negative sign since the demand for a product is negatively related to its own price. If a_1 is negative and/or a_2 is positive, the researcher may seriously question the data used to estimate the model or, in fact, even the model specification.

Having estimated and verified the model, the researcher may go in either of two directions: (1) accept the underlying theory using statistical tests (such as the standard error or t-statistic test), *or* (2) refute the underlying theory.

In the event the former occurs, the researcher has identified a (statistically)

Illustration 11.3
Econometric Forecasting

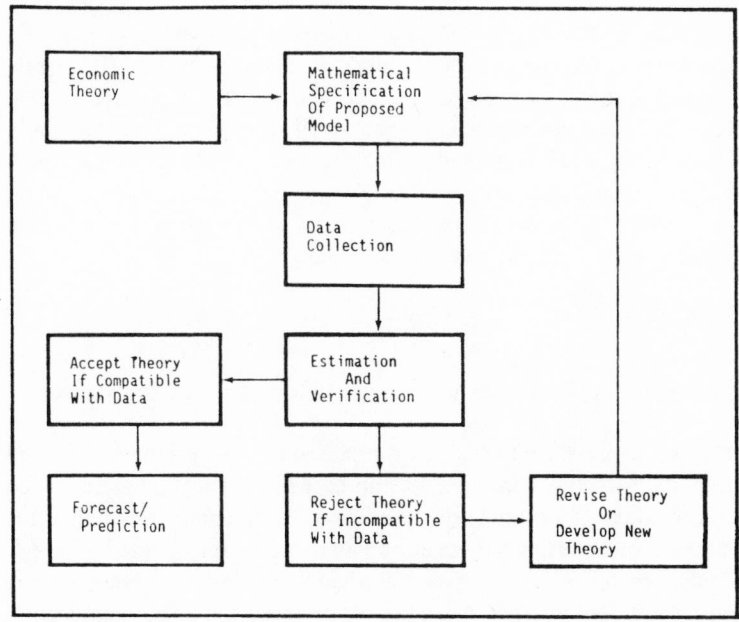

significant economic relationship based on the data and can use the equation for forecasting and/or sensitivity analysis. Alternatively, in the event the underlying theory is refuted, the theory will have to be revised and the whole process repeated starting with the specification of a new model and/or the collection of more reliable data (see Illustration 11.3).

Having explained the various methodological stages of econometric modeling, it is useful to examine the general concept of forecasting because one of the objectives of econometrics is to provide us with an acceptable model for forecasting purposes. The objective of forecasting is the prediction of future events or conditions. As such, the usefulness of a forecast is not as an end product but as input into the decision-making process. It is a prediction of what will happen under an assumed set of circumstances. Therefore, a forecast may include predicted future values of one or more explanatory variables under what is termed business-as-usual conditions or a baseline case. For example, assume that equation (3) is estimated using a historical set of data, and the following equation for the demand for widgets is derived:

$$D_t = .53 + .412Y - .5362P_o + .203P_s \tag{3$'$}$$
$$(.11) \quad (.052) \quad (.136) \quad (.236)$$

$$R^2 = .972$$
$$R^2\text{adj} = .953$$

Equation (3)' states that the demand for widgets is positively related to the level of consumer real income (Y) and the price of a substitute good (P_s), while negatively related to the its own price (P_o). This equation is a simplified version of the real world; there are numerous other variables that could conceivably affect the demand for widgets (including the price of complement goods such as bicycles if we assume that a practical use for widgets[8] arises when building bicycles). It is implicitly assumed that the effect of any variables not explicitly depicted in (3)' is truly random, and (3)' is actually:

$$D_t = .53 + .412Y - .5362P_o + .203P_s + e_t \qquad (3)''$$
$$ (.11) \quad (.052) \qquad (.136) \qquad (.236)$$

Where: e_t is an error term that includes the unsystematic effect of excluded variables.

An additional statistic, the adjusted R^2, is reported with the estimated equation (3)'. It is important to clarify the relationship between the R^2 and the adjusted R^2 within the context of econometric estimation. Econometricians will often judge the strength of an estimated equation based on the magnitude of the R^2. In fact, whether or not a set of extra right-hand-side variables belongs in a relationship depends on whether the addition of these variables significantly increases the R^2. This rule would, however, lead to a choice of a relationship with too many right-hand-side variables since the addition of new variables will never cause the R^2 to fall. Correcting the R^2 statistic for the degrees of freedom solves this problem. The corrected R^2 is the reported R^2adjusted in (3)'.

Adding another right-hand-side variable changes the degrees of freedom associated with the measures that make up the R^2 statistic. If an additional variable accounts for very little of the unexplained variation in the dependent variable, R^2adj falls (whereas R^2 rises). Therefore, only if R^2adj rises should an extra variable be seriously considered for inclusion in the model. This suggests that the researcher should search for the set of right-hand-side variables which produces the highest R^2adj.

The numbers in parentheses below the estimated coefficients of model (3)'' are the corresponding standard errors of the coefficients which are sometimes reported instead of the t-statistics.[9] The standard errors are used as an alternative to the aforementioned t-statistic test to measure the statistical reliability of estimated regression coefficients. Specifically, the rule of thumb states that if the value of the estimated coefficient is at least twice as large as the corresponding standard error at a 95 percent level of statistical significance, then there is at least a 95 percent probability that the coefficient is different from zero and should be included in the estimated model. Assuming that an estimated coefficient is statistically significant, there is a 95 percent probability that the true coefficient of the variable lies within two standard errors of the estimated value.

In the example of model (3)', using the coefficient of the income variable Y estimated at .412, there is at least a 95 percent probability that the value of the true coefficient lies within the range of $.412 - 2(.052)$ and $.412 + 2(.052)$ or .308 and .516.

A small standard error yields a smaller range within which the true coefficient lies, and, thus, the chances that the estimated coefficient is not far off from the true value are good.

A closer examination of equation (3)' shows that the constant term, as well as the coefficients of real income (Y) and price (P_0) are statistically significant and should be included in the estimated model. The price of the substitute good is clearly not statistically significant according to the standard error test developed earlier.

In this case, there are two routes the researcher can follow:

1. Eliminate the statistically insignificant variable from the model and reestimate the equation. Here the effect of the P_s variable on D_t would be included in the error term e_t.

2. Eliminate the statistically insignificant variable and search for data on another substitute good.

Option 1 is the most commonly followed. In the case of our demand model for widgets, reestimating (3)' without the variable P_s yields the following results:

$$D_t = .802 + .563Y - .8561P_o + e_t \qquad \qquad (4)$$
$$(.213) \quad (.023) \quad (.19)$$
$$R^2 = .968$$
$$R^2adj = .932$$

Note that all coefficients maintain the expected algebraic sign and continue to remain statistically significant.

Equation (4) can be used for forecasting. An implicit assumption is that the random component e_t remains truly random and that there is no systematic effect (other than the included variables) on the dependent variable. To illustrate this point, consider a case where e_t is not random. Assume that widgets are only produced in the country of Widgetstan and that information is leaked to the press that the widgets are dangerously unreliable and can lead to the construction of unsafe bicycles. This will lead to a decline in the demand for widgets due to a lack of confidence in the product. This is no longer a random effect on D_t and the estimated model can no longer be considered a baseline model for forecasting. Such an external shock can render forecasts and forecasting models unreliable.

This leads to an important conclusion concerning the forecasting value of a model. It is possible that a model may be economically meaningful and statistically correct for the time period for which it has been estimated. Yet the same model may not be suitable for forecasting due to rapid changes in the structural coefficients in the real world (a detailed description of structural coefficients and models follows later in this chapter). Therefore, the final stage of any applied econometric research is the investigation of the stability of the coefficient estimates.

The most common way of establishing the forecasting power of a model is to use the estimated model for a time period not included in the sample and compare the forecasted value with the actual (realized) value of the dependent variable. For example, assume that a model is estimated over a period of thirty years using annual data and that data on the dependent/independent variables become available for the thirty-first year. The post-sample forecasting power of the estimated equation can be examined by comparing the calculated value for the dependent variable (after substituting the data on the independent variables for the thirty-first year) with the actual value of the dependent variable. A t-test can be conducted to determine whether the calculated (forecasted) value of the dependent variable is statistically different from the actual value for the dependent variable. Alternatively, the researcher may have other criteria to evaluate the accuracy of the forecasted value (for example, an error of 1 percent or 2 percent may be considered acceptable).

There may be various reasons for a model's poor performance:

1. The estimates of the coefficients may be poor because of deficiencies in the data sample.

2. The values of the explanatory variables used in the forecast may not be accurate.

3. The estimates may have been "good" for the sample period but because of changes in the structural background conditions of the model they do not accurately depict the causal relationships in the post-sample period.

4. An incorrect mathematical specification (i.e., omission of crucial variables primarily because of the lack of data or incorrectly specified causal relationships between the independent and dependent variables) can also contribute to poor forecasting performance.

Whatever the reasons for a model's poor performance, the researcher must repeat the model-formulating process described in Illustration 11.2.

It must be emphasized that not all econometric models are developed for forecasting. Some models are developed solely for the purpose of establishing and explaining historical relationships between variables. Researchers building models strictly for explanatory purposes will not be concerned with the post-sample forecasting properties of constructed models.

AN EXAMPLE MODEL DEVELOPED FOR ECONOMETRIC FORECASTING

Before an example model is developed, some of the main differences between time-series and econometric forecasting will be reviewed.

As mentioned previously, a time-series data set is a set of chronologically ordered raw data points; an example would be the monthly sales figures of a product for several years. Time-series analysis helps identify trends that are repeated in this type of data. These patterns are usually related to changes in economic conditions—namely, expansions and contractions in economic activity (business cycles).

Econometric forecasting, on the other hand, is viewed more as a cause-effect approach. Its purpose is to identify and quantify the extent to which certain explanatory variables are responsible for the variation in the dependent variable.

Typically, time-series models involve relatively little investment of a forecaster's time and money. On the other hand, econometric models are generally more costly and not necessarily more accurate (Armstrong, 1978). However, they do have explanatory power which is missing from most time-series models. Econometric models are generally more useful for planning and policy analysis since they are flexible enough to allow for the existence of alternative scenarios.

Turning to an example of an econometric model, assume the following historical data on the sales of widgets (Y_t) in the (by now famous) country of Widgetstan (scrunched somewhere between the borders of Afghanistan and Pakistan) and the overall expenditures on durable recreational goods, X_t. Also, assume that the production of widgets is of national importance and pride with only one firm licensed for the production and sale of this product.

Given the data in Table 11.2 and following the estimation of a simple linear model of the form:

$$Y_t = a_o + a_1 X_t \qquad\qquad (5)$$

via ordinary least squares[10] the following results are obtained:

$$Y_t = 5.168 + .0009 X_t \qquad\qquad (5)'$$
$$\quad\;\; (2.345) \quad (170.07)$$
$$R^2 = .999$$
$$R^2 adj = .999$$

Where: The numbers in parentheses below the estimated coefficients are the t-statistics of the corresponding coefficients.

According to the t-statistic test developed earlier, both the constant term and independent variable X_t are statistically significant. In this case the R^2 indicates that a very high percentage of the variation in the independent variable (99%) is explained by the constant term and X_t. According to the estimated equation (5)', there is a positive relationship between the amount of national expenditures on durable recreational goods and the sales of widgets (an important raw input in the production of bicycles) in Widgestan. The model could be used to forecast the sales of widgets in the year 1981 if the actual value of X_{t+1} (i.e., the value

Table 11.2.
Widgetstan Data

Year (t)	Sales (Yt)	Expenditures (Xt)	PGAS	DUMMY
1961	206.3	226,600	$.52	0
62	216.7	238,300	.58	0
63	230.0	252,600	.59	0
64	236.5	257,400	.59	0
65	254.4	275,300	.60	1
66	266.7	293,200	.62	0
67	281.4	308,500	.62	1
68	290.1	318,800	.75	0
69	311.2	337,300	.79	0
70	325.2	350,000	.82	0
71	335.2	364,400	.84	0
72	355.1	385,300	.86	1
73	375.0	404,600	1.20	0
74	401.2	438,100	1.25	1
75	432.8	473,200	1.29	1
76	466.3	511,900	1.29	1
77	492.1	546,300	1.51	1
78	535.8	591,200	1.50	1
79	577.5	631,600	1.45	1
80	616.8	684,700	1.41	1

Units: Variables Yt and Xt are in thousands of Widgetstan dollars
(Widgedollars).

for national expenditures on durable recreational goods for 1981) is known with certainty. For example, assume that $X_{t+1} = 701,500$; then from (5)':

$$Y_{t+1} = 5.17 + .0009(701,500)$$
$$Y_{t+1} = 636.52$$

In other words, the forecasted value of widget sales for 1981 is 636,520 widgedollars. This forecast is known as a Type I forecast or unconditional forecast in which all values for the independent variables are known with certainty. There is also another type of forecast, the Type II (or conditional) forecast, in which the value of at least one of the independent variables is not known with certainty. To perform a Type II forecast, the value of at least one independent variable must be forecast.

It can be useful to test an estimated model's ability to forecast by comparing the actual values of the dependent variable with forecasted values. Such a forecast period is termed an ex post period, and in the previous example it would be the time period from 1981 to present. An ex post forecast must be distinguished from an ex ante forecast since the latter is a forecast to some future date from the present (see Illustration 11.4).

Returning to model (5)', it is important to note that since the R^2adj is equal

Illustration 11.4
Types of Forecasting

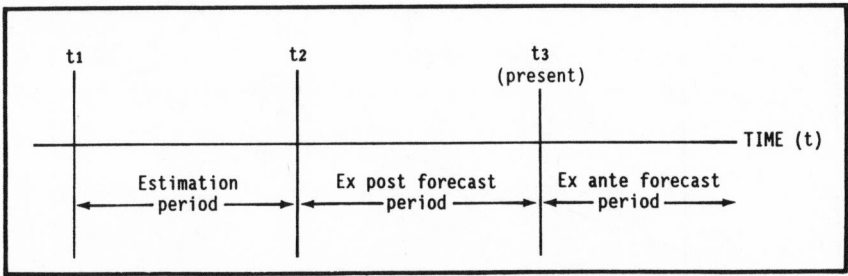

to .999 (i.e., 99.9 percent of the variation in the dependent variable is explained by the right-hand-side variable), it is almost impossible to improve on the fit of the estimated equation. Intuitively, there is no reason to further expand or investigate the validity of the estimated equation, or is there?

Model (5)' has been estimated using time-series data. A statistical problem known as autocorrelation is frequently encountered when using this type of data. Model (5)' was estimated as:

$$Y_t = 5.168 + .0009X_t + e_t$$

Here e_t is the error (or residual) term (i.e., the difference between the actual and the estimated value of Y_t). When the error terms of successive time periods are correlated, autocorrelation (sometimes known as serial correlation) is present in the estimated model.

Given this information, reexamination of model (5)' yields:

$$Y_t = 5.168 + .0009X_t \tag{5}'$$
$$\quad\ (2.345)\ \ \ (170.07)$$
$$R^2 = .999$$
$$R^2adj = .999$$
$$DW = 1.225$$

Note the addition of an additional support statistic called the Durbin-Watson (DW) statistic. The DW statistic helps identify whether autocorrelation is present in an estimated model.[11] It is routinely reported in econometric estimations and can take on a value anywhere from zero to 4.

As a rule of thumb, any DW statistic near the value of 2 indicates the absence of autocorrelation.[12] However, for positive autocorrelation (which is most commonly encountered) the Durbin-Watson statistic will be below 2. With fifty or more data points and around five independent variables, a Durbin-Watson statistic

Illustration 11.5
Autocorrelation

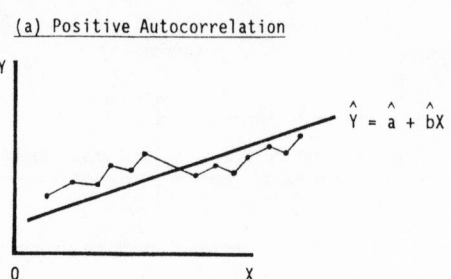

(a) Positive Autocorrelation

Positive autocorrelation exists when the observations in consecutive time periods tend to lie above or below the estimated equation line. Positive residuals tend to be followed by positive residuals and negative residuals tend to be followed by negative residuals.

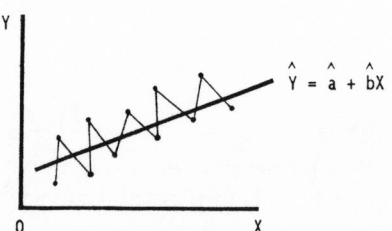

(b) Negative Autocorrelation

Negative autocorrelation exists when the observations tend to alternate below and above the estimated equation. Positive residuals tend to be followed by negative residuals, and vice-versa.

of approximately 1.5 is a danger sign. Negative autocorrelation (see Illustration 11.5) can exist only when the DW values are between 2 and 4.[13]

In model (5)′ the DW statistic is 1.225. Positive autocorrelation is present in the estimated equation. It is important to examine the consequences of autocorrelation within the context of model (5)′ since they can be severe and hamper the forecasting ability of the estimated model. In particular, in the presence of autocorrelation the standard errors (t-statistics) of the estimated coefficients are biased downward (upward). There is an excellent possibility the researcher may be happy with the statistical significance of the estimated coefficients, but, in reality, autocorrelation is leading to the incorrect acceptance of the variables.

Illustration 11.6
Relationship of Actual and Fitted Values

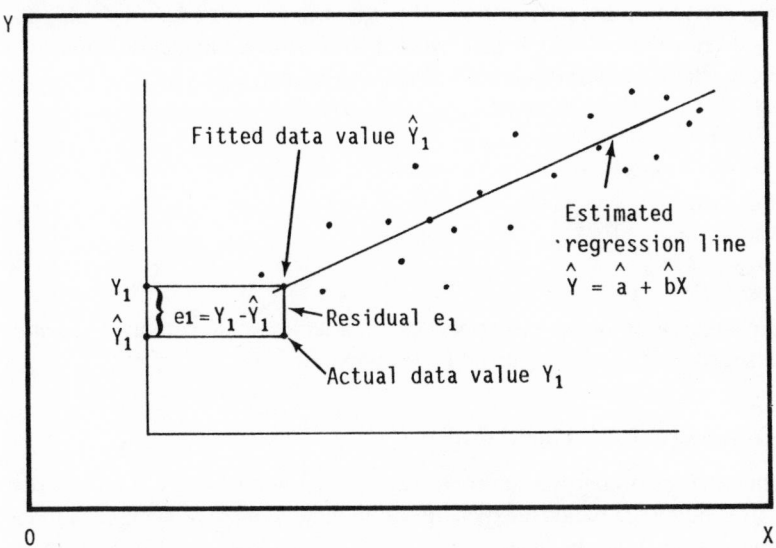

In model $(5)'$, the researcher cannot be certain X_t is a statistically significant variable in explaining the sales of widgets. The t-statistics may be misleading.

The most common cause of autocorrelation can be attributed to the existence of business cycles since many economic variables move cyclically. Other causes include incorrect mathematical specification of a model and the exclusion of important explanatory variables from a model.

In the presence of autocorrelation, the researcher is faced with the following dilemma: Is it best to attempt to correct for autocorrelation and salvage the original model, or is it preferable to attempt to estimate an alternative model? The ultimate decision lies with the researcher and is a function of the available resources and data. For expositional purposes, however, both approaches will be investigated in this section.

Correcting for Autocorrelation (Cochrane-Orcutt Technique)

The most popularly used technique to correct for autocorrelation is the Cochrane-Orcutt technique. First, this procedure estimates the specified equation using ordinary least squares (OLS). Then, it computes the residuals of the equation (i.e., the *actual* minus the *estimated* Y values in the data set) (see Illustration 11.6) and finds the best prediction of the residuals (e_t') from its own past values. A new dependent variable (Y_t') is then computed by subtracting the predicted residual from the original dependent variable Y_t. A second regression is then run using the new dependent variable Y_t' and the original independent variables.

A new set of residuals is formed and a new residual e_t'' is predicted. The process is repeated and continues until convergence or, in other words, until the same answer is derived from each iteration. The regression that is estimated using the converged error term is said to be corrected for first-order autocorrelation.

Applying the Cochrane-Orcutt technique on equation (5)′ yields:

$$Y_t = 7.53565 + .0008949X_t \qquad\qquad\qquad (5)''$$
$$\quad (1.9309) \quad (100.33)$$
$$\quad R^2 = .999$$
$$\quad R^2adj = .999$$
$$\quad DW = 1.877$$

Note changes in comparison to model (5)′. Variable coefficients and t-statistics have changed, and the DW statistic has improved.

An Alternative Model Specification

Assume the researcher has reason to believe that widget sales in time period (t) are affected by the national expenditures on durable recreational goods in the past time period (t-1). In other words, the effect of the variable X on Y_t is hypothesized to be subject to a one-year lag. In algebraic terms, model (5)′ now takes the form of:

$$Y_t = a_o + a_1X_{t-1} \qquad\qquad\qquad\qquad (6)$$

Using OLS to estimate (6) yields:

$$Y_t = -7.541 + .0009915X_{t-1} \qquad\qquad\qquad (6)'$$
$$\quad (-2.098) \quad (109.7017)$$
$$\quad R^2 = .998$$
$$\quad R^2adj = .998$$
$$\quad DW = 2.139$$

The coefficients of (6)′ are all statistically significant (based on the displayed t-statistics), and with a DW statistic of 2.139, autocorrelation is not a problem. The degree of variation of the dependent variable Y_t explained by the right-hand-side variables continues to be extremely high (99.8%). Overall, model (6)′ is judged to be preferred over models (5)′ or (5)″; that is, the national expenditures on durable recreational goods in the preceding year can be used to project widget sales in the current year. The nice feature of such a model is that the sales period (t + 1) can be projected without knowing x_{t+1}. This can be done by adding one time period to (6) to get:

$$Y_{t+1} = a_o + a_1X_t \qquad\qquad\qquad\qquad (6)''$$

Using (6)' and adding one time period yields:

$$Y_{t+1} = -7.541 + .0009915X_t \qquad\qquad (6)'''$$
$$\phantom{Y_{t+1} =} (-2.098) \quad (109.7017)$$
$$R^2 = .998$$
$$R^2adj = .998$$
$$DW = 2.139$$

Equation (6)''' contains statistically significant coefficients and could conceivably be used for forecasting. By substituting $X_{t=1980} = 684{,}700$ into (6)''' we have:

$$Y_{t+1} = -7.541 + .0009915(684{,}700)$$
$$= 671.27$$

In other words, the forecasted value of widget sales in 1981 using this transformed model is 671,270 widgedollars.

Assume now that additional data become available; presumably this data can enhance the explanatory power of model (6)' via the addition of variables that help explain the SALES of widgets in Widgetstan. Although model (6)' already has a very high R^2adj, the addition of more explanatory variables (provided that the R^2adj does not decline) may prove useful. It is within this context that the price of gas (PGAS) is hypothesized to have a positive effect on the sale of widgets (Y_t). In other words, it is postulated that an increase in the price of gas in Widgestan will lead to an increase in the purchase of bicycles as an alternative form of transportation. This will presumably lead to an increase in the sales of widgets since they are an input in bicycle production.

Similarly, assume that media exposure of the successes of the Widgetstan National Cycling Team has a positive effect on bicycle sales and, consequently, on widget sales. This variable is depicted through the use of a dummy variable.[14] This variable (called DUMMY) will take on the value of 1 in the years that at least one cyclist from Widgetstan's national team places in the top three of the International Cycling Championships and/or the Tour de France and zero if there was no such performance.

Given this information, model (6)' takes on the following form:

$$SALES_t = a_o + a_1EXPEND_{t-1} + a_2PGAS_t + a_3DUMMY \qquad\qquad (7)$$

Using the previous data set, ordinary least squares estimation yields:

$$SALES_t = -4.4066 + .000951EXPEND_{t-1} + 9.6387PGAS_t + \qquad (7)'$$
$$ (-1.2642) \quad (38.2164) \qquad\qquad (1.1539)$$
$$ 5.2851DUMMY + e_t$$
$$ (2.0938)$$

$R^2 = .998$
$R^2adj = .998$
$DW = 2.3225$

However, the DW statistic for model $(7)'$ is 2.322 which is sufficiently close to 2 to rule out any autocorrelation effect. Using the (absolute value of the) t-statistics in parentheses below the estimated coefficients, it becomes obvious that in equation $(7)'$ the variable $PGAS_t$ and constant term are not statistically significant. In other words, it can generally be said that the price of gas does not have a significant impact on the sales of widgets in $(7)'$; whereas the exposure of the victories of Widgetstan's athletes in international competition does affect the sales of widgets. The fact that the $PGAS_t$ variable does not have a significant impact on the sales of widgets means that the people of Widgetstan believe that bicycles and automobiles are poor substitutes and, therefore, do not turn away from the purchase of automobiles (and to the purchase of bicycles) when the price of gas rises. Since the weather in Widgetstan is uncomfortably cold and is not conducive to cycling, this argument is understandable.

The Case of Multicollinearity

Equation $(6)'$ remains the most acceptable model. Assume that information on an additional variable, $AUTOSALES_t$ (the current Widgedollar figure for automobile sales) becomes available. The researcher is convinced that including this variable in the $SALES_t$ equation will enhance the explanatory and potential forecasting power of the model. Based on theoretical expectations, AUTO-$SALES_t$ is expected to negatively impact the sales of widgets.[15] Specifying equation $(7)'$ with the additional variable yields:

$$SALES_t = 4.3869 - .000256EXPEND_{t-1} - 1.95PGAS_t + \qquad (8)$$
$$(2.985) \quad (174.8976) \qquad (10.023)$$
$$.0563AUTOSALES_t - .28396DUMMY + e_t$$
$$(87.5497) \qquad (1.47)$$

$R^2 = .978$
$R^2adj = .956$
$DW = 1.893$

Based on the t-statistics in parentheses, all variables except the DUMMY variable are statistically significant. However, something just doesn't make sense here; the estimated equation tells us that when expenditures on durable goods rise, there is a drop in widget sales. Moreover, there is a negative correlation between the price of gas PGAS and the sales of widgets which is counterintuitive. One would expect that when the price of gas increases, then more bicycles would be bought (the SALES of widgets would rise) since it costs more to drive automobiles.

When the researcher encounters such counterintuitive results using time-series data and has corrected for the possibility of autocorrelation, then closer attention must be paid to the model specification itself. If two or more right-hand-side variables are systematically correlated, then the cause of the problem is probably multicollinearity. In the event that the researcher suspects such a problem is present, then the partial correlation matrix[16] of the independent variables will lend insight to the magnitude of the problem. For absolute values above .80, one can conclude that a strong degree of multicollinearity is present. Another indication of strong multicollinearity is a high R^2 associated with an equation that also has statistically insignificant coefficients.

Correcting for multicollinearity is unfortunately quite difficult. One way is to simply drop the independent variable thought to be the culprit. Problems may disappear in the reestimated equation. This, however, may be a case in which the cure is worse than the disease; if there is strong justification for the variable to be in the model in the first place, then dropping it will result in an error in model specification. In the previous example of the $SALES_t$ equation, the researcher may suspect that the added variable $AUTOSALES_t$ is correlated with the $EXPEND_{t-1}$ or $PGAS_t$ variables. This is a case where additional information (i.e., an added variable, $AUTOSALES_t$) does not necessarily improve the explanatory power of the model and may actually hamper its forecasting ability.

From these results, model (6)′ appears as the most appropriate model to use for scenario analysis and forecasting.

Estimation Using Cross-Section Data

Preceding models have been estimated using historical (time-series) data. It is now time to turn to a brief example of estimation using a cross-section data set and to explore the associated difficulties.

First, it may be useful to lay out a sample of ten observations of time-series and cross-section data, side by side, to contrast their differences (see Table 11.3).

Time-series data are information on variables over time. Cross-section data are information on variables across firms or individual agents at a certain point in time. With this in mind, consider the following equation which has been estimated using a cross-section data set containing ninety observations of family consumption patterns in 1982:

$$C_{1982} = .013 + .0065INC + .019CHILD - .0048RACE + e_i \tag{9}$$
$$\phantom{C_{1982} = .013} (2.03) \quad (10.146) \quad (3.518) \quad (-1.19)$$

$R^2 = .485$

R^2 adj. $= .429$

DW $= 2.138$

Where: C_{1982} = the consumption of recreational bicycles in the year 1982 (in current widgedollars)

INC = the income of the sampled families in the year 1982

Table 11.3.
A Comparison of Time-Series and Cross-Section Data

SAMPLE 1 - Time Series Data			SAMPLE 2 - Cross-Section Data (1982)		
YEAR	SALES(000s)	EXPENDITURES	FAMILY ID#	FAMILY CONSUMPTION	FAMILY INCOME
1971	$335.2	$364,400,000	1	$1,288	$55,900
72	355.1	385,300,000	2	1,435	59,560
73	375.0	404,600,000	3	1,875	66,634
74	401.2	438,100,000	4	1,770	63,900
75	432.8	473,200,000	5	1,800	65,210
76	466.3	511,900,000	6	1,955	69,800
77	492.1	546,300,000	7	1,990	77,900
78	535.8	591,200,000	8	1,870	72,400
79	577.5	631,600,000	9	1,910	74,780
80	616.8	684,700,000	10	2,020	75,510

CHILD = the number of children in the (non-driving) cycling age group (considered to be between five and fifteen years of age)

RACE = a dummy variable indicating the race of the family (where Caucasian families = 0 and all families of other ethnic origin = 1)

According to equation (9), the consumption of recreational bicycles in Widgetstan is (as economic theory would postulate) a direct function of the level of family income (INC) and the number of children in a family (CHILD). Both variables are statistically significant since the t-statistics in parentheses under the estimated coefficients are over the value of 2. At the same time, the constant term is also statistically significant indicating that even if all variables were to take on the value of zero, there would still be some consumption of bicycles.[17] Examining the coefficient of the income variable, it becomes evident that the marginal propensity to consume[18] is .0065. An increase in family income of 1,000 widgedollars would lead to an increase in the consumption of bicycles by 6.5 widgedollars. Similarly, the effect of an increase in children between the ages of five and fifteen by 1,000 would result in an increase in the consumption of bicycles by 19 widgedollars. Meanwhile, the variable RACE is not statistically significant. The implication is that the consumption of recreational bicycles in 1982 was not related to the ethnic origin of purchasing families.

Equation (9) was estimated using data for ninety families. The equation can be used to predict bicycle consumption for families that were not included in the sample. For example, given data for the important independent variables for the 91st family, that family's bicycle consumption can be predicted. This is unlike time-series forecasting where forecasts are made for the dependent variable for periods not included in the sample. Although not covered here, there are pooling techniques used in equation estimation and forecasting. These techniques combine the use of time-series and cross-section data.

A review of the support statistics for equation (9) will contrast differences in the estimation of cross-section and time-series equations. The R^2 is .485 in this example. At first, this may seem low compared to the customarily high values of R^2 encountered in the estimation using time-series data. In cross-section data estimation, such a value is considered quite good. In fact, it is not unusual to encounter publications in economic journals that provide an R^2 of between .20 and .30.

The Durbin-Watson statistic in this cross-section sample estimation is 2.138. This shows a lack of autocorrelation which is rarely a problem in cross-section data. What is frequently a problem in cross-section estimation is heteroscedasticity. The variation of the error term around its zero average should not depend on the values of the independent variables. There should be a random dispersion of the error within a constant distance about the estimated regression line. In simple terms, the squared difference between the actual Y's and the estimated Y's (which is a measure of dispersion around the "fitted" regression line) is, on average, constant.

Whenever heteroscedasticity is present, this dispersion is no longer random (see Illustration 11.7). Illustration 11.7(a) shows a random dispersion of data points within a relatively constant distance from the estimated regression line. This is known as homoscedasticity (the exact opposite of heteroscedasticity). The increasing and decreasing variance of the dispersion around the regression line depicted in Illustrations 11.7(b) and (c) show heteroscedasticity.

The consequences of heteroscedasticity are quite severe. Although the estimated value of coefficients is unaffected, the tests (standard error, t-statistics) are inapplicable because of the variance of the error term. The tests of statistical significance cannot be applied with any degree of confidence. In the context of equation (9) and in the presence of heteroscedasticity, it is not certain that the RACE variable is statistically insignificant or that the INC and CHILD variables are significant.

How can heteroscedasticity be detected? There are two widely used tests: the Park-Glejser and the Goldfeld-Quandt tests which make the task of detecting heteroscedasticity fairly routine.[19] It is a different story, however, when attempting to correct for heteroscedasticity. If the pattern of the heteroscedasticity is known, then the variables of the model must be redefined and the new model, presumably free of heteroscedasticity, must be estimated.[20] In the event that the variances of the error terms are unknown, it may be difficult to correct the problem.

To summarize, simple equations have been specified and examined using both time-series and cross-section data. The statistical difficulties associated with the particular data were also explored. It was then shown how such equations can be useful for forecasting. Difficulties associated with the estimation and the forecasting process were also discussed.

MULTI-EQUATION MODELS

Previous sections have dealt with single equation models and shown how they can be used for forecasting. The focus in this section will be on models that

Illustration 11.7
Homoscedasticity and Heteroscedasticity

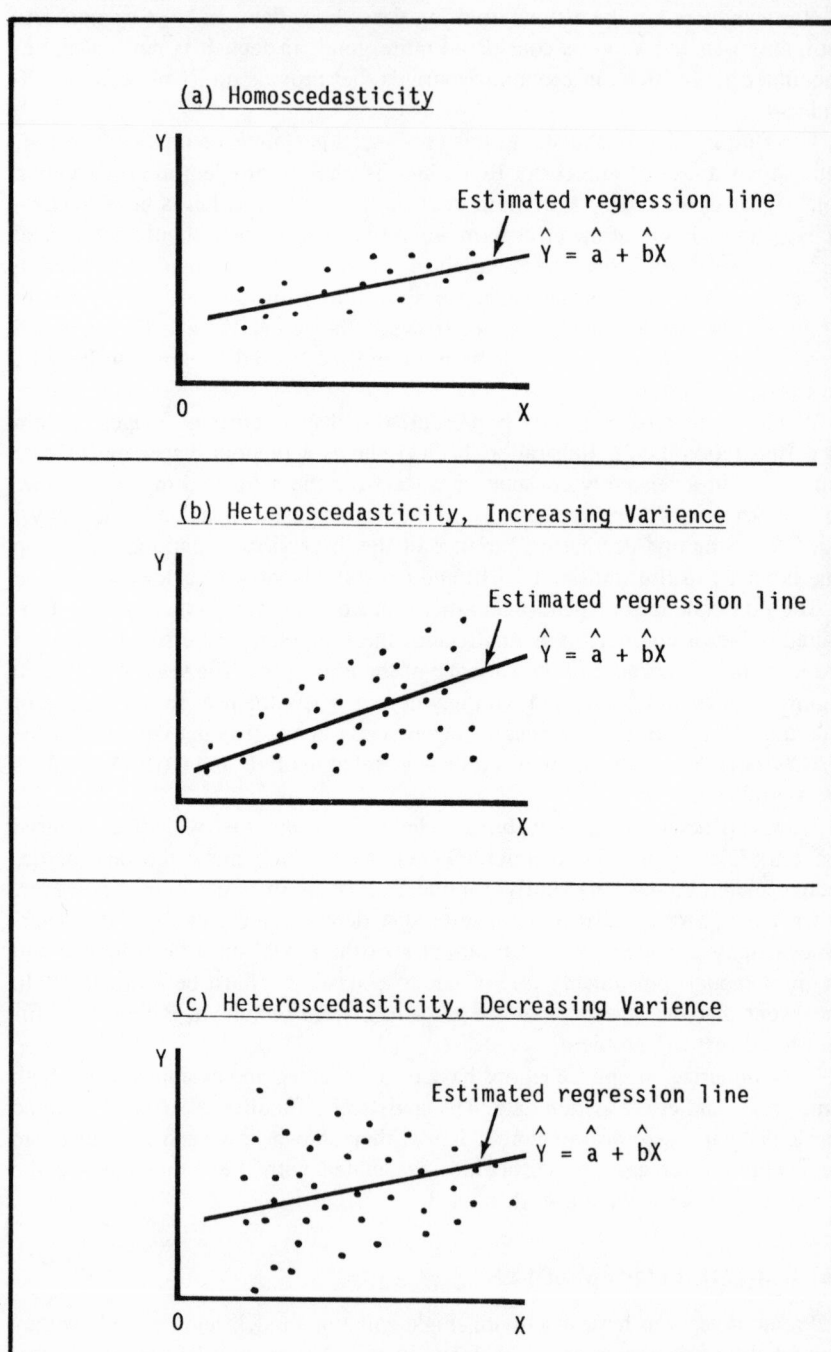

include more than one equation and the examination of the difficulties associated with multi-equation model estimation.

There are two types of multi-equation systems: recursive and simultaneous equation systems. The following examples are presented to help illustrate the differences between the two systems.

Example I

Consider the following system of equations.

$$Y_1 = a_0 + a_1 Y_2 + a_2 Y_3 + b_1 X_1 + b_2 X_2 + e_1 \tag{10}$$
$$Y_2 = a_3 + a_4 Y_1 + a_5 Y_3 + b_3 X_3 + e_2 \tag{11}$$
$$Y_3 = a_6 + a_7 Y_1 + a_8 Y_2 + b_4 X_1 + b_5 X_3 + e_3 \tag{12}$$

In this example, the Y's represent the endogenous variables—variables that are determined within the system of equations. The X's represent the exogenous or predetermined variables—variables that are determined outside the system of equations and are considered as given.

In equation (10), Y_1 is a function of both Y_2 and Y_3 while in equation (11) Y_2 is a function of both Y_1 and Y_3. Similarly, in equation (12) Y_3 is a function of the other two endogenous variables Y_1 and Y_2. This is a simultaneous equation system since the parameters of one equation cannot be estimated without considering the information from the other two equations.

Example II

Now consider the following multi-equation model.

$$Y_1 = a_0 + b_1 X_1 + b_2 X_2 + e_1 \tag{13}$$
$$Y_2 = a_1 + a_2 Y_1 + b_3 X_3 + e_2 \tag{14}$$
$$Y_3 = a_3 + a_4 Y_1 + a_5 Y_2 + b_4 X_1 + b_5 X_2 + e_3 \tag{15}$$

This system may appear to be a simultaneous equation system, but it is actually a recursive system of equations. It is different from the simultaneous equation system since at least one equation can stand alone. In particular, the dependent variable Y_1 in equation (13) is solely a function of exogenous variables and can therefore be treated as a separate equation from (14) and (15). The researcher can estimate Y_1 from equation (13) and substitute the estimated values into (14) to estimate Y_2. The estimated values of Y_2 along with Y_1 can then be substituted into (15) to estimate Y_3; thus the recursiveness of this multi-equation system. Each equation can be independently estimated using a sequential ordering.

Recursive systems do not present any major difficulties and will, therefore, not be dealt with further. Simultaneous equation systems do, however, present certain estimation difficulties which warrant closer examination.

Simultaneous Equation Systems

Consider the following simple model for the market of Brand Z Ontario wine, consisting of a demand and supply equation and the market clearing condition (condition where supply equals demand and the market is in equilibrium):

$$D = a_0 + a_1P + a_2I + u \tag{16}$$

$$S = b_0 + b_1P + b_2T + v \tag{17}$$

$$D = S \tag{18}$$

Where:
- D = demand equation
- S = supply equation
- P = price per ton
- I = Ontario provincial income
- T = rainfall index for the year

This econometric model is said to be a complete model since it contains at least as many independent equations as endogenous variables (three equations, three endogenous variables—D, S, and P). Equations (16) and (17) are structural equations forming a structural model; whereas equation (18) is the market clearing condition and always holds true when there is equilibrium in the market (this is also called an identity). The coefficients a_0, a_1, a_2, b_0, b_1, and b_2 are called structural parameters and show the direct effect of each explanatory variable on the dependent variable.

A structural model is a complete system of equations describing the structure of the relationships of the economic variables involved. Structural equations show the relationship between the left-hand-side (endogenous) variables and other endogenous and predetermined (exogenous) variables.

Variables that do not appear in an equation of a structural model are not precluded from having an effect on the dependent variable of an equation, albeit in an indirect fashion. Indirect effects, however, can only be computed by solving the structural system. The reduced form of a structural model is the model in which the endogenous variables are algebraically solved for as a function of the exogenous variables. Therefore, substituting (16) and (17) into (18) and solving for the endogenous variable P yields:

$$P = (b_0 - a_0)/(a_1 - b_1) - a_2/(a_1 - b_1) I + [b_2/(a_1 - b_1)]T + (v - u) \tag{19}$$

Substitution of (19) into either (16) or (17) (in this case (16)), and given the appropriate algebraic manipulations, yields:

$$Q = (a_1b_0 - a_0b_1)/(a_1 - b_1) - [a_2b_1/(a_1 - b_1)] I$$
$$+ [a_1b_2/(a_1 - b_1)]T + [a_1v + (1 - a_1)u] \tag{20}$$

Equations (19) and (20) are reduced form equations and constitute the reduced form model. Rewriting (19) and (20) to simplify notation:

$$P = c_0 + c_1 I + c_2 T + e_1 \tag{19}'$$
$$Q = c_3 + c_4 I + c_5 T + e_2 \tag{20}'$$

Where:
$$c_0 = (b_0 - a_0)/(a_1 - b_1) \tag{21}$$
$$c_1 = -a_2/(a_1 - b_1) \tag{22}$$
$$c_2 = b_2/(a_1 - b_1) \tag{23}$$
$$c_3 = (a_1 b_0 - a_0 b_1)/(a_1 - b_1) \tag{24}$$
$$c_4 = -a_2 b_1/(a_1 - b_1) \tag{25}$$
$$c_5 = a_1 b_2/(a_1 - b_1) \tag{26}$$

The reduced form coefficients c_0, c_1, c_2, c_3, c_4 and c_5 measure the total effect, direct and indirect, of a change in the predetermined variable on the endogenous variables after accounting for the interdependencies among the jointly dependent endogenous variables. These coefficients are, therefore, very important for forecasting and policy analysis since it is the total effect of a change in the exogenous variables on the dependent variable(s) that is of interest to the policy maker.

Having discussed the particulars concerning structural and reduced form models, it is time to turn to the estimation techniques frequently used to quantify these theoretical models.

Two methods of estimating reduced form models will be presented.

Method I

Express the endogenous variables as a function of all the predetermined/ exogenous variables and proceed with the estimation of the coefficients. For example, given the variables shown in the model (16) through (18), the reduced form equations would be:

$$P = c_0 + c_1 I + c_2 T + e_1 \tag{27}$$
$$Q = c_3 + c_4 I + c_5 T + e_2 \tag{28}$$

Ordinary least squares estimation may be used to estimate the reduced form parameters c_0 through c_5. This method of obtaining the c's is called Least-Squares-No-Restriction (LSNR) estimation since it does not use any restrictions imposed by the structural equations (16) and (17). For example, a restriction in structural equation (16) is that the coefficient of the variable T is equal to zero since variable T is not included in this equation. LSNR estimation does not take this into account. Therefore, this method does not require complete knowledge of the structural system, only knowledge of the predetermined variables appearing in the whole system of equations.

Table 11.4.
Data for the Estimation of Demand and Supply for Ontario Wine

YEAR	Quantity (Q)	Price (P)	Income (I)	Rainfall (T)
1970	12,917	2,260	1,089	100
1971	17,920	2,150	1,169	110
1972	18,475	1,970	1,281	110
1973	28,180	1,620	1,335	112
1974	26,330	1,380	1,388	105
1975	31,029	1,200	1,452	107
1976	41,430	1,310	1,516	110
1977	48,924	1,080	1,536	100
1978	52,739	1,180	1,558	105
1979	55,009	1,390	1,587	105
1980	50,100	1,340	1,625	98
1981	67,559	1,350	1,693	105
1982	61,986	1,360	1,774	95
1983	55,986	1,250	1,826	88
1984	60,311	1,210	1,899	95

Method II

Obtain the reduced form of the structural model by solving the structural system of endogenous variables in terms of the predetermined variables, the structural parameters, and the error terms.

For models (16) through (18) this would involve substituting equations (16) and (17) into (18) and solving for the endogenous variable P. This variable would then be substituted into either (16) or (17) to obtain an equation for the endogenous variable Q. This method yields equations (19) and (20).

Since there is a definite relationship between the structural parameters and the reduced form parameters, it is possible to first obtain estimates of the reduced form parameters (using the OLS estimation technique) and then substitute these values into equations (21) through (26) to indirectly obtain the value of the structural parameters. This technique is called indirect least squares (ILS).

Applying ordinary least squares to the reduced form equations (19) and (20) and using the data from Table 11.4 yields:

$$P = 5,491.09 - 1.54I - 16.38T \qquad\qquad R^2 = .676 \qquad \textbf{(19)}''$$
$$Q = -108,849.81 + 77.47I + 325.15T \qquad\qquad R^2 = .875 \qquad \textbf{(20)}''$$

Using the estimated coefficients of (19)″ and (20)″ and substituting into (21) through (26) yields:

$$c_0 = 5,491.09 = (b_0 - a_0)/(a_1 - b_1) \qquad\qquad\qquad \textbf{(21)}'$$
$$c_1 = -1.54 = -a_2/(a_1 - b_1) \qquad\qquad\qquad \textbf{(22)}'$$

$$c_2 = -16.38 = b_2/(a_1 - b_1) \tag{23}'$$
$$c_3 = -108,849.81 = (a_1 b_0 - a_0 b_1)/(a_1 - b_1) \tag{24}'$$
$$c_4 = 77.47 = -a_2 b_1/(a_1 - b_1) \tag{25}'$$
$$c_5 = 325.15 = a_1 b_2/(a_1 - b_1) \tag{26}''$$

Solving this system of six equations with six unknowns yields the value of the coefficients of the structural equations (16) and (17):

$a_0 = 149.18$

$a_1 = -19.85$

$a_2 = 46.89$

$b_0 = 167,376$

$b_1 = -50.30$

$b_2 = 498.77$

Equations (16) and (17), estimated through this method of indirect least squares, are:

$$D = 149.18 - 19.85P + 46.89I + u \tag{16}'$$
$$S = 167,376 - 50.31P + 498.77T + v \tag{17}'$$

An examination of equations (16)' and (17)' shows that the coefficient of the price variable (P) in (17)' has a counterintuitive (negative) sign. Economic theory states that an increase in the price of a good leads to an increase in the supplied quantity of the good. There is therefore, room for troubleshooting in this estimated model. This example has been presented for illustration; therefore, further analysis of counterintuitive results will not be pursued.

Although the method of indirect least squares is more tedious than LSNR estimation, it has certain advantages:

1. Calculation of reduced form parameters is more efficient (i.e., it takes into account all the information provided in the structural model).

2. When structural changes occur, they can be taken into account by the structural coefficients in formulas (21) through (26). This cannot be done in the LSNR estimation since the relationship between structural and reduced form coefficients is not firmly established and formally identified.

3. Other information can be incorporated into the estimation as it becomes available from other studies. Such information could not be used in the absence of the reduced form coefficient formulas.

These are useful in terms of identifying the various estimation methods and characteristics of multi-equation models. What follows is an analysis of the problem that researchers face when attempting to estimate them.

A difficulty that may frequently arise using this estimation technique (or any multi-equation estimation technique) centers on recovering the value of the structural coefficients from the reduced form coefficients. In fact, there are instances when the coefficients of the structural model cannot be calculated from formulas similar to those in (21) through (26) and (21)' through (26)'. To contrast this scenario, there are also instances when more than one value of the structural coefficients may be obtained. The former case describes the problem of under-identification, and the latter that of overidentification. The ILS estimation example is an exactly identified system since a unique set of structural coefficients was derived from the reduced form parameters.

The question arises as to what exactly it means to have an identification problem, how it arises, and how it is handled in estimation.

Identification is considered to be more of a problem of model formulation than that of model estimation. For a multi-equation system to be identified, each equation must be identified. To illustrate the significance of the (lack of) identification problem, consider the following simple example:

$$D = a_0 + a_1P + u \tag{29}$$
$$S = a_2 + a_3P + v \tag{30}$$
$$D = S \tag{31}$$

Where:
$\quad$ D = Quantity demanded
$\quad$ S = Quantity supplied
$\quad$ D = S

Equation (29) is the demand equation, (30) is the supply equation, and (31) is the market equilibrium condition. This is a complete model, since there are three equations and three unknowns (endogenous variables D, S, and P). Is this an identified system, or in other words, is each equation identified? To answer this question, first consider the type of data used in the estimation of such a model. Typically, time-series market data are used, and the quantity registered at a certain price is, in fact, both the quantity supplied and the quantity demanded. In other words, it is the transacted quantity Q at the prevailing market price P. Using these data for estimation, the coefficients of a function of the general form $Q = f(P)$ are being measured. This could be a demand, supply, or even a hybrid equation.

Consider Illustration 11.8 which depicts the P and Q data points that will be used to estimate the functional relationship $Q = f(P)$. One could conclude that the scatter of data in Illustration 11.8(a) depicts a supply curve, Illustration 11.8(b) a demand curve, but Illustration 11.8(c) depicts neither relationship. This is not necessarily true since, in order to identify a demand or supply relationship, one needs to know the changes in the other variables (excluding the price variable) that determine the supply and demand relationships. It is statistically impossible to estimate a model such as the one depicted in equations (29) through (31) where each equation contains the same explanatory variables.

Illustration 11.8
Price and Quantity Data Points

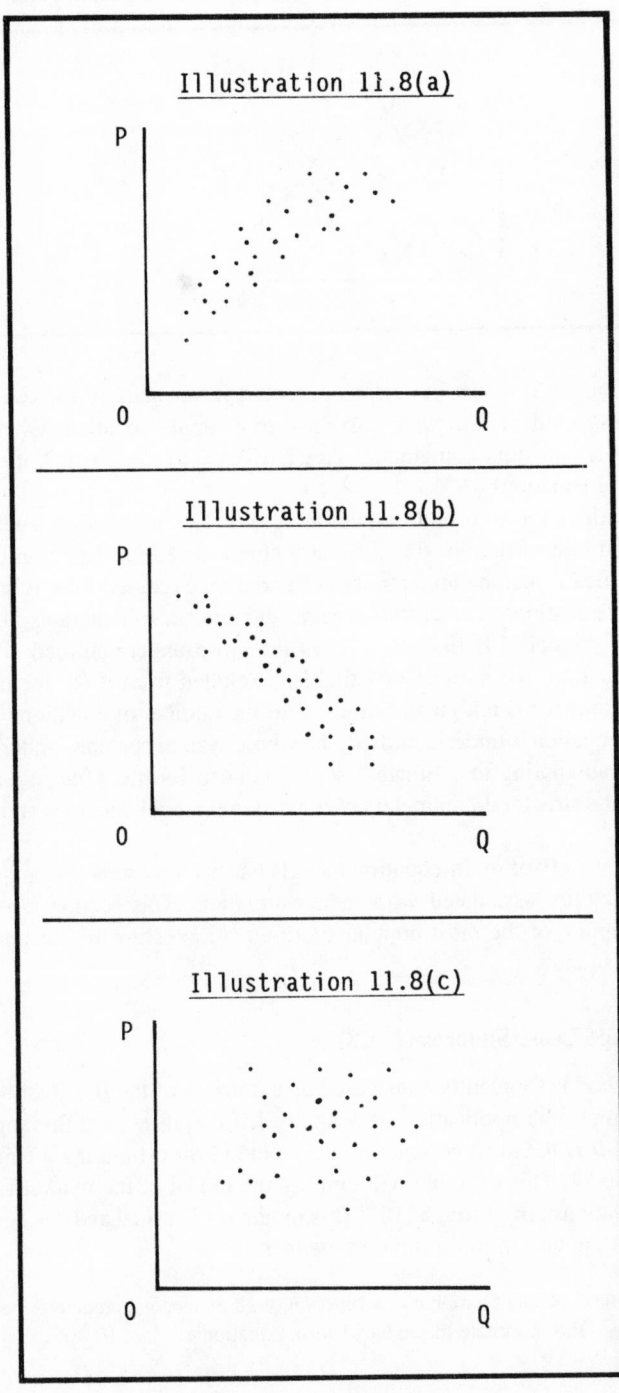

Illustration 11.9
Observed Data Points Originating from Changes in Both Demand and Supply

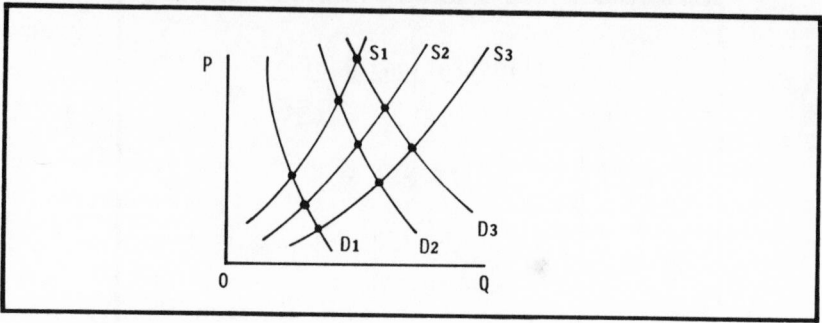

Illustration 11.9 shows the error one could have made in the event that the data in Illustration 11.8(a) were attributed to a supply equation. Obviously, the observed price/quantity combinations are attributed to changes in both the supply and demand equations.

The identification of a multi-equation system aids in avoiding such potential errors. As a rule of thumb, the necessary condition for an equation of a model to be identified is that the total number of variables excluded from it but included in the other equations is at least as great as the number of equations in the model minus one. Model (19) through (21) is therefore underidentified since in the demand equation, the number of variables excluded from it but included in the other equations (0) is not greater or equal to the number of equations minus one (2). If one equation is underidentified, the whole system becomes underidentified. Therefore, attempting to estimate a set of reduced form coefficients and trying to recover the structural parameters of the original model becomes an impossible task.

So far, a variety of multi-equation models has been presented along with some of the difficulties associated with their estimation. This section closes with a brief description of the most popular multi-equation estimation technique: two-stage least squares.

Two-Stage Least Squares (2SLS)

This method is frequently considered an extension of the ILS method. In fact, 2SLS is simply the application of ordinary least squares (see the appendix) in two stages. It is the most commonly used method for estimating a simultaneous equation model. This example will employ the model of the market for Ontario wine in equations (16) through (18). This model is identified and can be estimated using 2SLS applied in the following manner:

1. Express the dependent variable as a function of all exogenous/predetermined variables and, using OLS, estimate the reduced form equations:

$$P = c_0 + c_1 I + c_2 T + e_1 \tag{27}$$

$$Q = c_3 + c_4 I + c_5 T + e_2 \tag{28}$$

2. Having estimated the coefficients of (27) and (28), substitute the actual data values of I and T into equations (16) and (17) to derive the estimated price (P-hat) and quantity (Q-hat) values.

3. Using the calculated values of P-hat and Q-hat as the new data values for the price-quantity combinations in the structural equations (16) and (17) and applying OLS yields:

$$Q\text{-hat} = a_0 + a_1 P\text{-hat} + a_2 I \tag{16}'$$

$$Q\text{-hat} = b_0 + b_1 P\text{-hat} + b_2 T \tag{17}'$$

The estimated coefficients a_0 through b_2 in the demand equation (16)$'$ and supply equation (17)$'$ are the two-stage least squares estimates of this model and should be identical to the ILS estimates since this system of equations is exactly identified and only one set of structural parameters can be retrieved from the reduced form parameters.

SUMMARY

The objective of this chapter has been to serve as a guide to understanding some of the fundamental concepts of econometric estimation and forecasting. An attempt has been made to examine the most relevant and pertinent methods and techniques as well as the associated statistics. Since the area of econometrics is vast, this examination is in no way considered exhaustive. The concepts should, however, provide the planner with enough analytical tools to be able to evaluate the accuracy and interpret an estimated equation or system of equations.

Economic forecasters attempt to predict the past as well as the future. At first, this may seem nonsensical; however, consider the following: A weather forecaster at least knows if it is raining or sunny today, yet economic forecasters must start by predicting the immediate past. It takes years before they know whether they are correct, since published data are subject to constant and major revisions. It takes Statistics Canada a minimum of three years of revisions to report ''reliable'' data on measured variables.

It has been suggested that one can't forecast what one can't measure; accordingly, if one cannot measure accurately, chances are one won't be able to successfully forecast either. It is nearly impossible for economists to forecast accurately when imponderables such as terrorism, oil embargoes, world trade wars, and government policies are key elements. Nevertheless, economic forecasting has progressed considerably and has performed fairly well given all of these difficulties. Therefore, the determination of fundamental trends, the understanding of critical assumptions, the interpretation of forecasts for a particular business, and the use of alternative scenarios make economic forecasting an integral part of any business information bank and aid business executives in preparing for that uncertain tomorrow. Therein lies the usefulness of business forecasting. After all, even though forecasting is considered an art and not a science, it is an art that has proven to be a useful input into the science of economics.

NOTES

1. Trend is the tendency of a measured variable to consistently grow or decline over a period of time.

2. This is known in the statistical literature as a linear trend model. *Linear* because all the variables are raised to the exponential power of one or, alternatively, because the equation is the algebraic expression of a straight line; a *trend* model since its only right-hand-side variable is TIME.

3. A detailed explanation of this curve fitting technique will be presented later in this chapter.

4. This can be interpreted as the derivative of SALES with respect to TIME, d(SALES)/d(TIME).

5. The derivation of fitted values for the dependent variable entails substituting the actual data values of the right-hand-side variables into an estimated equation. As an example, assume an estimated equation $y = 5 + .3x$, where the actual value of x for time period one is 5.3. Substituting this value into the estimated equation yields $y = 5 + .3(5.3) = 5 + 1.59 = 6.59$ which is the fitted value of y. If the actual value of y in period one is known to be 7.1, then it can be said that the fitted value diverges from the actual value by $6.59 - 7.1 = -.51$. This is also known as the residual of the estimated equation for period one. As these residuals approach zero, and the fit of the equation improves, the R-Square approaches the value of one.

6. Degrees of freedom are defined as the number of sample data points minus the number of independent (right-hand-side) variables—excluding the constant term.

7. If the problem of data availability is quite severe, then time-series forecasting may be an alternative.

8. At last, a practical use for widgets!

9. The reader may find it confusing that both the standard errors of the coefficients and/or the t-statistics are used in this chapter to test for the statistical significance of the independent variables. It is, however, quite useful to accustom the reader to these measures since both are used in econometric literature.

10. See the appendix for a detailed exposition of ordinary least squares estimation and the formulas used to derive coefficients and some associated support statistics.

11. In addition to using the Durbin-Watson statistic to test for autocorrelation, a different method can be used. This involves the use of the residuals of the estimated model. In particular, when testing for first order serial correlation, the model $e_t = a_0 + \rho e_{t-1} + u_t$ is estimated. If the coefficient (ρ) of the lagged residual term ρe_{t-1} is statistically significant, then there exists first order serial correlation in the original model. In other words, the error term of the past period (t-1) is systematically related to that of the current period (t).

12. This is not necessarily true; all it means is that there is no serial correlation of the first degree. There may still exist autocorrelation of a higher order. For a more detailed description of the various orders of serial correlation, see any econometric textbook.

13. For a more detailed and formal description of the Durbin-Watson test for auto-correlation, see Kmenta, pp. 295–297.

14. The use of dummy variables is quite extensive in econometric estimation. They are used to test the significance of various external shocks in a market as well as the statistical significance of seasonal variations or socioeconomic status on the dependent variable. For example, dummy variables could be used to test the significance of the impact of war years on the dependent variable. The dummy variable would be set equal to 1 for war years and 0 for nonwar years. If the dummy variable is statistically significant, then the war has had an impact on the dependent variable.

15. Widgets are an essential input in the production of bicycles. Thus, when the variable AUTOSALES, goes up, it is expected that the purchase of bicycles (and therefore the sales of widgets) will go down.

16. Computer printouts of most econometric software packages include a matrix of simple correlation coefficients between all pairs of independent variables. The off-diagonal elements contain the simple correlation coefficients (i.e., coefficients showing the degree of correlation between variables) for the given data set; moreover, the diagonal elements are all equal to one since each variable is perfectly correlated with itself. See Pindyck and Rubinfeld, pp. 94–96.

17. Most likely to be used as a means of transportation out of the country and into neighboring Afghanistan or Pakistan to find work and get out of the zero income position.

18. This is the effect of a change in income on the consumption variable when all other variables remain constant (i.e., dC_t / dY_t).

19. For an excellent exposition of the tests for heteroscedasticity, see Pindyck and Rubinfeld, pp. 146–152.

20. Ibid., pp. 142–146.

APPENDIX: Ordinary Least Squares Estimation

Assume data exist for variables Y and X, as shown in Table 11.5.

Table 11.5.
Hypothetical Data

Y_i	X_i	$Y_i X_i$	$(X_i)^2$	
2	9	18	81	
2.5	6	15	36	
2.5	12	30	144	$\Sigma(X_i)^2 = 11,664$
3	12	36	144	
3	15	45	225	$\Sigma Y_i/N = \bar{Y} = 24/8 = 3$
3.5	15	52.5	225	
3.5	18	63	324	$\Sigma X_i/N = \bar{X} = 108/8 = 13.5$
4	21	84	441	
$\Sigma Y_i = 24$	$\Sigma X_i = 108$	$\Sigma Y_i X_i = 343.5$	$\Sigma X_i^2 = 1,620$	

Also assume that variables Y and X are linearly related according to this equation:

$$Y = a + bX \tag{1}$$

Coefficients a and b can be calculated using ordinary least squares estimation. This technique estimates the coefficients by attempting to fit a straight line through the data while simultaneously attempting to minimize the sum of squared deviations of the actual from the fitted values of Y. In other words, OLS estimation of a and b minimizes:

$$\sum_{i=1}^{n} (Y_i - a - b_i)^2$$

The OLS solution formulas for the coefficients are:

$$\hat{b} = \frac{N \sum X_i Y_i - \sum X_i \sum Y_i}{N \sum X_i^2 - (\sum X_i)^2} \tag{2}$$

$$\hat{a} = \frac{\sum Y_i}{N} - \frac{\hat{b} \sum X_i}{N} \tag{3}$$

Where:

N = number of observations
$\bar{Y}$ = the average (mean) of the dependent variable
$\bar{X}$ = the mean of the independent variable

Use of (2) yields:

$$\hat{b} = \left(8(343.5) - 108(24) \right) \div \left(8(1,620) - 11,664 \right) = .12 \tag{2'}$$

and similarly from (3):

$$\hat{a} = 3 - .12 (13.5) = 1.38 \tag{3'}$$

Therefore, the ordinary least squares method yields the following estimated equation:

$$Y = 1.38 + .12 X \tag{4}$$

The $\sum (\hat{Y}_i - \bar{Y})^2$ which was minimized in the previous OLS procedure is also called the residual sum of squares (RSS). Similarly, the sum of squared deviations of the calculated Y values from the mean of Y (i.e., $\sum (Y_i - \bar{Y})^2$) is called the explained sum of squares (ESS).

The total sum of squares (TSS) is equal to the RSS + ESS. Since the R^2 is the proportion of the total variation in Y, which is explained by the regression equation $Y = a + bX$, it is defined as:

$$R^2 = RSS/TSS = \Sigma (\hat{Y}_i - \bar{Y})^2 / \Sigma (Y_i - \bar{Y})^2$$

or

$$1 - \Sigma \hat{e}_i^2 / \Sigma (Y_i - \bar{Y})^2 \tag{5}$$

The adjusted R-Squared $(\bar{R}^2) = 1 - (1 - R^2)\dfrac{N\text{-}1}{N\text{-}K}$ $\hspace{2cm}$ **(6)**

where: N = number of observations

$\hspace{1.5cm}$ K = number of independent variables

Note: When comparing the explanatory power of two regressions by virtue of the R^2adj, the dependent variable must be the same for the comparison to be meaningful. Also, the adjusted R^2 may take on a negative value. In such cases it is interpreted as the value zero. R^2 and R^2adj are not valid statistics if the associated regression equation does not include a constant term.

The standard error formulas for the estimated coefficients in a two-variable model such as (1) are:

$$S_{\hat{b}} = \sqrt{\frac{\sum (Y_i - \hat{Y}_i)^2}{(n - 2) \sum (X_i - \bar{X})^2}} \tag{7}$$

$$S_{\hat{a}} = \sqrt{\frac{\sum (Y_i - \hat{Y}_i)^2 \sum X_i^2}{(n - 2) n \sum (X_i - \bar{X})^2}} \tag{8}$$

Finally, in the t-statistic test of statistical significance of a coefficient the formula used is:

$$t = \frac{\hat{b} - b^*}{\sqrt{S^b}_2}$$

where: $\hat{b}$ $\hspace{0.3cm}$ = OLS estimate of b

$\hspace{1.5cm}$ b^* = hypothesized value of b (i.e., if the hypothesis being tested is that

$\hspace{2.5cm}$ b = 0, then b^* = 0)

$\hspace{1.5cm}$ S_b^2 = variance of b

n = sample size

k = total number of parameters (in this model k equals 2 because there are two parameters a and b)

REFERENCES

Armstrong, J. S. "Forecasting with Econometric Methods: Folklore versus Facts," *Journal of Business*, 51 (1978): 549–564.

Kmenta, J. *Elements of Econometrics*. New York: Macmillan Co., 1971.

Koutsoyiannis, A. *Theory of Econometrics*. 2d ed. New York: Harper & Row, 1977.

Levenbach, H., and Cleary, J. *The Beginning Forecaster*. Belmont, Calif.: Lifetime Learning Publications, 1981.

Pindyck, R., and Rubinfeld, D. *Econometric Models and Economic Forecasts*. 2d ed. New York: McGraw-Hill, 1981.

Index